GOLDEN KEYS TO ASCENSION AND HEALING

REVELATIONS OF SAI BABA AND THE ASCENDED MASTERS

JOSHUA DAVID STONE, Ph.D.

Volumes in the series
The Easy-to-Read Encyclopedia of the Spiritual Path
by Joshua David Stone, Ph.D.
published by Light Technology

1 THE COMPLETE ASCENSION MANUAL
   How to Achieve Ascension in This Lifetime

2 SOUL PSYCHOLOGY
   Keys to Ascension

3 BEYOND ASCENSION
   How to Complete the Seven Levels of Initiation

4 HIDDEN MYSTERIES
   ETs, Ancient Mystery Schools and Ascension

5 THE ASCENDED MASTERS LIGHT THE WAY
   Beacons of Ascension

6 COSMIC ASCENSION
   Your Cosmic Map Home

7 A BEGINNER'S GUIDE TO THE PATH OF ASCENSION

8 GOLDEN KEYS TO ASCENSION AND HEALING
   Revelations of Sai Baba and the Ascended Masters

9 MANUAL FOR PLANETARY LEADERSHIP

10 REVELATIONS OF A MELCHIZEDEK INITIATE

11 YOUR ASCENSION MISSION
   Embracing Your Puzzle Piece

Golden Keys to Ascension and Healing

Revelations of Sai Baba and the Ascended Masters

Joshua David Stone, Ph.D.

THE EASY-TO-READ ENCYCLOPEDIA
of the SPIRITUAL PATH
✦ **Volume VIII** ✦

Published by
Light Technology Publishing

© 1998 by Joshua David Stone, Ph.D.

Cover design by
Fay Richards

ISBN 1-891824-03-1

 Published by
Light Technology Publishing
P.O. Box 1526
Sedona, AZ 86339
(800) 450-0985

Printed by
MI**SS**ION
PO**SS**IBLE
COMMERCIAL
PRINTING
P.O. Box 1495
Sedona, AZ 86339

Contents

Dedication to Sai Baba
by the Inner-Plane Ascended Masters
of the Planetary and Cosmic Hierarchy

Sai Baba is light and Sai Baba is love. Sai Baba is the Shiva embodiment of Brahma and Vishnu. He is also Shakti. It is the joining of the energies of his holiness the Lord Sai Baba with ourselves, the inner-plane ascended masters, that is the inspiration for the writing of this book. Thus it is fitting that we introduce it. We also seek to share the fundamental truth that for all who seek us with sincerity of heart and mind, we stand ready to be in telepathic communion. So we wish to address how we can be accessed telepathically.

The world has advanced and evolved most quickly in recent times. There is a great telepathic network that exists throughout all of humanity, although it is focused most greatly among the disciples, initiates and self-realized masters of the world. This telepathic network is an aspect of the group consciousness that you, the children of the one God, manifest as never before. This is between those of you who are working in the physical realm of embodiment and can be referred to as being in horizontal telepathic communication.

There is another most wonderful telepathic link that has been activated to a degree never before possible to the masses. This is the vertical energy connection between humanity and the higher realms of planetary masters, cosmic masters, the archangels, angels, the elohim and various other planetary cultures whose function it is to aid humanity. We of the celestial hierarchy, dear beloveds of our heart, exist and embrace you from both of these realms. We walk among you as one of you and therefore are in telepathic connection with you via the horizontal spiritual link that exists person to person within humanity. In some cases we are you, for you have reached the heights of being that allow you to be God's very own representatives on Earth. In truth, we, the inner-plane hierarchy of ascended masters of the most sublime light, love and power, live most of our existence in these expanded realms of being so that we ever maintain an open channel of communication with all who seek us via the vertical spiritual link.

This special book is about the bridge that exists between Sai Baba, ourselves of the celestial realms, the inner-plane hierarchy, the author and each and every one of you. It is a tribute and an honoring to his holiness the Lord Sai Baba and also to all ascended beings. It speaks to the pervasive unity of all life, and in joyous devotion celebrates the grace of Sai Baba!

Let it be known that the love, grace and wisdom of Sai Baba embrace all who embrace him and all who love God by any name. All who call to his holiness in love and devotion likewise call to us. Sai Baba has come to Earth to be with you all, for he is of the all and the very essence and substance of that which is, and therefore there is nowhere that he is not, no person he cannot speak to, no prayer he does not hear.

Thus he comes and he is, and he does his cosmic work on the hallowed soils of planet Earth. Thus every man, woman and child is embraced within his heart of hearts. Where love abides there Sai Baba is known—and known by many names. For he is of the heart of love itself. To whose hearts shall he speak? To any and all of you who but love, for love is both the giver and the receiver. Love is the seed, the flower, the fruit and the hand that waters the vine.

What, then, is the great difference between the one who pens the master's inner guidance as he speaks within the heart, mind and spirit, who adores the master's beingness without following the traditions—and the one to whom the master comes as healer in a shower of vibhuti upon a picture, whose path and calling are to follow the master's work along the footprints of Hindu tradition? There is no difference between these, beloved ones. You are all the same, for love will always speak unto love. The vehicle of expression will find the most appropriate outlet, but it will always be that One voice of love that the heart and mind follow and pay heed to.

Expand, then, your vision of him that he might reveal more of his very self to you. That is what the words within this book seek to do: to break down the walls of division and expand the ultimate vision. What indeed is that vision if not one of unity—unity between man and man, woman and woman, man and woman, humanity and God? The form of his holiness the Lord Sai Baba has been brought into manifestation, not that he might be limited by form and conceptions or held singularly apart from the celestial hierarchy, but that you, dear ones, might see through his form in action just how limitless and transcendent form truly is. All bodies are but the dense manifestation of God, and the forms you wear—your embodiments—are, in fact, vehicles for the expanding expression of God upon Earth, and that is what he has come to bear witness to and reveal.

His guiding, loving presence, his light, his wisdom are all here for the asking, for the taking, if only you will reach for them. He is in India in a semblance of human form, yes, but he is also beyond India. He is beyond your imaginings of who he is, and yet he is right here within each and every one of you. Some he calls to make the journey of many, many miles to where he physically resides in form. To others he comes in less than a blink of an eye, for he is already with and within you all. So be not confused or unsettled if you find his guidance within your mind or his touch within your heart, for even as he calls some of you to where he physically resides, so is he called by some, and hopefully more and more of you, to where you physically reside. And then, behold—there he is!

There is no way to limit him, even as there is no way to limit or confine the limitless vastness of the All That Is. Many hearts, one love; many paths, one truth; many voices, one sweet song of glorification of the One. Be then open to the vastness of his holiness the Lord Sai Baba. Wonder not how one particular person or group of people can hear him and bring through their message of his guidance and love. Rather wonder why you do not avail yourself of this also.

The further into unity one expands, the more pervasive one becomes. Baba has come to Earth already expanded, already pervading; all-pervasive is he. Therefore, follow the path that best guides you to him if you seek to know him. But remember that although that path may indeed involve the journey of many, many a mile, it also may be that with a journey of just one breath, one sigh, you will see him and know that you have been one, even as you ever shall be one with Baba and all of the inner-plane ascended masters. Therefore, no division of heart or revelation has in truth ever existed. Where he is and we are, there God is also. Where thou art, there God is also. In this truth is revealed the secret of his and our accessibility and the glories of our sacred communion.

This book was brought forth from within, not in Puttaparthi, India, but in the heart and experience of Joshua, a devotee who called upon his holiness the Lord Sai Baba and found that he was indeed there. Many books have been written by those who have made the physical journey to his outer ashram. These books reveal a great many miracles and open many a heart.

Here in these pages is the story of an inner journey to Baba to his inner-plane ashram, where also a great many miracles take place and manifest solidly upon the physical. This story is told so that others will know that this journey is available to them also—a journey that requires no airplane trip or passports save one: the passport of love and sincerity. That is why Baba has asked that this unique book take shape and form—so that everyone everywhere and of every faith and path could hear the truth of divine oneness and know how Baba is, literally, but a prayer away from your knowingness of him and his miracles of love. Read this book; then know that this pilgrimage of the heart is one that you can take, even this very second, and that he is in truth already at one with and within you. Even as he does call some of you specifically to come to him, so it is equally true that for the rest of you he simply awaits your call to manifest the love and wisdom and the miracles that life would unfold. He is here and waits only to be of service to you.

Ever in the love of the One, we are the voice of the inner-plane ascended masters.

Preface

This book is about how to heal and manifest one's ascension, prosperity and health on all levels through Sai Baba and the ascended masters. Before presenting my 420 golden keys, I would like to lay a foundation and provide a context for a number of the keys presented in the book.

During a certain phase of my adult life I experienced some very serious physical health lessons. In retrospect, I see this experience as a wonderful teacher and catalyst for not only my spiritual growth, but also as training in my development as a psychotherapist, wholistic health advocate and spiritual teacher. Since the golden keys that you will read in this book are ones I have used to heal myself on all levels and to manifest my ascension and leadership, you will see that some of them have an autobiographical flavor.

I have written many books of a more didactic nature. This book is unique in that Sai Baba asked me to write a more personal account of how I applied in my own life all of the information from my books and workshops. I refer often in this book to the health lessons I had to overcome and how I did it; therefore, this is one of the themes of the book. Since in my other books I had not written about my personal life, I wanted to provide my readers with an understanding of how I approached the writing of this book.

I have tried to consolidate the heart of my previous books, and much more, into one concise, easy-to-read, practical volume. This book, then, is the quintessential teachings of the ascended masters as I have applied them in my personal life.

My goal was to write a book that would be a guideline for helping people to heal themselves, achieve ascension and move into spiritual leadership—even if they had not read any of my previous books. This book will also provide insights and serve as a resource guide for working with the more in-depth coverage of certain topics in my other books. To you, my beloved readers, I offer this book with great love. May the words and energy from this book provide inspiration and benefit to you on your spiritual journey.

Foreword
Inspired by Sai Baba and the Ascended Masters

Sometimes it is not enough for humanity to be asked simply to have faith. While faith is indeed an attribute to be cultivated, humanity needs a foundation upon which to cultivate that faith. As is evidenced all around us, the world is in a stage of great and rapid transition. Humanity is being called home to unite the small self with the greater Self, the atman, and the atman with Brahman, the One. This is no small matter, this rebirthing of a planet; and so Sai Baba, the man of miracles, the God avatar, has come to function as a foundation upon which faith can be the substance of things seen, known and felt as reality upon the Earth.

There has been much confusion regarding Sai Baba as well as great elevation and devotion. From the ascended master and esoteric perspective, Sai Baba is a manifestation of the cosmic Christ. He embodies more light and love than any being who ever has incarnated upon the Earth. He is here because humanity is ready for him and, in a very real sense, has called forth his beingness. Part of this is due to the natural process of evolution, which has moved Earth forward to where she now stands, a sacred planet embodying more of the God energy than ever before. Yet humanity itself has played a great role in this evolution through the invocation of light and love, and so has accelerated itself through its own efforts.

Sai Baba then comes forth from transcendent cosmic spheres born of the God-self and the call of the God-self. He comes forth to show the way and the vast potential inherent in humanity, otherwise he would not have taken a human form. He comes forth as a healer, a wayshower and the embodiment of light and love, which he radiates. He comes to teach by word, by the very presence of his sublime essence and by being a living example of humanity's potential. Even though he is incarnated in Indian form and lives in the little village of Puttaparthi, this in no way confines his cosmic mission either to the Hindu tradition or to a specific locality upon the planet. Many devotees seem to know him well who have never met him upon his native soil, for they have met him through the heart light that burns within.

Sai Baba's mission is not only global but cosmic. He is referred to as both Shiva and Shakti, and he is indeed both. As the Earth births herself, the old is destroyed or, more aptly put, transformed, making room for the creation of the new. This is seen all around us daily in every nation, for there is indeed a great upheaval occurring as the old gives way to the new. It is as if humanity as a whole, with lightworkers at the fore as prototypes, is passing through the birth canal again and again as each level and initiation is transcended, only to be faced with the next level as the process repeats itself. Thus do Shiva and Shakti dance, destroying and re-creating, moving humanity to heights never before within reach of the seeking hand and heart. Shiva and Shakti are pure energy. Shiva is the energy of destruction and transformation; Shakti is the creative principle, the energy of manifestation itself, and the feminine to Shiva. Together Shiva/Shakti form a perfect balance of which Sai Baba is the divine representative.

The pure energy of the divine Mother is yet another name for Shakti energy, the coiled serpent at the base of the spine that rises up through the spine and through the head to unite that which we call man with that which we call God. The advent of Sai Baba is the revelation in matter of the coexistence of these two principles and is thus the true embodiment of hu-man, God-man. Sai Baba is, in full and total realization, the divine representative of both humanity and God.

It is important to realize that Sai Baba is an avatar in the truest sense of the word. He was born enlightened, born awake in the full and total realization of his God-being. He is not your average guru, master or even ascended master. He comes forth as grace incarnate that we might know the future of our own becoming; that we, as devotee or initiate or indeed master upon Earth, might see within ourselves a greater potential for more love, more light, more truth and for God actualization. Yet we are not there now, not in the realm of realization or actualization or even in understanding. Yet because Sai Baba is, and is here, we are graced to see, touch, feel and sense the glory that awaits us within our cosmic evolution.

How, then, is one to look at Sai Baba? Naught but through the eyes of love. How then is one to view his miracles? Certainly not through analysis, for they defy any means we might think we have to analyze them. They too are gifts of love. What we have been graced with is a being so utterly pure and divine and God-realized that to try to know him in any other way save the way of the heart is a useless endeavor. Think on love itself. Is not love complete in the act of loving? Does not one demonstrate love through the virtue of its own merit, its own gift? This is Sai Baba, Sai Ram.

Certain devotees are called to follow the traditional Hindu/Indian path of devotion. Others are not, but likewise are called through love by Sai Baba. Know that he cares not by which manner you are devoted to him or how you know him—only that you know him as love. That love is your shrine and your altar and that which is worshipped upon that altar. Sai Baba comes in form, but who he is so transcends that form that to limit him thusly is to limit love, to limit God. To know him, though, and love him is grace; for it is therein that humanity has the opportunity to see the face and form of love itself, unaltered and unveiled.

So it is that Sai Baba has graced the Earth at this time to bring more light and love to lightworkers, and to awaken the sleeping to the truth that God is and that God abides within all. The forces of light and love would awaken each and every one of us, even as they would further awaken the already awake! Thus comes Sai Baba, the avatar of love and light, who awakens humanity to God and who gives to each and every one of us who is open to him even a little, the exact thing we need to take our next step into greater knowingness, lovingness and beingness. For some, miracles are required—and they are offered in abundance. Even those who claim to believe in miracles often are awestruck when in the presence of one, be it the manifestation of vibhuti or an amulet, or the answer to a prayer.

Sai Baba is the manifestation of all of this and more. He is Shirdi Sai Baba of the past and Prema Sai Baba of the future. He is now, as he was and will be, the highest manifestation of God on Earth ever to grace our planet. This in no way negates the divinity of Christ, Buddha and other great masters. This is simply to say that an avatar from cosmic spheres has chosen to come upon our Earth at this heightened time of evolution to help nurture her—and all of us contained within her many realms—along the lighted path. Even as Earth embodies more love and light than ever before, so does Sai Baba bring into manifestation in form more love and light than ever has been anchored upon our planet.

This prelude seeks conclusion now, but therein lies the hidden key: There is no conclusion, no ending either to who Sai Baba is or to humanity's potential. Therefore, we simply say, feel with your heart. Sai Ram.

Introduction
My Personal Experiences with Sai Baba

The Glory of Sai Baba

This is the story of my journey with Sai Baba. In my first book, *The Complete Ascension Manual*, I wrote what I feel is an inspiring chapter about Sai Baba's life and teachings. It is one of my favorite chapters in the book. Now I am going to share my more personal experiences.

The two spiritual teachers who have had the most profound effect on my life are Sai Baba and Djwhal Khul. Even though my entire life is focused in Djwhal Khul's ashram and will be so even after I leave this earthly plane, Sai Baba still seems to be functioning in my life as a cosmic guru, so to speak. Whenever I have any significant spiritual experience in the dream state, it is always Sai Baba who is present. I do not spend a great deal of time devoting myself to him the way his true devotees do, nor do I spend a lot of time thinking about him since I am so busy in DK's ashram. But Sai Baba in his omniscience knows my heart and can feel the infinite love and devotion I feel for him.

It must be understood that Sai Baba is no average ascended master. I am not sure if there ever has been an incarnated spiritual master of this magnitude living on the Earth. Most ascended masters on Earth are at the sixth, seventh, eighth, maybe ninth initiation at most, in the Alice Bailey system of initiation. Sai Baba is functioning somewhere between the twelfth and twenty-fourth initiation.

I have been involved with nearly every mystery school, spiritual path and religion on the planet. I never have come across anyone of the magnitude of Sai Baba. In saying this I am not suggesting that he be your guru or that you change your spiritual path, nor does Sai Baba. Keep the spiritual teachers and path that you are on, for he is in all of them. Sai Baba has been referred to by some channels as a spiritual regent. I would recommend that you use him as a support system for the spiritual path you are already on.

Sai Baba is the highest spiritual being living on Earth. The two highest beings living on the planet are Sai Baba and the Lord Maitreya. Lord Maitreya is the planetary Christ and head of the Spiritual Hierarchy. Sai Baba is the cosmic Christ. Lord Maitreya might be termed a galactic avatar. Sai Baba is a universal avatar. The term "avatar" is used quite loosely in metaphysical circles. What I mean by the term is a being who is totally God-realized at birth. By this definition, Jesus, Buddha, Mohammed and

Krishna were not avatars. None of the great masters who started all of our known religions was truly an avatar as I am defining the term. I don't mean this as a judgment, just a simple fact.

One thing that is unique about Sai Baba is that he is physically incarnated now, which in a way makes him more readily available. Lord Maitreya also is physically incarnated, but he will remain in seclusion until his time of open declaration. This is not to say that he is not available in a spirit sense, but he is not readily available in the sense that Sai Baba has been for the last sixty-seven years on Earth. Sai Baba is literally a walking God on Earth. He can walk on water, raise the dead, turn water into wine and materialize things at will. Sai Baba actually could materialize things out of thin air when he was a child. He never had a guru or any spiritual training, for he was God-realized at birth. Sai Baba has said that there are fifteen signs of a self-realized being. The sixteenth sign manifests only in a true avatar. The sixteenth sign is absolute omnipotence, omniscience and omnipresence. This is the glory of Sai Baba.

I have never been to India. I would have gone in an instant; but since I was recovering from hepatitis and was on a strict diet, there was no way I could have withstood the trip. By the grace of God and his holiness the Lord Sai Baba, my desire was fulfilled—for Sai Baba came to me. I have made a deal with my core group that as soon as we learn how to teleport effectively, the first place we are going to is Puttaparthi, India, to visit Sai Baba.

I am amazed that I had not known anything about Sai Baba until about five or six years ago, even though I was constantly searching out spiritual paths to study. A great many people have told me the same thing. Perhaps each person is guided to tap into his energy at the appropriate time in their lives. For those of you who don't know much about him, consider that you are now being initiated. For in truth, I don't think there is anything in the world I enjoy more than turning on people to Sai Baba. With this preface I will begin my personal odyssey with his holiness Sathya Sai Baba.

The Journey into His Glory Begins

I first became turned on to Sai Baba while dating a woman in Los Angeles. The woman had a brother who had just come back from India. She told me the following story. Her brother had traveled to Sai Baba's ashram and spent ten days trying to receive a personal interview. There were thousands and thousands of people there, and after ten days he finally gave up. He went hiking that day about ten miles from the ashram to a large mountain. He sat on the mountain and prayed to Sai Baba, and passionately told him that he accepted him as his guru even if he never received an interview. He opened his eyes and Sai Baba had materialized ten packages of vibhuti ash in his lap. (Three days later this man was nice enough to give me one of these packages.) The next day on returning to the ashram Sai Baba picked him out of the crowd and he received his first interview.

I was intrigued by this story and began to read Howard Murphet's *Sai Baba, Avatar*. I also wrote a letter to Sai Baba shortly after this. Sai Baba says that he reads all letters although he doesn't necessarily open all of them. In the letter I asked for his help in achieving liberation and self-realization. It was a number of months later that I had my first dream about him. Prior to this I had attended a one-day workshop given by Patricia Diegel, though I had met her ten years earlier through my father.

Patricia is a spiritual teacher and psychic who specializes in helping people chart their level of soul evolution. She has developed a scale from one to one thousand, and she tunes in psychically and tells you where you are spiritually, mentally and emotionally. I was intrigued by her program and had a reading with her. She told me where my evolution was according to her scale, and I felt intuitively that she was probably accurate. Patricia had some background in the Alice Bailey material, so she was familiar with the concept of spiritual initiations. But she had not connected this concept to her system, so her scale didn't tell where liberation is achieved.

I began to play with her material intuitively to try and figure out how many points on her scale I needed in order to achieve liberation from the wheel of rebirth. It was while I was doing this that I had my first Sai Baba dream. In the dream Sai Baba came to me and said that I needed seventy points on Patricia Diegel's scale to achieve liberation in this lifetime. You can't get any clearer than this.

At that time I still didn't realize fully who Sai Baba was. I didn't know that he was a cosmic avatar. I thought that he was one of the many self-realized masters from India. I was deeply moved by this dream, however, and became even more focused on my spiritual path. Sai Baba has said in his books and lectures that no one ever dreams about him without his willing it, so I had been contacted. About two or three weeks later he appeared to me again in the dream state sitting on my crown chakra in a lotus position. He stepped out of my crown chakra and began performing miracles of a most amazing nature in front of a large group of people.

Sometime after that I received a healing treatment from a friend who is very clairvoyant and clairaudient. During my healing she received a message that the masters were calling me. I asked, "What masters?" The guidance was that one of them was Sai Baba. Mr. Dense here finally got the message. From that point on I became immersed in Sai Baba, and this became one of the most amazing periods of my life. I read every book I could find on him. I attended Sai Baba meetings. I visited the Sai Baba book store in Tustin, California. At the meetings and the bookstore I bought many wonderful books and pictures of him.

Each book I read about Sai Baba was more amazing then the last. It was only then that I began to understand his profundity. Very few people truly understand the magnitude and blessing the Earth is receiving at this time. Sai Baba has said that he is the incarnation of the Lord Attatreya, who in Hinduism is the incarnation of Brahma, Shiva and Vishnu living in the same body. He also has said that he is the incarnation of Shiva and Shakti living in the same body. This is his second incarnation of a triple avatarship. In his last life he was the God-realized saint, Shirdi Sai Baba, and in that life he was the embodiment of Shiva. My fifth book, *The Ascended Masters Light the Way*, gives an account of his past as this awesome saint.

Sai Baba has said that he will live to the age of ninety-six and then pass on. He will return again in two years as Prema Sai Baba. To one devotee he even gave a medallion of how he will look in that future incarnation.

Inner-Plane Encounters with Sai Baba

It was during this period that I attended a fire initiation led by Earlyne and Robert Chaney. At that time I made vows of spiritual commitment and purity, which I purposely timed to go into effect at the time of this fire initiation. That night after the fire initiation I dreamed that I was in a classroom with Sai Baba and about a hundred other people. A lot of us in this classroom were going to have personal interviews with Sai Baba. Sai Baba came to me first and tapped me on the head. I went into his office and had my first interview. I wasn't able to travel to India to have an interview, so Sai Baba was kind enough to give me one on the inner plane.

I had many more dreams about Sai Baba during this period of my life. In one of them I was visiting him in his ashram in Puttaparthi, India, and he was showing me around. In the dream I remember saying to him that I couldn't believe that I was actually visiting him like this. In another scene I was in a room with him and some other people. I was overwhelmed with love and devotion for him. I started to cry as I told him how much I loved him. He got a tear in his eye and came over and brought me a tissue, which I thought was sweet. This is a common experience that many of Sai Baba's devotees have. This has been called "bhakti tears," or devotional tears.

In the next scene I performed what is called padnamaskaram. It is the spiritual practice of touching one's head to the master's feet, as a sign of surrender to God. In the dream I remember feeling a little awkward because I am not Indian and wasn't quite sure how to do it. I then had a soul-travel experience that was incredibly sweet in which Sai Baba showed me how his devotees did it. Sai Baba is the epitome of love, selflessness and egolessness.

Another experience with Sai Baba related to a channeled reading I had from a spirit being, Dr. Peebles, who is quite popular in Los Angeles. In this reading I asked Dr. Peebles if he could send a message to Sai Baba, though I don't know what made me think of this. The message was, "I humbly request to be your devotee and student on my path of liberation and God realization." Dr. Peebles took the message to Sai Baba, and Sai Baba sent the message back through him that I was accepted. He added that within a week I would find something that would cement our bond.

The next day I was meditating with a dear friend, Athena. She is clairvoyant and clairaudient, and we would often meditate together. In this meditation she said that she had just received a message that I would find something under my pillow. I was skeptical and didn't give it much credence. However, two hours later when I remembered the message, I looked under my pillow. There was the medallion that I had lost several months before and which was one of my most valued possessions! It was gold and had a picture of Jesus with a dove, a symbol of the Holy Spirit, descending upon him. I had told no one that I had lost it. Sai Baba had materialized my lost medallion for me as an anchor for my connection with him. Now I was connected with Sai Baba hook, line and sinker.

Later I went back to see Dr. Peebles and asked him to deliver another message. I asked Sai Baba for help in achieving my liberation. I knew that I was getting close; a year and a half or two years had passed since that first dream about needing "seventy points." From my calculations I was not too far away. Sure enough, Sai Baba responded and said that I would achieve liberation in April and that he would come to me at that time. It was January when I had the spiritual reading.

On the last day of April I was meditating with Athena again, and Sai Baba appeared and told me that my long-awaited goal of liberation had been achieved. He even performed a ceremony, using Athena as the vehicle and channel to honor this occasion. I was enormously moved. It wasn't until much later, upon getting immersed in the Alice Bailey material, that I realized that at that moment I had taken my fourth initiation. In the Alice Bailey system, the fourth initiation includes liberation from the wheel of rebirth. It wasn't ascension, but it was liberation. At that point in my spiritual evolution I did not yet understand or use the seven levels of initiation.

The Healing of My Pancreas

On another occasion while meditating with Athena, I prayed to Sai Baba for help in healing my pancreas. I still had serious problems with it, including a low-grade chronic pancreatitis. Sai Baba came to us and placed a golden ball of light in Athena's hand. Athena said that it actually burned her hand—that it felt as if an egg was frying in her hand. Sai Baba, using Athena's body, placed the golden ball of light right on my pancreas. He then put a second ball of light in her hands and did the same thing again.

Within a week's time I was able to eat grain and starch and get back to a more normal diet. Sai Baba miraculously had healed my pancreas. There still was a little weakness left, but my pancreas was now functioning within a normal range for the first time in years. This truly was a miracle.

Sai Baba and the Soul-Evolution Scales

One other story has to do with Patricia Diegel. I found out later that Patricia had an appointment with one of Sai Baba's secretaries, who apparently was very taken with her work. Patricia offered to do one of her soul-evolution workups for Sai Baba as a gift to him. The secretary apparently went back to India and asked Sai Baba if he was open to receiving such a gift. He said that he was, and Patricia did a spiritual workup for him.

Patricia told me that Sai Baba was scheduled to give a lecture to a very large group of people. During his lecture he said that he had just received a gift from "the white magician in the West," Patricia Diegel, and that the reading was accurate. Needless to say, this was the best compliment Patricia ever had received. I found this story interesting, since the first dream I had ever had with Sai Baba related to the seventy points I needed to achieve liberation. Sai Baba had personal knowledge of this process.

Later I was able to calculate approximately how Patricia's scale correlated with the Alice Bailey system of initiation. During this period of my life I began receiving inner guidance on my own as to where I was on this numerical scale. I was able to figure out how much I was evolving each month. I found this helpful because usually spiritual growth seems like such an abstract thing. Once I began working more closely with Djwhal Khul, I switched over to using the seven levels of initiation rather than Patricia's scale. However, Patricia had served as a helpful catalyst before I found Djwhal Khul. (I believe that Patricia is living in Las Vegas, Nevada, if you should ever desire to contact her.)

Sai Baba came to me one other time, using his own soul-evolution scale when he appeared to me in a dream. I was in a classroom again and he told me I was at the 800 level. This was about a year before I actually ascended. In the dream in this classroom, I was the most evolved of those in attendance, and Sai Baba was showing us the evolutionary level of different people in the group. This scale definitely was different from Patricia's, but I intuitively knew what he was talking about.

In this same dream I was told I was on the right track and that I should just be sure to stay balanced within the four-body system. I took this to mean to be sure to stay grounded, eat right, get enough physical exercise and not spend all my time writing, which I was inclined to do.

A Summary

These are just a few of the most outstanding experiences I have had with Sai Baba, and they illustrate the profound effect he has had on my life. My three years of complete immersion in Sai Baba were one of the happiest periods of my life. If Sai Baba had not healed my pancreas, I believe that eventually I would have died of pancreatic failure. To this day, any time I need help in any aspect of my life I call on Sai Baba. I will always consider him my cosmic guru.

Nothing compares to his awesome love and power. There never has been a universal master of his stature on the planet. It would be as if Melchizedek, the universal logos, chose to incarnate on Earth. This is the magnitude of the being known as Sai Baba.

Sai Baba Honors All Paths

Whatever your path, you can call on Sai Baba for help. You do not have to go to India and you do not have to accept him as your guru to take advantage of his cosmic powers. He is a cosmic master that is not interested in having you switch loyalties. Most of the time he will actually guide you *not* to switch, the way he did with me. He is a cosmic advocate for all on the spiritual path and a brother to Melchizedek on the universal level.

My life is completely devoted to Djwhal Khul, Lord Maitreya and Sanat Kumara. However, Sai Baba stands as a cosmic beacon of light supporting these masters in their work. It is significant that the medallion he rematerialized for me had a picture of Jesus. He was giving me a message that it was not my path to be focused on him and the Eastern traditions. My path instead lay in the ashram of the Christ where I presently work. Sai Baba actually was pointing me toward my true work before I had fully found it. So use him as a support to whatever spiritual teacher, religion or mystery school you already are involved in.

Sai Baba isn't looking to get all those he contacts into his ashram, as is the case with many gurus. In fact, he does exactly the opposite. No matter to whom you pray, Sai Baba will be there, and he will respond. Take advantage of his holy presence, for never has there been another like him incarnated on Earth. We live in a most blessed time in Earth's history, for God has graced the Earth with his holiness the Lord Sai Baba and his holiness the Lord Maitreya.

One time I asked Sai Baba why he did not speak of the ascended masters. He said that his mission was a global one in which he sought to reach the masses of all religions. However, he said that through this book, he wanted to show his alliance with those he calls his brothers and show his support of the ascension movement. Most of all he wanted me to let people know how he could be contacted by anyone on the planet and how no one needs to travel to India or become his devotee to do so.

How You Can Call on Sai Baba

Sai Baba is with me the second I call, and he miraculously answers my every prayer. He also will do this for you only for the asking. My first contact with him occurred through writing him a letter. Send him a letter if you are so inclined, and pray to him for help. To paraphrase a quote from the baseball movie, *Field of Dreams*, "If you call him, he will come." Tune in to him in meditation. Ask in meditation to go and sit in the love seat of Sai Baba in his ashram. Bathe in the sweet succor of his love. There is nothing quite like the glory of Sai Baba. Once you are smitten, you are smitten for life.

Sai Baba wants you to know that he is here for all. All are special to him. All will be taken under his omnipresent wing for the asking. The combination of your personal power joined with the power of Sai Baba and the ascended masters can raise the dead. This is an unbeatable team. Ask for Sai Baba's grace and help in every aspect of your life. Sai Baba is incapable of turning down a sincere and loving call for help. He is happy to answer any sincere spiritual request. Whatever is your cross to bear, whether health lessons, financial problems, relationship problems, career problems—call on him. With this power you can climb any mountain and overcome any obstacle.

Other Examples of Help

It is Sai Baba who remains with me now as my protector and benefactor, helping me in my mission and removing all stumbling blocks. One example of this was that my publisher was procrastinating with signing a certain document involving my worldwide agent for translating all my books around the globe. This had been going on for three months. Finally I called to Sai Baba for help, and on the inner plane he grabbed the pen and contract from the woman and signed it. Two days later I spoke to her and she had signed the contract.

I asked Sai Baba's help in filling up the Wesak festival in 1995 with 300 people. I ended up having to turn away 200 people. In 1996 I asked Sai Baba's help in gathering 1200 people—and, again, we had to turn people away. Melchizedek, Lord Maitreya and the other masters are helping also, which of course adds to this power. As you can see, I call on Sai Baba for everything.

One time a friend wanted a few more clients, so she petitioned Sai Baba, and within the next few days her flow of clients increased. Another time she prayed to Sai Baba for some vibhuti. Two days later a friend gave her some for her birthday. We don't have to wonder who inspired the gift. Truly you have a wonderful advocate waiting to help you.

Asking and Determination Are the Keys

The key here is that you must ask Sai Baba for help as you must ask the ascended masters. I have been blessed in my life and have overcome enormous obstacles for two reasons. One is because of my tremendous will to live, achieve liberation and serve. The second is that I have not been afraid to ask for help and ask questions every step of the way. As Djwhal Khul said in the Alice Bailey books: "Sometimes the average man surpasses the genius." I am very much an average man.

What I have gone through in this life could have destroyed me. Instead I think of myself as the luckiest man on Earth. If I hadn't experienced these health lessons, I wouldn't be the person I am today. I feel grateful now for the adversities and seeming losses, for I have come many times farther by following the path I have. Through my challenges I was forged in the fires of life. My choice was either to crumble and be destroyed or to become a man of steel. There was no in-between. Sai Baba has said, "It is the mind that creates bondage and the mind that creates liberation."

God stripped me of everything—or I stripped myself of everything —so I would rely only on God. I have given my all to God and the masters, and I have given my all to humanity. As *A Course in Miracles* says, "To have all, give all to all." I have held absolutely nothing back from you, my brothers and sisters, in my books and lectures and workshops and daily life. To hold back anything, I knew, would be to hold back on myself, for in truth we are the same Self. By the grace of God I have given everything and, by the grace of God and Sai Baba, I have been given everything back. For this I am eternally grateful.

Learning More about Sai Baba

I would love to see every person on the planet check out Sai Baba. His teachings are some of the clearest and most beautiful I have found. Only the teachings of Djwhal Khul and Jesus/Lord Maitreya have I found comparable. There is a chapter in *The Complete Ascension Manual* that provides the flavor of Sai Baba's life and teachings. This is an easy place to start. Then there are many wonderful books about and by Sai Baba. Ones that I have read and love include: *Voice of the Avatar*, a collection of quotations; *Baba, the Breath of Sai* by Grace McMartin; and Howard Murphet's two books, *Sai Baba, Man of Miracles* and *Sai Baba, Avatar*. This will give you a comprehensive overview of his teachings. Read these and other Sai Baba books and you will be hooked for life.

I also recommend calling the Bodhi Tree Book Store in Los Angeles to order a video tape called "The Aura of Divinity." Whatever it costs, it is worth it. It is one of my most prized possessions. It is a two-hour video telling the story of Sai Baba's life and mission. It shows him materializing things and performing other miracles right before your eyes. I have watched the video many times, and I am always awestruck by the glory that is Sai Baba.

Sai Baba Resources

Book Stores

Sathya Sai Book Center of America
305 West First Street
Tustin, CA 92680
(714) 669-0522, Fax (714) 669-9138

This center has all of Sai Baba's books and wonderful pictures for your altar. If you are ever in Los Angeles, visit the store. There is a small room that contains one of his orange robes and other belongings where you can meditate. A mail-order catalog is available.

The Bodhi Tree Book Store
8585 Melrose Avenue
West Hollywood, CA 90069-5199
(800) 825-9798 or (310) 659-1733
A mail-order catalog is available

Newsletter

There is a quarterly Sai Baba newsletter that is only $5 a year.
Sathya Sai Newsletter
1800 East Garvey Ave.
West Covina, CA 91791

Sai Baba's Ashram

I recommend writing to Sai Baba at his ashram in India. Sai Baba has said that he answers all letters, not necessarily physically, but spiritually. This was how I made my first connection with him. After that you can simply call him in while meditating and he will come instantly, as will any of the ascended masters. Sai Baba's address in India is:

Sri Sathya Sai Baba
Prasanthi Nilayam P. O.
Anantapur District,
Andhra Pradesh 515134
South India

In closing this introduction, I would like to share two more recent Sai Baba experiences. The first was a telepathic message I received right after the 1996 Wesak celebration for 1200 people. The Wesak celebration turned out to be a tremendous success; however, one of the highlights for me came a couple of weeks after the festival was over. Sai Baba came to me and told me he was very pleased with my presentation at Wesak and with the most recent book I wrote as a gift of devotion to him and the ascended masters. I was very honored, humbled and touched by this feedback, especially coming from Sai Baba, whom I love so dearly.

The last Sai Baba experience I would like to share was another inner-plane dream experience. I was driving on a highway and turned off the road to the right to find myself on a small cliff above the highway. I found myself waiting for Sai Baba. He arrived and I gave him a type of Hallmark greeting card with a beautiful printed message. I found myself thinking that I should also have written a personal message on it. Sai Baba went through his mail. I thought he forgot about my card because he left after he was done. As soon as I thought that, I found my shirt front covered in blood. I was not hurt in any way, and this was not my blood.

I immediately knew this was a great blessing. It was the blood of Christ. Sai Baba holds the position of the cosmic Christ in the spiritual government. I again felt greatly humbled and honored that he would bestow such a wonderful blessing on me. In a somewhat cosmically humorous way, he also gave this blessing at just the moment I thought he wasn't going to respond to my card, which made it even more impactful.

GOLDEN KEYS TO ASCENSION AND HEALING

1

CORE SPIRITUAL PRINCIPLES
Keys 1-53

UNCONDITIONAL LOVE

VIEW ALL WITH THE CHRIST MIND

THE HEART OF COMPASSION: RECOGNIZE THE ONENESS OF ALL LIFE

POWER

SEEK ONLY GOD

SURRENDER AND DETACHMENT

SELF-INQUIRY AND GETTING RIGHT WITH YOURSELF

BALANCE

SERVICE

LIVE LIFE AS A SPIRITUAL WARRIOR

SPIRITUAL VOWS

Unconditional Love

1   The Foundation of Life and All Spiritual Practice

Unconditional love is the premier golden key. It has been the heart of the manifestation of my healing, ascension and leadership. Sai Baba teaches that love is the most important spiritual practice of all. He says that the way to live is to "start the day with love, fill the day with love, spend the day with love and end the day with love—for this is the way to God." This is the foundation of all spiritual practice.

Sai Baba has also said that our physical bodies are a house rented to us by God. We live in the physical body as long as God wills it, and we pay God rent by demonstrating faith, devotion and spiritual sadhana, or spiritual practice—and the number-one spiritual practice is unconditional love. Sai Baba says that the way to immortality is the removal of immorality. Since being one with God is being one with all in love, this is the foundation of everything. Tied in with unconditional love are the qualities of generosity and graciousness.

There are spiritual teachers who have great information and who are great channels or psychics, but if love is not the foundation of everything they do, faulty thinking has entered in. If someone does all of the other golden keys in this book and does not demonstrate love, then they've missed the boat, and true God-realization will not be attained.

2   Transform All Attack Thoughts to Love

The next golden key is an aspect of love that has been a guiding light for me from *A Course in Miracles*. This is to release all attack thoughts. I have made a vow to myself and God never to attack even when I am attacked by others. I will go to any lengths to maintain an attitude of love no matter how I am attacked or ripped off. This is not to say that I don't need to stand up for myself and stand in my own power. But I do it with tough love. This can be a challenging lesson for some people. It is tied in with the quality of humility and what Christ said about turning the other cheek and loving your enemies. It also relates to seeing everything through your Christ mind.

3   Remain in Love, Oneness and Peace in All Situations

This golden key has been my commitment to remaining in love, oneness and peace at all times, in all situations. Remaining in love, oneness and peace is the guiding precept of everything I do. I try to maintain this attitude in dealing with people who are competing or comparing themselves with me or who are dealing with me in an egotistical manner. This leads to an instant attitude of forgiveness at all times—forgiveness both of others and myself. I look at every situation in life as a spiritual test to see if I can remain in this state of consciousness.

4   Practice the Presence

The next golden key has been what I call practicing the presence. This description came from a sweet book of that title by Joel Goldsmith. Every day I would get up and try to practice the presence of God. I realized that if I wanted to be God I had to act like God. Every person, animal, plant and mineral is God incarnate. I would practice greeting every person as if they were the Master Jesus or Buddha or Sai Baba—which, in truth, they are. This helped me also to develop tremendous love for animals. Here I used the "fake it till you make it" approach. I figured if I kept practicing being an ascended master, eventually I would be one. This turned out to be an excellent spiritual practice. It is not enough just to think about God or just feel God. We each must *be* God. This may be the most important sadhana or spiritual practice of all.

5   Holy Instants

This golden key has been the understanding of the "holy instant" as described in *A Course in Miracles*. In this holy instant I am the Christ, you are the Christ, we are all perfect and we are all one with each other and one with God. In reality all else is illusion. This is why *A Course in Miracles* says, "Nothing real can be threatened; nothing unreal exists. Herein lies the peace of God." You do not have to try and become God. You already are God. The spiritual path is undoing or cleaning off the mud on the diamond. Our own faulty thinking has identified with the mud instead of the light. In the holy instant this is all released as a bad dream that was never real in the first place.

6   Holy Encounters: See God in Every Person

The next golden key has been what I call the holy encounter. This also is a term from *A Course in Miracles*, which states that every meeting with a brother or sister is a holy encounter. Every exchange between two people is Christ meeting Christ, God meeting God. This, in combination with what I call innocent perception—seeing the innocence in each person, that which is divine—has been one of my main spiritual sadhanas.

This ideal leads to unconditional love; for if each person is God and the eternal Self, then nothing but love can follow. This ideal is a commitment to

seeing beyond the appearances of the physical, emotional and mental bodies and to seeing the true core of every person. The world is a mirror of our
own thinking. What we see in our brothers and sisters is, in truth, what we
are seeing in ourselves. To heal oneself one must see God in every person
as well as oneself. This also applies to how one sees the opposite sex. Do
you see a person as a physical body first—or as God living in a physical
body?

View All with the Christ Mind

7   *Attitudinal Healing: Think with the Christ Mind*

This golden key involves attitude and perspective. It is our thoughts
that create our reality, and there is always a perspective on life that will
bring you inner peace no matter what your outer situation. This is the science of attitudinal healing. My commitment to thinking at all times with my
Christ mind and not my ego mind has been, I would say, one of the major
keys to my success in life.

When I would get unclear I would write in my journal, for many hours if
necessary, until I would get myself and my life in proper perspective. In
earlier stages of my life I had to do a lot of journal-writing. Now I have had
so much practice that I can do it about as effectively with my mind. Thinking with the Christ mind leads to clarity, steadiness and stability. This mastery helps to produce emotional stability, for our emotions often are an out-
growth of our attitude.

Related to thinking with the Christ mind is the understanding that there
are only two emotions, love and fear. Love-based emotions are expressions of
the Christ mind; fear-based emotions are expressions of the ego. The ego
perceives itself as separate, and therefore fear arises as it tries to protect itself. When you view all through your Christ mind, you see all as one and part
of God, so love-based emotions are what arise. Therefore, your experience of
life depends on whether you interpret life from your negative ego mind or
from your Christ mind. This is the foundation of all spiritual growth.

8   *Be a Love-Finder, Not a Faultfinder—Seeing*
through Christ Eyes

This golden key is also is one I learned from *A Course in Miracles*—to
be a love-finder instead of a faultfinder. I always try to see the best in others
as well as the best in myself. Everything in life is perception. We see with
our minds, not just with our physical eyes. All people are beautiful when we
choose to see life through our Christ eyes.

This gets to the importance of being nonjudgmental. It is okay in life to make spiritual discernments and spiritual observations, but this is done from the heart, not just from the mind. Love-finding instead of faultfinding is a practice of seeking goodness and beauty beneath appearances. Seeing the glass as half full or half empty is a matter of perception. Beauty is in the eye of the beholder.

The Heart of Compassion: Recognize the Oneness of All Life

9   *The Suffering of One Is the Suffering of All*

This golden key has been a major focus for me in the development of compassion. My studies of Buddhism and my devotion to Quan Yin and the Virgin Mary have greatly inspired me in this regard. I learned to really understand that other people's suffering is, in truth, my suffering. The suffering of animals and plants is my suffering. We do not need to take on the suffering of others so that it is debilitating, but we can have the utmost compassion for their suffering. I consider compassion to be one of the most important Christ/Buddha qualities a person can develop.

10   *Oneness with All Life: Sai Baba Stories*

This golden key is that of knowing that we are one with all life and that all life needs to be honored as a part of God. This key is illustrated by two of my favorite Sai Baba stories. The first occurred during Sai Baba's past incarnation as the avatar Shirdi Sai Baba. One day one of his devotees went to the market to get Shirdi Sai Baba some dates, figs and nuts as an offering. She returned home and left the plate of food on the table. When she left the room to change her clothes before taking the offering, her dog climbed up on the table and ate it all.

When the woman saw what had happened, she was aghast and proceeded to beat and kick the dog. She then went back to the market in an angry fit and bought more food for the offering. This time she walked straight to her guru, Shirdi Sai Baba, and offered him the gift. With disdain, Shirdi Sai Baba said, "I don't want it. I have already eaten." The woman was shocked and said, "What do you mean, master? It is still early." He replied, "I already ate, but then you beat me and kicked me."

This story had a great effect on me, and I have tried to remember at all times that I live in all things and all things live in me. What I do to another is literally what I do to myself. The Golden Rule states, "Do unto others as you would have others do unto you." If our true identity is the eternal Self and all of creation is a part of that eternal Self, then anything we do to any other part of creation we literally are doing to ourselves. By the same token, to give something to another is literally to give love to oneself. If humanity would deeply understand and practice this one law, the entire world would change in an instant.

In another Sai Baba story, someone was driving him down a highway and Sai Baba had his eyes closed in meditation in the back seat. The car was going around fifty miles an hour, when all of a sudden the driver saw a snake crawling across the highway. The driver didn't want to slam on the brakes and disturb Baba, so he ended up running over the snake. After doing so, the driver looked back at Sai Baba in his rear-view mirror. Sai Baba's eyes were still closed and he hadn't moved in the slightest. When they arrived at their destination, the driver opened the car door for Sai Baba—who got out of the car and proceeded to take off his shirt. As Sai Baba walked away, the driver saw tire marks across his back. Sai Baba never said a word!

Every person, every animal, every plant, every rock, is God. There is only one identity in the universe for all of life throughout creation—and that is God. We all share that one identity. We must let go of glamour, illusion, maya and appearances so that we can see the true reality of life. Our true identity as the eternal Self lives within all creation. All creation is a part of you. Strive to be harmless and defenseless in all things.

Your brothers and sisters share your identity as the Christ with you. God had only one son and one daughter and we are all part of that sonship or daughtership. We each are apprentice gods who are in the process of realizing this on deeper and deeper levels. This is the initiation process. Learn from Sai Baba's example.

Power

11   Own Your Personal Power

This golden key has been a core tenet of my life. I give it equal status with unconditional love, which no other golden key in this book achieves. This key is owning your personal power. I have made a commitment to owning my power at all times. When I asked the ascended masters what was the key to leadership, they said "empowerment." Owning your power generates inner fortitude and steadiness, both essential for effective leadership.

The only reason I am still in this physical body is because I did not give my power to my physical body when I went through all of my health lessons. I have trained myself over many years never to let go of my power, even when I am sleeping. It has become much easier in my life now than it was in the past because it has become a habit. However, this does not mean that vigilance is not still required at all times. If you heed nothing else in this book, remember these two golden keys: *personal power* and *unconditional love*. Combined, this is first- and second-ray energy, the foundation of God's kingdom.

12 Don't Give Away Your Power

This golden key in my spiritual progression was learning not to give my power away to anything. This is a corollary to owning your personal power. Do not give away your power to other people, outside situations, your emotions, thoughts, physical body, subconscious mind, inner child, ego, lower desire body or sexuality. Do not give away your power to astrology, your dreams, the rays, to any spiritual science or path or to the ascended masters. Do not give your power even to God. God does not want it. God wants you to use it and your love and your wisdom to become a master.

Pray with power, not like a weakling. Your prayers will be much more effective if you do. Astrology is wonderful, but the bottom line is that you are God and God has created astrology. Dreams are wonderful, but don't give them your power and let an unsettling dream wreck your day.

13 Don't Give Your Power to Channels

Expanding on the previous key, do not give your power to any external channel even if it is a person channeling the ascended masters. With all channeling, no matter who is doing it, the information is filtered through the personality and information banks of that person—even if we are talking about Edgar Cayce, Alice Bailey or other great channelers. Also, information may be valid at the time it was given, but not necessarily at a later time.

Remember that even the ascended masters do not have all knowledge. They are only one-tenth of the way toward full God realization. I am not saying that using external channels is not okay at times, for it is. And certainly there are many valuable channeled books. But I am saying to *trust your own guidance and intuition above anything outside yourself*. And do not give your power to the channeling process itself. Above all else, to thine own self be true.

14 Be at Cause in Your Life

The next golden key has been the attitude and practice of being at cause in my life and not at effect. This is the ideal of being a master, not a victim. Being at cause in your life is a major component of maintaining your personal power at all times. Being at cause in my life has been a major key to my success in manifesting. By remaining at cause at all times and using my personal power, prayer, affirmations, visualizations and positive actions, I have been able to manifest everything I need on an ongoing basis.

I have used the power of the Hermetic law, "As within, so without; as above, so below." The mastery of my mind has led to the mastery of my emotions, which has led to the mastery of my subconscious mind and four-body system. This level of personal power has attracted and magnetized all I have needed, because the superconscious, conscious and subconscious minds have been in accord. This, in combination with prayer and using the power of Sai Baba, the ascended masters and God, has provided miracle after miracle. In truth, however, there are no miracles, but rather the natural byproducts of using universal laws.

Obviously I do not have complete control over everything that comes into my sphere of life and influence; but what I do have complete control over is my attitude toward what comes into my life. By committing myself to thinking with my Christ mind at all times and not my ego mind, I am able to magnetize and attract to my life only that which is the highest and most sublime.

Seek Only God

15   *Desire for God Realization*

This golden key has been my total commitment to achieving liberation and being of service. The Eastern religions talk about giving up desire. The ideal of life isn't to give up desire, but rather to have only higher-self desire. My all-consuming desire in life has been to attain God realization, liberation and ascension, and to be of service. I have been completely on fire for these and only these. I have been so completely focused in this direction that I have not allowed my lower self to steer me away. I have sought to strengthen the Christ quality of being focused and maintaining that focus. In Eastern religion this is called following your dharma. I have followed my dharma like a drowning man wants air.

This spiritual fire, in combination with owning my personal power and practicing unconditional love, has cultivated in me the unceasing quality of enthusiasm that is so pervasive in my personality and my books. I love God with all my heart, soul, mind and might, and I am not afraid to demonstrate this. Underlying all of this is my commitment, which I have fortified with an untold number of spiritual vows. I hold onto these vows as my own personal tablets of creation. My personal commitment is not just for planetary ascension, but for complete cosmic ascension for myself and all of my brothers and sisters.

16   Devotion to God

This key has been love for God and love for the masters. This sometimes has been referred to as devotion. I think my greatest inspiration for this quality has come from the incomparable Paramahansa Yogananda. Devotion and purity pervade and shine forth from this great soul. This is true of Sai Baba as well. Devotion in essence is love of God and God's creation. All love begins with love of God. Jesus summed up the whole law with, "Love the lord thy God with all thy heart, soul, mind and might, and love thy neighbor as thyself."

One can give devotion without giving away one's power, and this is important. Djwhal Khul told me that the masters feel and appreciate my love for them. Love for God and the masters has been the keynote of my life. God is my only interest. Beware of false gods and hence idol worship. Some of these false gods are money, sexuality, power, fame and romantic relationships. Examine your life with devastating honesty and see if you are putting anything before God. If you are, forgive yourself and make the appropriate attitudinal correction.

17   A Thirst for Spiritual Knowledge and Wisdom

The next golden key has been my incredible thirst for spiritual knowledge and wisdom. I am sure most of you reading this book can relate to this. I never was interested in filling my mind with meaningless facts. However, anything relating to divine knowledge and to my service has driven me with an insatiable thirst. Spiritual reading has had an enormous effect on my life. Spiritual reading in combination with meditation, prayer, journal-writing, self-inquiry, affirmations, visualizations, repeating the names of God and devotional music all have had an enormous impact on my life. These have been my basic sadhana or spiritual practice.

Surrender and Detachment

18   Surrender to God's Will and Give Thanks in All Situations

This golden key for me has been learning to look at everything that happens in life as lessons, challenges, opportunities to grow and—most of all—as spiritual tests. Look at everything that happens as a gift, and bless every person and situation. This attitude is quite foreign to the ego, but it is one of the real keys to developing inner peace. To everything that would happen in life I would say, "Not my will but thine, oh Lord. Thank you for this lesson." This simple attitude has had a revolutionary effect upon my life. You can surrender to God and still retain your personal power. They are not mutually exclusive. The idea is to do both simultaneously. It works. Try it.

19   Have Preferences Rather Than Attachments

The next golden key has been the attitude of having preferences rather than attachments. Buddha stated in his four noble truths that all suffering comes from one's attachments. During one period of my life, my health—and at times even my physical existence—were seriously in jeopardy. I have called that period my Job initiation. During that time I had to let go of all attachments or I would have been unable to find inner peace.

Letting go of attachments is one of the tests of the fourth initiation, which is the initiation of renunciation. It is very important in life to have preferences, even strong ones. But attachments keep you unhappy, fearful and off-center. The difference is that with preferences you are happy whichever way a situation turns out; but with attachments and expectations you lose your inner peace if things don't go the way you had wanted. This attitude has had an enormous effect on my life.

20   Divine Indifference

This golden key is the cultivation of the quality of divine indifference This is a quality of being the witness, objective, detached, yet still involved. It is the difference between sympathy and compassion. In sympathy you take on the other person's stuff. Compassion retains boundaries and a healthy psychological immune system. An effective person and leader must have this quality. This allows one to respond to life instead of reacting.

Self-Inquiry and Getting Right with Yourself

21   Get Right with Yourself First

This golden key has been the understanding that the most important relationships in my life are, first, my relationship with myself and, second, my relationship with God. If I am not right with myself, then I will not be right with anything in my life including God. Get right in these two relationships first and all other relationships will come into divine order. Before we are ready to serve others, we need to self-actualize. There are many people who are trying to serve from a place of not being right with self and right with God. It is noble that they want to be of service, but they would be better off getting right with themselves first.

22   True Self-Worth Comes from God

The next golden key relates to self-worth. The key insight here is that true self-worth comes from God. It is our spiritual inheritance. Can a son or daughter of God be unworthy? Self-worth is enhanced by focusing on your victories instead of your defeats. It also is very important to compare yourself only with yourself. Do not compare yourself with others, for each of us carries within us a special puzzle piece of God's plan.

23   Commit to Self-Inquiry and Monitoring Your Thoughts

This golden key has been an unflinching commitment to self-inquiry. I see self-inquiry as the commitment to monitoring one's thoughts and being spiritually vigilant at all times. This means never going on automatic pilot. This also means not allowing any fear thought or any other thought that is not of God to enter one's mind. This spiritual practice is so important that Sai Baba says it is 75 percent of the spiritual path. It is the practice of recognizing that there are no neutral thoughts. All thoughts are either from the higher self or from the ego. It is the ego that fears, for the higher self knows that it is eternal. It is up to each one of us to choose who we will serve.

24   Examine Your Motives

This key has been my intense examination of my motives. This is something I would recommend that all lightworkers do in a thorough and honest manner. The negative ego is very tricky, as we all know. In the deepest recesses of our subconscious mind, what is it that truly motivates us to do what we are doing? It takes great courage to fully examine this. To truly realize God and move into the highest levels of leadership, the conscious and subconscious minds must be cleansed of the impurities of the ego: selfishness, narcissism, lower-self desire, hedonism and materialism. The study of motives in the field of psychology needs much more focus than it has been given to date.

25   Commit to Living with Integrity

This golden key has been my commitment to living with integrity. This can also be seen as consistency between my mighty I Am Presence, higher self, conscious mind, subconscious mind, emotional body and physical body. One of the most common weaknesses I see in lightworkers is an inconsistency between levels. The conscious mind thinks and responds one way and the subconscious mind thinks and feels something else. The conscious mind says that it wants to do something, but the physical body doesn't end up doing it. The importance of having integrity and never speaking a single word that the rest of yourself does not follow through on is very important on the spiritual path. When the ascended masters say they are going to do something, they do it. Integrity applies to keeping time commitments, returning phone calls, handling money and every other aspect of Earth life.

How can we expect to be placed in positions of leadership for a whole planet, solar system, galaxy or universe if we cannot stay in integrity with the people on Earth? We need to watch our every thought, word and deed. Everything is written into the soul records. Everything is recorded by our permanent atom in our own being. To be selfish and rip someone off or be inconsiderate or insensitive is to do this to God, for our brothers and sisters are God. The integrity with which you deal with your brothers and sisters is literally how you are dealing with yourself.

The world and other people are a projection screen for our own thoughts. When we learn to project onto life only thoughts of God, Christ or Buddha consciousness in a consistent manner, we graduate—for that is what we are on this Earth to learn. Earth life is a school for practicing being God. What we are really talking about here is having an immaculate, flawless character. The question is, how we are going to choose to live? Many people use the excuse of being human for their lack of integrity. This is another ploy of the negative ego. It is also a misconception of what it means to be human, for human at its highest is hu-man or God-man. To identify yourself as God living in a physical body is ascended master consciousness.

26   Sacred Sexuality

The next golden key has to do with sexuality. One of the keys to my physical healing and spiritual acceleration has been my commitment to be moderate in the use of my sexuality. I am not a prude by any means; however, the more spiritually mature I became, the more sacred became the use of my sexual energies. I began to raise this energy more and use it for other things such as creativity, meditation and brain illumination (ojas). I began to relate to my sexual partners in a more tantric manner. In essence, expressing my sexuality became a much more sanctified act. Sexual energy is life energy itself. My commitment has been to master this energy and never use it in service of the carnal or lower self but rather in a sanctified way.

This takes enormous commitment, focus and self-discipline, but it is well worth your attention. In the attainment of God realization and total self-mastery, sexuality is one of the most difficult areas for many lightworkers to master, and this was a challenge for me earlier in my life. The proper use of sexual energy has a great healing and spiritually accelerating effect on your life.

27   Practice Nonviolence

This golden key involves the principle of nonviolence. This includes for me a vow of nonviolence not only on a physical level, but also on the mental and emotional levels. The ideal here is to transmute all violent thoughts and emotions. When they come up, don't listen to them, for they are a product of negative-ego thinking. It is the negative ego that creates all negative emotions. When you think with your Christ mind, your emotions remain loving, joyful and peaceful. God lives in all things, even insects. If insects invade your home, you have the right to protect your space. Outdoors, however, you must respect their space. Try to avoid violent movies, television and books, for they are vexations to the soul and spirit.

28   Commit to Decisiveness

The next golden key relates to decisiveness. This is one of the most important qualities that every ascended master and leader must develop. The ideal is to be decisive in all you do. Whatever you do in life, do it with 100 percent of your energies. It is better to be decisive and make the wrong decision than to make no decision at all.

29   Develop a Healthy Psychoepistemology

This golden key has been a foundation in my spiritual work and a key to my success—developing a healthy psychoepistemology. This is a term most people are not familiar with. There are certain thoughts that form the basis for our view of the world. These thoughts are called *psychoepistemological thoughts*; they are the thoughts through which all other thoughts are filtered. A major key to being successful is to have a clear and balanced psychoepistemology. I have called this having one's head screwed on straight. If your psychoepistemology is askew, then everything in your life will be askew.

In the ideal state of God realization, one looks at life through the full-spectrum prism of the seven rays, and eventually through the higher rays as well. Most people see life out of a lens of only a small fraction of this God-realized prism. Your psychological lens is determined by the psychoepistemological thoughts that are filtering your experience. The ultimate goal of life is to see life through the lens through which God sees it. Many people view life primarily through such lenses as the inner child, negative ego, desire body, mental body, astral body, physical body, parental upbringing, victimization, cultural programming, educational programming and religious programming. You can see how viewing life through these lenses will cause one's view to be highly distorted and skewed into a very narrow vantage point.

I wrote a masters thesis on this most important subject. The subject of developing a healthy psychoepistemology is one of the most important subjects in the field of psychology and spirituality and probably the least understood. Early in my life I was able to develop a healthy psychoepistemology, which led to my developing a type of Midas touch.

When your own personal lens is in accord with your higher self, your mighty I Am Presence and universal laws, your consciousness will be aligned with the consciousness of God. Then you will manifest abundance on all levels, for abundance is the vantage point of God. Focused work in bringing clarity to your psychoepistemology will be worth its weight in gold.

Balance

30   Live in the Tao

This golden key has been a real guiding light for me. It is *living in the tao*. There is a tao to everything in life. This has to do with the balance of the yin and yang. When surfing a wave, if you get ahead of the wave, you will get dumped. If you go too slow, you will miss the wave. There is a tao to every aspect of life. Learning to remain in this tao is one of the real keys to health, balanced living and success. Learn to listen to this tao and remain within its sublime rhythm. It is one of the keys to developing the Midas touch.

31   Commit to Balance, Integration and Moderation

The next key has been my commitment to these three principles. Early in my life this was a very hard lesson for me to learn, for I was very much a Type A overachiever. Nothing like a bout of hepatitis and pancreatitis to change that modus operandi. My physical body has been my great teacher about the middle path, of which Buddha spoke so eloquently. It is not necessary to be an ascetic. The spiritual path is the path of balance and moderation.

The physical, emotional, mental and spiritual bodies must all be respected, balanced and integrated properly. If what you are doing in your life is hurting your physical body, then stop. The physical body is a face of God. My mind would like to work 24 hours a day, but my physical body rebels when my Type A overachiever acts out. I needed this karmic lesson, because earlier in my life I was not obedient to God's laws. I now listen to the wisdom of my physical and emotional bodies and do not try to override them. I would be lying if I said that I was not still a workaholic, but now I can proudly say that I am a balanced workaholic, not a Type A workaholic.

32   Balance the Masculine and Feminine

This golden key in my evolution has been the focused work I have done in learning to balance the feminine and masculine aspects within myself. This is one of the prerequisites to achieving ascension. This ties in with the need to balance the four bodies and three minds and coming into a proper relationship with the inner child in firmness and love. These are core aspects and the nuts and bolts of the spiritual path.

33   The Hermetic Principle of Gender

This golden key is the principle of gender. This Hermetic principle states that gender is in everything; everything has its masculine and feminine principle; gender manifests on all planes. This Hermetic law, in combination with the law of polarity, has been an incredible golden key in my life, for I have applied this to everything. By understanding the opposites in life I have learned and trained myself over time to balance them. In *The Ascended Masters Light the Way*, pages 130 to 132, I have compiled charts showing comprehensive lists of these balances. Study these and see where you might be too yin or too yang. Do not judge yourself. Simply forgive yourself and set up a program or battle plan of attitudinal healing to make the appropriate character corrections in your personality structure. This chapter also will serve as a guide to provide you with a deeper understanding of the seven great Hermetic laws.

34   Balance Selflessness and Selfishness

This golden key has been my understanding of the balance of spiritual selflessness and selfishness. Many spiritual people are often too much one or the other. The ideal is to be both in the appropriate moment. Being spiritually selfish is an important quality in its place. Many lightworkers get trampled on and then are filled with resentment because they don't understand this precept. The common belief is that it is egotistical to be selfish and spiritual to be selfless.

However, selfishness has a positive and negative component, as does selflessness. People often are turned off to the idea of being saintly because of this misunderstanding. The true saint knows how to be spiritually selfish when necessary. The second lesson here is to be decisive with whichever aspect of this continuum you are choosing. If you are selfish and not decisive about it, you will be filled with guilt. If you are selfless and not decisive about it, you will be filled with resentment. The key is to tune in and follow your inner guidance as to the appropriate decision in each situation.

35   Transcend Duality

This golden key came from the *Bhagavad-Gita* and from Sai Baba. It relates to the understanding of duality. Third- and fourth-dimensional consciousness is filled with duality. There is profit and loss, pleasure and pain, sickness and health, victory and defeat, praise and criticism. In God consciousness, one remains in even-mindedness, equanimity, inner peace, unchanging joy and unceasing love. Duality is transcended and one's consciousness does not become an emotional roller coaster. The psychology of the future is a transcendent psychology and philosophy of life that is higher-dimensional.

36   Transcend Top Dog/Underdog

This key is to transcend all thoughts of superiority and inferiority, for they are two sides of the same negative-ego coin. Fritz Perls called this the top-dog/underdog complex. His guidance was that whenever the top dog or underdog comes up in your mind, laugh it off the stage. Sai Baba and the masters could not have said it better. Most people on this planet are caught in the never-ending flip-flop between top-dog emotions and underdog emotions. They have not been educated to see that inner peace lies in transcending duality and living in the centered spiritual Christ/Buddha attitude. Read *Soul Psychology* for more help with this lesson.

Service

37   The Law of Service

The next golden key is the law of service. Your powers of manifestation are increased a thousandfold if your life is focused on serving God and serving your brothers and sisters in Christ. There is an ancient proverb that states, "One who is pure of heart has the strength of ten." I experienced this in putting on and hosting the Wesak celebrations. The number of cosmic and planetary ascended masters and angels that came to my aid and guided people to come from all over the globe was astounding.

When prayer and manifestation are raised from the personality level to the soul and monadic levels in total dedicated service, the power is increased exponentially. When doing manifestation work, pray and work for the benefit of others as well as yourself, for in truth, the "other" is yourself and the "other" is God.

You are not limited by the boundaries of your third-dimensional body because you are not a third-dimensional being. Currently I am working on becoming a tenth- to twelfth-dimensional being. Sai Baba and Melchizedek are something like 30th- to 36th-dimensional beings. The higher you go, the more you realize that you live in all things and that all people and things live within you. Dedicate your life to the service of humanity, and the entire God force will come to your aid upon your every request.

38   An Attitude and Lifestyle of Service

This golden key can be expressed in the statement from *A Course in Miracles*, "To have all, give all to all." I honestly can say that I have given 100 percent effort on my spiritual path in this lifetime. I also have given my all to help my beloved brothers and sisters. I have held back nothing. I have given all of my love and effort and any small amount of wisdom I might have gathered. I have saved nothing for myself. I can honestly say with a clear conscience that I have given you, my beloved brothers and sisters, everything. I often have given even more than the inner-plane ascended masters might have wanted me to give.

From a very early age I have had a desire to be of service to people in whatever capacity I could. This service has taken many forms besides counseling, teaching and writing books. Sometimes it would simply be helping someone push a stalled car or carry groceries. I became deeply aware as a young adult that anything I held back from my brothers and sisters I was really holding back from myself and God—for the three, in truth, were one.

I didn't care about money; I was just grateful to have the opportunity to serve. When I would counsel, sometimes my sessions would last for four hours even though I would charge the person for only one hour. Money was not my god; helping people was. Jesus also said in *A Course in Miracles*, "Helping my brothers and sisters is my true church." In reality, who was being helped the most was myself. For in giving my all I was receiving all back from God. God was already giving me everything; now I was learning to give everything to myself by sharing it.

I am not saying here that I have not made mistakes, because I have made tons of them. All I am saying is that I have given my best effort and that God has graced me by giving me back all that I have given and far more. I did not give it for this reason, but this is God's law in action. As *A Course in Miracles* says, my salvation is up to me. This statement had a most profound effect on me. It was this insight in action that has gotten me to where I am now. This spiritual practice is tremendously healing to oneself, and it is also a key to manifestation, for it builds an ongoing attraction and magnetism of good karma. Being of service is one of the best ways to release karma and build one's spiritual bank account. When one develops a life-style of giving instead of taking, the gifts flow back in untold abundance. This was also my way of paying back all of those who had helped me so greatly in my life.

It is important to let go of the myths and glamours of ascension and to focus increasingly on world service. The advanced ascended-master abili-ties of teleporting, materializing and dematerializing will come in due time, but should not be obsessed about. The quickest way to accelerate your as-cension is to dedicate your life to serving and fulfilling your part of God's divine plan.

39   *Random Acts of Kindness: A Story*

The next golden key was gaining an understanding of how small acts of service can create a ripple effect and produce major shifts in conscious-ness. One particular occurrence early in my life touched me in a most pro-found way. I had been studying *A Course in Miracles* and was filled with the spirit of God. One day I was driving my car on the freeway and I saw a man whose car had stalled. He was trying to push his car onto the emergency embankment. I immediately pulled over and got out to help him. I ended up driving him for about forty minutes back to his home, and he was very ap-preciative. When we got to his house he invited me in, but I declined. He offered to give me money, which I also declined. I said that I was just grate-ful to have the opportunity to be of service.

He was very moved and said that he wanted to tell me a story. The man was Filipino, and he said that when he had first come to Los Angeles six years ago, he hated it. He had a tow truck and had started a small garage business. But his business was not doing well and he kept encountering enormous prejudice wherever he went. About a year after he had moved there his car broke down and a man stopped to help him in much the same way I had. That man drove him around for two hours helping him take care of things. The Filipino tried to pay him and invite him over, but the man wouldn't even tell him his name. After finishing helping him, the man just left, asking for nothing in return.

The Filipino man was deeply touched that a human being who didn't even know him would do this for him. So he started doing the same thing for people all around the neighborhood where his garage was. Soon this man became extremely well-liked in his community because of the help and service he rendered to people, and it wasn't long before his business started thriving. During the next few years he made hundreds of friends and became one of the most beloved people in his community. As we sat in the car and talked, the man said to me that this other man had helped him five years ago, and now I had done the same thing for him again. I was blown away. I felt so grateful to be an instrument of God in this small way.

Just last night on the news I saw a story where someone was playing one of the McDonald's sweepstakes games and ended up winning a million dollars on one of the tickets. This person immediately sent the ticket to Saint Jude's hospital and didn't even leave his name or address. It was totally anonymous. The McDonald Company usually doesn't allow the transfer of tickets, but of course they allowed that one. I am always moved by such stories. Never underestimate the effect we can have on the lives of people through random acts of kindness. With the ripple effect that these acts generate, we can change the world.

I remember one incident when I was twelve years old. I was in line at a cafeteria and the man in front of me didn't have enough money to pay for his food. Someone behind me offered to pay for his meal. I was extremely touched by this, and I wanted to kick myself for not offering to do this myself. Even at that young age I vowed to myself that if this ever happened again in a restaurant or market, I would be the one to offer to pay. I always have remembered that experience and have kept that promise many times.

Stories of selfless service such as these provide great inspiration for me. This is the real world and the real work. As Sai Baba has said, "Hands that help are holier than hands that pray." Jesus said, "My true church is helping your brothers and sisters." It is amazing how we can touch people's lives if we allow ourselves to be creative and open to the opportunities all around us. I believe that it is these little things that are most important to God.

40 Recognize the Joys of the Path of Service

The next golden key has been the understanding that the spiritual path is not hard work or a sacrifice. As *A Course in Miracles* says, "True pleasure is serving God." I have always related to this within the deepest core of my being. In the earlier stages of my life when I would get out of tune with serving God, I would feel terrible. There was no worse feeling. I learned through suffering and karma that making such choices was not in my best interest. By the grace of God I finally learned this lesson of happy obedience.

I never feel anymore that I am losing anything by following this path, but just the opposite. I feel that I am gaining everything, including health and wealth. In the early stages of the spiritual path, the negative ego may tell you that you are making a sacrifice, that you are giving up something. This is an illusion. This is like saying that trading a grain of sand for infinity is losing something. If you are not serving God, what else would you be doing with your life?

The spiritual path does entail much hard work at times, but there is fun as well—and I wouldn't trade it for anything in the world. The most important thing to remember is that the spiritual path is the path of balance and integration. You have the best of both worlds. You don't have to give up earthly enjoyment to be on a spiritual path. You do have to give up lower-self earthly enjoyment, but not higher-self earthly enjoyment.

An example of this might be the need to give up pornography but not sexuality. Sex between two consenting adults when love is present is a most wonderful thing, from God's perspective. It is meant to be enjoyed in a balanced manner. The spiritual path is not the rejection of the Earth, but just the opposite. Becoming one with the Earth is what ascension really is.

41   Planetary Service Work: Healing the Earth

This golden key has been a commitment to healing the Earth through both spiritual methods and positive action. I frequently end individual and group meditations by focusing on healing the Earth, humanity and all of creation. We do this by sending light and energy around the globe to people, cities and countries that need help. Use all spiritual methods, including the power of prayer, light, sound, visualization and affirmation. And take action by getting involved in environmental causes. An aspect of this work is a commitment to keeping abreast of world affairs.

Once one's complete planetary ascension is realized, there is much less focus on personal spiritual growth and much more focus on planetary service and leadership. This is one of the nice features of achieving liberation.

Live Life As a Spiritual Warrior

42   Be a Spiritual Warrior, Both Tough and Loving

This golden key has been the attitude of being a spiritual warrior in life. Earth life is a very tough spiritual school, one of the toughest in the universe. The theme for our entire universe, in terms of the cosmic day we live in, is courage. To be successful in life and to own one's spiritual power, I learned early on that I had to be very tough as well as loving. It is the integration of this archetype in its positive, uplifting aspect that truly has made me unstoppable. No matter how many times I would get knocked down, I would get back up and fight on toward spiritual victory. I have used all of the adversities that have happened to me to strengthen me on all levels. I believe that this has prepared me for my current mission. The masters know they can trust me and that I am absolutely unstoppable in my efforts.

This becomes easier as time goes on. It becomes an ingrained habit once you have attained mastery over, and integration of, the subconscious mind, inner child, the physical, mental, emotional bodies and the ego. Djwhal Khul has called this the subjugation of the dweller on the threshold. Once this has been accomplished, life becomes a lot easier. Lessons will always arise, but once you are the captain of your ship, setbacks are temporary. Djwhal Khul has said that I have moments where I lose it but that these usually last only a short time, and then I am right back on track. This relates to mastery in terms of the science of attitudinal healing.

43   Recognize That Earth School Is a Spiritual War

One of the most important golden keys for me has been the understanding that life in this Earth school is like a spiritual war. Anyone who doesn't believe this is naive, and I say this with no judgment intended. I learned this lesson very early on in life at around age twenty-two. That may be the number-one key insight that has allowed me to climb and reach the top of the mountain, so to speak. This was reaffirmed by Paramahansa Yogananda in his writings when he said that life is a battlefield. It was reaffirmed by Krishna in the *Bhagavad-Gita* when he told Arjuna to give up his unmanliness and get up and fight, and that his self-pity and self-indulgence were unbecoming of the great soul that he was. Krishna also said in the *Bhagavad-Gita*, "When you fight with love in your heart, no karma is incurred!"

The spiritual war in which all of us are involved is the battle between the lower self and the higher self; the battle between truth and illusion; the battle between negative-ego thinking and Christ thinking. The term "spiritual warrior" is a most useful tool to get you to the higher levels of initiation and beyond. The spiritual teacher Paul Solomon said that the spiritual path was like climbing a mountain. It was up five steps, then knocked down two. Up seven steps, knocked down five. Up four steps, knocked down two. This was how it was even for the most advanced initiates. Since the theme for this cosmic day of our universe is courage, the spiritual warrior archetype is inherent in the way this universe was created.

There are a great many lightworkers who do not embrace this concept enough and who are hence beaten up by life's lessons. I never was naive about what I was dealing with, and every morning I prepared for battle by putting on my spiritual armor. My spiritual armor is my personal power, my unconditional love, my protection, my faith, my trust, my patience and my forgiveness.

The battle we are all in is to climb this mountain known as God realization. It is not an easy mountain to climb, especially on this planet. It is not easy to master the mind, emotions, physical body, negative ego, inner child, emotional body and sexuality, to name a few. Lightworkers also have to deal with negative extraterrestrials and the Dark Brotherhood. The Dark Brotherhood is nothing to fear unless you are weak. The very first step on your spiritual path is when you begin to own your personal power. The kind of war I speak of is not the war waged by the negative ego. That type of war needs to be abolished.

This spiritual war is the fight to hold true to our spiritual ideals under enormous obstacles. It is the fight to remain loving under all circumstances. It is the fight to transcend negative-ego consciousness at all times. It is the fight not to go on automatic pilot, but instead to remain vigilant for God and His kingdom at all times. It is the fight to bring one's brothers and sisters out of the seduction of glamour, maya and illusion. It is the will to live instead of giving in to the will to die. It is the fight to remain in absolute mastery at all times in service of God and the Christ consciousness.

If there is one key to my success in this lifetime, it has been to declare war in the service of God every morning for the last twenty years. This has been the reclaiming of my personal power and the reaffirmation of my spiritual vows. My spiritual war is to retain my spiritual vows no matter what happens in my life. As Jesus said, "Be ye faithful unto death, and I will give thee a crown of life."

I am the ultimate spiritual warrior. It is no accident that my name is Joshua. Joshua was the spiritual warrior king who took over for Moses and led the Jewish people to the promised land. Joshua is also the Hebrew name for Jesus. It is my job in this lifetime to be God's spiritual warrior again and help lead the disciples of all faiths back to the promised land. I am prepared, for I am strong and I do not waver in my convictions. The other requirement is love. My heart is filled with love for God, the masters, my brothers and sisters and myself. You must have both strength and love to be integrated and self-actualized.

44   Positive Anger and the Spiritual Warrior

This golden key relates to coming to a proper understanding and relationship to anger. Much anger is of the negative ego. However, there is a Christ quality that Edgar Cayce spoke of as positive anger—what I like to call the fervor or righteous indignation of the spiritual warrior. When anger arises, instead of squashing it, channel it into personal power, tough love and the spiritual warrior archetype. There is enormous personal power in anger. It is only negative if it is misdirected. Use that energy to right wrongs, exercise, clean the house or meditate. Then it becomes transformed and has a positive effect.

Spiritual Vows

45   Make Spiritual Vows

This next golden key for my life has to do with the practice of making spiritual vows. This has been an integral part of my spiritual work and a major key to my spiritual progress. I have made numerous vows. Usually in the beginning I would make them as part of my journal writing. These vows would bring me great inner peace. I would stick to them like my own personal Ten Commandments. These spiritual vows were the ideals and precepts that I lived by. As the master Jesus said, "Be ye faithful unto death and I will give thee a crown of life." I have been faithful to my spiritual vows and ideals above all else. That is why, by the grace of God, I have been given the crown.

This is not unique to me. It is available to any person who is willing to demonstrate this level of commitment. Your salvation is not up to God; it is up to you. God has given you everything. What of yourself are you willing to give? The key to my success has been that I have not been wishy-washy or indecisive. I chose God 100 percent. By doing this I gave God to myself. God does not create our reality—we do. The key question in life every moment is always the same: Do you want God or your ego to rule in this situation? Make up your mind to choose God every moment for the rest of your life, holding to this conviction like a drowning man or woman wants air, and you shall soon realize your heart's desire. Apply these golden keys I have outlined, and the outcome is as inevitable as the sun rising in the morning.

46   The Bodhisattva Vow

This golden key in my life was taking the vow of the bodhisattva. This is a vow I have made to remain on Earth to be of service to all sentient beings even after I have attained total liberation. I can honestly say that even though I completed my personal planetary ascension, I am fully committed to remaining on Earth and being of service. I truly love people, and I see all beings as God. I want to do everything in my power to help relieve suffering and bring enlightenment to all.

I would not be in the position I am in now if certain key people in my life had not come to my aid, and my heartfelt gratitude toward them is unbounded. With God as my witness, I have and will dedicate my total energies and last breath to returning this blessing that was given me. This is the vow of the bodhisattva as I personally relate to it.

47   Vow to Use All Time and Energy Wisely

This golden key is a spiritual vow I made early in my life. It is never to waste a single bit of time or energy. By the grace of God, I have kept this vow. This doesn't mean that I don't have fun and enjoyment, for this is not wasting time. Fun and enjoyment are an important part of the spiritual path. This spiritual vow has to do with not losing sight of my priorities and staying on the mark.

48   Be a Master of Choice

This golden key has been to become a master of choice. By this I mean that I vowed to remain conscious at all times and not to think, say or do anything I do not choose to do. When the intuitive mind, feelings and instinct are integrated properly, this process can work very quickly.

49   The Vow of Saintliness or Godliness

This next golden key is one in which I've had an interest from a young age. I call this my vow of saintliness. To some this word might have a negative connotation, but it shouldn't, because saintliness is ascended master consciousness. This is a commitment to be loving at all times and never to attack. It is a commitment to live a godly life of service and to be egoless at all times. If you prefer another word, you can call this the vow of godliness.

50   A Vow of Purity, the Brahmacharya Vow

This golden key on my spiritual path was a vow of purity, or what I call my brahmacharya vow. This applies to purity on all levels. This includes purity in the mental body from impure thoughts; purity in the emotional body from impure, negative emotions and lower-self desires; and purity on the physical level in terms of diet, proper use of sexuality and proper action at all times. We are speaking here of maintaining an immaculate mental, emotional and physical diet within and without. This ties in with a commitment to be always vigilant and never to go on automatic pilot. This vow is a commitment to maintain mastery at all times even when you are feeling physically fatigued and/or emotionally exhausted.

51   Vow of Renunciation

The next key was another vow I made, which I call my vow of renunciation. A renunciate is one who renounces the material world and gives first priority to the spiritual world. However, this does not mean that one does not remain involved with the material world. The distinction is that after this renunciation I was involved but not attached. The key is to let go of all material attachments, for that is what leads to suffering. As Buddha says, "All suffering comes from wrong points of view."

The idea here is to remove suffering by grace instead of waiting for life to remove it by karma. If you remain on your spiritual path, all attachments will ultimately be removed because this is necessary for you to realize God. So why not, in this moment, make this vow and put material life—including all relationships—on the spiritual altar and surrender them to God. Tell God and the masters that you put your spiritual life first above all else, that you release all false gods and idols. By doing this you will save yourself much suffering. Make material things preferences and no longer attachments. Once they are preferences, your happiness and inner peace no longer are tied in with them.

52   Vow to Make Your Life Count

This golden key is what I have called my *Readers Digest* initiation. It relates to the stories in the *Readers Digest* of the incredible things people had done that demonstrated the triumph of the human spirit. I would also watch television shows about such people or see stories on the news. I then made a spiritual vow that I would live such a life, not for ego purposes but for the glory of God. It would not matter what I would go through or how great the obstacles. I vowed that I would have a positive impact on the world. When I made this vow and others like it, little did I know what this seed would bring to fruition ten or fifteen years later.

53   Vow to Be of Service and Attain Growth

This golden key was a vow I made early in my life. I vowed that I would make as much spiritual growth as I possibly could in this lifetime, and that I would help as many people as I could. I would live a balanced, integrated life, but spiritual growth and service would be the driving force of everything I did. Spiritual vows such as these have a profound effect on a person's life, especially if you mean them for a whole lifetime and even on into eternity as I did. Making spiritual vows such as these will catapult you in your spiritual evolution as much as the activations from the ascended masters. Together they are an unbeatable combination.

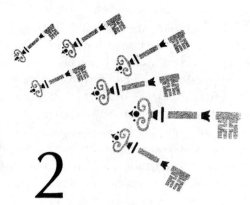

GOLDEN KEYS
TO ASCENSION
AND HEALING

2

HEALING FROM THE
HIGHER DIMENSIONS
Keys 54-76

ARCTURIAN TECHNOLOGIES
HIGHER-DIMENSIONAL HEALING TEAMS AND TEMPLES
HEALING ON ALL LEVELS

Arcturian Technologies

The Arcturians are a godsend. Working with them has been a major key to the resurrection of my physical body, and they have had an enormous effect on the acceleration of my ascension. Following are some of the many wonderful love and light technologies that have come forth from the Arcturians. They use the highly advanced computers on their ships to do this work. Once you are on line, so to speak, in the computer banks of the Arcturian ships, the slightest request is instantly answered. I have found that the Arcturian technologies have produced more healing for my physical body than anything else I have used. It is as if I have my own private healers available anytime I need them. I am much indebted to Lord Arcturus and the Arcturians for their help.

54   *Increase Your Light Quotient and Strengthen the Physical Body*

This golden key has been so indispensable in my manifestation that I use it every day. I call to Lord Arcturus and the Arcturians for a 100 percent light-quotient increase, along with a healing and strengthening of whatever parts of my physical body need attention. Sometimes I ask for strengthening of my pancreas or liver. Other times I request strengthening of my vocal cords or immune system. At still other times I ask for help in balancing all the meridian flows in my body. I do this sometimes before bed and find I sleep better. I also do it after typing for four or five hours. You all know the feeling of how the body can ache after typing or sitting at a computer for a long time. I make this request and usually within fifteen to thirty minutes I feel my entire etheric system come back into balance.

55   *Call on the Arcturians in Extreme Situations*

This golden key is for people with chronic health problems. For those of you with this spiritual challenge, I recommend running the Arcturian energies 24 hours a day on a consistent basis. Keep praying to the Lord of Arcturus and the Arcturians for a 100 percent light-quotient increase and healing of the physical body part that you're having trouble with. If the energy doesn't feel strong enough, ask them to increase the frequency. Keep asking over and over again for an increase until they do it to a level at which you can really feel yourself percolating, so to speak.

If you feel yourself beginning to fade and not feel well again, call them back in and ask for more light and healing in that area. Call in the Arcturian liquid-crystal technology every day followed by the golden cylinder a half hour later. This will keep your field clear and energized.

In extreme situations when I am not feeling well, I will ask to go to the mechanism chamber on the Arcturian ships to be worked on. When I am extremely fatigued and in emergencies, I ask the Arcturians for a total revitalizing and energizing of my physical body. I have found this to be an invaluable tool. I also meditate or take a catnap when I feel tired. In extreme situations you also can call upon Dr. Lorphan and the galactic healers (see Golden Key 66).

56   Arcturian Liquid-Crystal Technology

This Arcturian tool is their liquid-crystal technology. Upon request, the Arcturians will isiphon nto your four-body system and chakras a type of liquid crystal that will immediately deactivate any and all negative energy. Often I will use this process first and then call in the golden cylinder.

57   The Arcturian Golden Cylinder

The Arcturian golden cylinder can be called for directly from Lord Arcturus, and it will be lowered down over your four-body system. It will remove all kinds of toxic energies, and I have used it to remove unwanted implants, elementals, etheric mucous, parasites and any other imbalances on any level. It is like a huge magnet that draws out impurities. Then as the cylinder is lifted up off the body, it pulls out any remaining residue. I have found that combining this with the liquid-crystal technology completely clears my field every time. These tools have been a godsend in the healing of all my bodies and in my ongoing clearing process. They are also ascension accelerators. I use these tools especially during the sleep state anytime I feel myself getting unclear or becoming contaminated from involvement with life lessons.

58   The Arcturian Prana Wind Machine

This golden key is their prana wind machine. I have found this tool to be invaluable. Call for the Arcturians to anchor this into your energy field. It is a fan that is lowered into the heart chakra, and it blows all negative energy right out of your energy field. It realigns and clears your nadis, or etheric wiring, and your whole etheric light grid. It also helps to clear your veins and arteries. It has had a very strengthening effect on my physical vehicle. I have used this anytime I have felt any negative energy in my energy field.

59   The Arcturian Joy Machine

Their joy machine is another amazing Arcturian tool. It has a wonderfully beneficial effect on the emotional body. Anytime I feel emotionally low, I call for the Arcturian joy machine. I'll make you a bet. If you call right now to the Arcturians for their joy machine to be activated, I will bet you ten light-quotient points that you will not be able to stop smiling and even laughing. I have shared this with friends and they have been completely blown away. The Arcturians will send you pure ninth-ray joy, and you will not be able to be depressed even if you want to. Nothing is more healing than joy. Ascension, joy and love are all connected. Use this tool to help cultivate the Christ/Buddha quality in your daily life.

60   Arcturian Voltage Increase

The next golden key has been the use of the Arcturian voltage-increase technique. Often when I'm standing in line at the market or post office and want to utilize the time, I will whisper to myself or telepathically say, "Lord Arcturus and Arcturians, increase the voltage." I will feel an increase in the flow of spiritual current running through my body. It is simple, effective and can be done quickly in the midst of any activity.

61   The Arcturian Plating System

This is a key dispensation I received from Lord Arcturus. This was an anchoring of the Arcturian plating system into our chakra systems. Lord Arcturus said that this advanced technology could, metaphorically, mail a letter in 18 seconds that normally would take the chakra system three months. These advanced technologies, which one by one were anchored in over time, literally resurrected my entire being.

62   Arcturian Reprogramming of Your Etheric Biochemical Makeup

The next golden key is to ask Lord Arcturus and the Arcturians to reprogram your biochemical etheric makeup to make sure it is in accord with your physical body structure. In my case, at one point my spiritual, mental and emotional bodies were evolving faster than my physical vehicle, so the Arcturians had to upgrade my etheric biochemical makeup to create consistency within my four-body system.

Higher-Dimensional Healing Teams and Temples

63   The Inner-Plane Healing Masters

The next golden key is working with the inner-plane healing masters. These healers have been the other major key to the resurrection of my physical body. When calling forth this group of inner-plane healers, invoke your Christ self and your monad along with the inner-plane healing masters. I call them in or feel myself in one of their healing chambers anytime I'm not feeling well, no matter what the symptoms or cause. When I needed them the most, I would call them in many times a day. After you call them in, tell them what you want them to work on. Lie down and rest or meditate and let them work on you for up to an hour.

Following are some special requests that you can make of the inner-plane healing masters:

- Request a complete cleansing and repairing of all of your vehicles: spiritual, etheric, mental, emotional and physical. This includes asking them to repair any leaks or holes in your aura.
- Request to be given shots on the etheric level of the substances you need such as vitamins, minerals, hormones and so on under the guidance of the ascended masters. This is like giving these to yourself radionically or like the request for etheric acupuncture. It works because everything is energy.

I used to get a lot of healings from other practitioners until I realized that nearly everything I needed I could access on my own. This is the finest group of healers available to humanity. The inner-plane healing masters and the Arcturians are an awesome one-two punch for staying in good health on all levels.

64   Restore Your Divine Blueprint

The next golden key was asking the etheric healing team to repair my etheric damage from past lives and this life. This is most important, because otherwise the physical body is working from an imperfect blueprint, and complete recovery cannot occur. Call this team in and ask them to repair your etheric body and bring it to a state in which it outpictures only your perfect monadic blueprint. Working with this team, in conjunction with calling for the anchoring of my monadic blueprint body and my mayavarupa body, greatly accelerated both the healing of my physical vehicle and my ascension.

65   The Acupuncture Healing Masters

This golden key is to ask the ascended master acupuncture healing team to put etheric acupuncture needles in your body to help correct any physical health problems you are having. Ask them to remove the needles when you are complete.

66   Dr. Lorphan and the Galactic Healers

An invaluable golden key in my healing was working with Dr. Lorphan and the galactic healers. This is a highly advanced group of healers you can call upon in extreme health situations. Because my health lessons were so severe, I called on Dr. Lorphan, and he did wonders with recircuiting my energy field and strengthening my digestive system. I use Dr. Lorphan and the galactic healers in serious situations when I need resources in addition to the wonderful healing gifts of the Arcturians and the inner-plane healing masters.

67   Color Baths in the Inner-Plane Healing Temples

With this golden key, request to go to the healing temples on the inner plane and bathe in the color baths. These are pools of liquid light and color. They are the most glorious healing spas. Call to your angels of healing and request to have a healing bath in a healing pool of whatever color you desire. This is a wonderful thing to do before bed because it is so relaxing and rejuvenating.

Healing on All Levels

68   Healing Must Be Done on All Levels

This golden key is to remember that physical healing cannot be completely manifested without first healing the etheric body, emotional body and mental body. Use the tools I have provided in this book to heal these bodies, which are the cause of all disease in the physical body.

69   Clear Using the Fear-Removal Program

This golden key, the program for removing your core fear, has been a godsend. This technology is a process whereby all of the core fears you have stored in your four-body system—from this lifetime and all of your past lives—can be removed with help from the ascended masters. Call forth Djwhal Khul and Vywamus to anchor this latticework technology into your energy field, and request their help in removing your core fears. This can be done in regard to overall fear or with specific fears.

This matrix also can pull out all astral entities, astral disease, gray fields and mental and/or etheric disease and help to mend and realign your etheric light grid with the help of the holographic computer in DK's ashram.

Over a period of about nine months I had enormous amounts of core fear removed from my four-body system. All of the health lessons I had experienced had caused fear to be stored in my organs. Clearing and removing all of these black weeds from my system catalyzed a resurrecting and regenerating effect on me. In just one weekend workshop that I led, the masters removed 45 percent of my core fear for my entire life. This is quick therapy! This technology is available to all. I go into this in more detail in a chapter in *Beyond Ascension.*

70   Remove Etheric Toxic Debris

The next golden key in my healing was to request the removal of all etheric darts, needles and bullets. These negative aspects have usually been deposited from past lives, but they can also be acquired from this life. I was involved in one relationship where the person had a lot of anger and at one point it was directed at me. Dr. Lorphan and the inner-plane healing masters had to spend two days pulling out the darts and needles lodged in my liver.

Every time people attack or get angry at others, they are sending them psychic darts such as this. All this stuff needs to be cleansed and removed. You can see now why people get so sick and why there are so many diseases relating to a breakdown of the immune system, such as cancer. To a great extent it is because all of this inner-plane stuff has not been cleansed and removed. This is why conventional medicine is so ineffective with chronic diseases. They deal with just 10 percent of reality and are missing 90 percent of what is going on in the rest of the twelve-body system.

71   Clear the Etheric Filter through Your Personal Color Coding

This golden key came from an insight that my friend shared with me concerning what the masters referred to as the *etheric filter.* They said that every etheric body has a filter that works much like a lint filter in a clothes dryer. It was built to work automatically, but in most people it has become clogged over time. Thus light has not been able to pour through properly. Melchizedek said that it is of the highest importance to clear this filter. This is done through calling forth one's personal color coding.

Each person has his or her unique color coding. For example, Melchizedek told me that my personal color coding is the platinum ray, the golden ray, the blue ray and the red ray. Melchizedek said that the platinum ray is the direct God-source energy; the golden ray is his ray from the Golden Chamber; the blue ray is the ray of Djwhal Khul's ashram; and the red ray is El Morya's first-ray ashram dealing with leadership. To clear your filter, call forth from the masters your own personal color coding, which will help to clear your etheric filter. I would recommend doing this once a month as a tune-up.

72   Adjust the Etheric Web

This golden key is to ask Djwhal Khul and Lord Arcturus for an adjustment of the web of the etheric body. For those who are too empathic, a tightening of the etheric web may be in order. For those who are too closed down emotionally or psychically, a loosening of this web may be needed. Leave this up to your own mighty I Am Presence and the wisdom of the ascended masters. Most people need a tightening of the etheric web, for it provides more protection.

73   Clear Pets

This golden key has come from understanding the need to clear from pets all alien implants and negative elementals. This was brought home to me after I had had my implants cleared. I had forgotten to have my two cats, Patches and Rags, cleared in the process. Clearing pets is an easy procedure. Just call in the liquid-light technology and the golden cylinder from Lord Arcturus and the Arcturians and make a specific request that all negative alien implants and negative elementals be neutralized and removed from the animals you want worked on.

74   Clear Old Imprints from the Energy Field

The next golden key has been my request to Djwhal Khul and Vywamus for the removal of all negative imprints from my aura. Negative imprints usually are carried over from past lives. They include such things as a sword or knife wound in the energy field. Also request that all irritations and spots in the aura be healed and cleansed. All of these things are very easy to heal and remove if we just know what to ask for.

75   Request a Complete Genetic Clearing

The next golden key was a series of cosmic clearings that literally revo-lutionized and resurrected my entire four-body system. In the first part of this process I requested from Djwhal Khul, Lord Maitreya, Melchizedek and Lord Arcturus a complete genetic-line clearing of all sickness and weakness within the physical body in this life and all past lives.

As part of this, also request to the Arcturians the complete removal of all cancers and disease of all kinds that have formed within the etheric, mental and emotional bodies. Call for a complete removal from the physical and etheric vehicles of all that is not of perfect, radiant health. Request this for your entire bloodline—past, present and future.

76   Cosmic Cellular Cleansing

This golden key is to call forth to Melchizedek, Metatron and Vywamus for a cosmic cellular clearing. This will clear your entire cell structure back through your first inception and incarnation on Earth.

I think you are beginning to see that by calling forth these different spiritual technologies, no matter how sick we are physically, emotionally, mentally or spiritually, we can be literally brought back to life. These are the advanced spiritual technologies of the future that are available now. And the purpose of this book is *to make them available to you right now*. The most amazing thing is how simple they are to use and how effective. The spiritual path should be simple, I think you will agree.

I recommend that you go through this book, key by key, in a systematic fashion, requesting and practicing each one of these procedures. In doing this your entire twelve-body system will be completely cleansed, purified and refined so that there will be no possibility of disease manifesting. This is because you are cleansing the subtler bodies where all disease begins.

These tools can be used for healing, health maintenance and preven-tion. I am showing you a way to heal and evolve on your own without having to pay money to other practitioners. Why should I give you fish when I can teach you how to fish? All disease manifests in the etheric, emotional and mental bodies first. By keeping these bodies clear using these tools and in-sights, you can maintain health in your physical vehicle. Do you have any idea how much money I am saving you? Save your money and come to the next Wesak celebration!

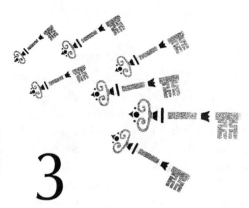

GOLDEN KEYS TO ASCENSION AND HEALING

3

Becoming Who We Truly Are:
EVOLUTION AND INTEGRATION ON ALL LEVELS
Keys 77-118

ASCENSION
ASCENSION SEATS
THE CHAKRAS
EVOLVING THE FOUR-BODY SYSTEM
SOUL AND MONAD EVOLUTION
THE RAYS
HIGHER EVOLUTION

Ascension

77   *Build Your Light Quotient*

This golden key has been the understanding of the light quotient. I have come to understand that building the light quotient is the key to manifesting the completion of one's initiations. The amount of light one holds is paramount. Once I uncovered this truth, I began focusing a great deal of my time on building my light quotient. Sitting in the ascension seats was one of the ways I did this.

The second way was to ask directly for a light-quotient increase during every meditation. I would call for this from the Arcturians, Metatron, Melchizedek and the other masters I work with. I also called to Djwhal Khul and got involved in his "second-ray light-quotient intravenous drip program" (this is the only thing I can think of to call it). Ask Djwhal Khul for this and he will know what you are talking about. Each initiation requires a different level of light quotient to complete.

Another way was to call for the light of a thousand suns to pour into my being. All the light and energy in the universe is available for the asking. You can also ask Lord Maitreya to place within your crown chakra one of his golden rods of light. This will be absorbed into your four-body system and will serve to accelerate the increase in your light quotient.

78   *Stabilize Your Light Quotient*

This golden key is working to stabilize your light quotient. There is a great fluctuation of the level of light within the four-body system and within different moments of your daily life. For example if you are meditating and doing a lot of light activations, your light quotient will rise considerably. You might be at the 80 to 83 percent light-quotient level ordinarily. In a given meditation you might rise as high as 93 percent for a few minutes. Then in daily life it might drop back. But each time you meditate, a fraction more is added to your overall average. The key is not just to attain a high light quotient in meditation, but to stabilize your light quotient at the highest level possible in all four bodies consistently. This is where the real work comes in.

For example, you might be a great meditator, but if you are not psychologically balanced and clear, this will drain your light quotient somewhat. Your every thought, word and deed affects your light. Sometimes people get confusing readings from spirit on light quotient and initiation level because this fluctuation process is not being taken into consideration. Ask the masters what your stabilized light-quotient level is and how much it fluctuates.

79   Call Forth Your Next Level of Light

The next key is to keep calling forth to the masters to stabilize your light quotient at the next level above where you are now. Again, the key is to achieve stabilization. When I stabilized at the 99 percent light-quotient level, I transferred over to the cosmic light-quotient scale. This put me back to a 10 to 11% level on the cosmic scale. No matter what level you achieve, there is always another step to climb on the ladder.

80   Build the Antahkarana

The next golden key has been building my antahkarana, or rainbow bridge. The antahkarana is the bridge of light you create between your personality, soul, monad and God. This basic spiritual work is crucial. The antahkarana is, first, the key to connecting your personality with your higher self. Then it connects you to your monad or mighty I Am Presence. Finally it serves as the bridge to help create the integration of these three aspects of self.

Once this bridge of light is complete, finish building your antahkarana all the way back to God. This is your cosmic antahkarana. This light bridge allows more light to come into the four-body system, which is healing on all of these levels. Building the antahkarana is a key aspect of the ascension process. I recommend working with the chapter on this subject in *The Complete Ascension Manual*.

81   Connect the Antahkarana to the Ascension Column

The next golden key was taught to me by Djwhal Khul. This was a request to the seven chohans or masters of the seven rays to shine through the third-eye center and connect the force of the rainbow bridge—the antahkarana—into the light of the ascension column, through the soul and all the way back to the monad. By doing this the chakra column, ascension column and antahkarana, or rainbow bridge, all blend and merge into one integrated column of light.

82   Widen and Clear the Antahkarana

Another golden key has been the use of meditations to widen and clear out the antahkarana and the central canal. In *The Complete Ascension Manual* I gave specific meditations on how to do this using the spiritual vortex meditation and the corkscrew meditation. It is important to widen the central canal, the planetary antahkarana and the cosmic antahkarana, for then a greater amount of spiritual current can flow through. The more spiritual current that flows through, the faster your light quotient will build and the greater your physical health will be. Be sure to use these two meditations all the way back to Source.

83   Call Forth Your Ascended Spiritual Self

This golden key is calling forth your ascended spiritual self, who already has achieved ascension in nonlinear time/space realities. Ask to merge with it on a permanent basis. The heart of the spiritual path is concerned with healing the separation between higher and higher levels of cosmic dimensions and light. Once you see how the process works, you see how you can use the same tools over and over again, not only in your planetary ascension, but also in your cosmic ascension.

84   Call for the Weaving of the Ascension Fabric

This golden key is an essential one. Call forth to the ascended masters of your choice and request the weaving of the ascension fabric into your physical, emotional, mental and spiritual bodies. Eventually, as you progress into your cosmic ascension, this ascension weaving will be moved to your solar, galactic and universal bodies. This takes you up through the twelve dimensions of reality. Don't limit yourself to just fifth-dimensional consciousness.

85   Angels of Ascension

This golden key was calling forth my angels of ascension to help me in this process. Specific angels in charge of the ascension process can be of enormous value. Ask them for help in completing your seven levels of initiation and in achieving your ascension. Ask them for help in expanding your service work and moving you into your full, true and complete mission on Earth.

86   Ground Spiritual Energy into Your Physical Body

The next golden key is calling forth to Archangel Sandalphon and the Gaia Earth Mother to help you ground all of your spiritual energy into your physical body. Remember that ascension is descension.

Ascension Seats

87   Work with Ascension Seats

A major golden key to manifestation on all levels has been working with the various ascension seats. In *The Complete Ascension Manual* and *Beyond Ascension* I listed as many as 20 different ascension seats throughout the cosmos that I have uncovered in my spiritual research. These ascension seats have had an enormous impact on both the acceleration of my ascension and the healing of my physical body.

Prior to my ascension, I found the ascension seats at Mt. Shasta and Luxor to be particularly useful. After my ascension I most often used the Arcturian light chamber and the Golden Chamber of Melchizedek. I would sit in these chambers during regular meditation. I also sat in them while watching television, going for walks and talking on the phone. At these times I often experienced a bilocation effect from doing the two things simultaneously. When you use these ascension seats, you will be tapping into universal energy.

Following are some of my favorite ascension seats.

- Sai Baba's Love Seat. Travel on the inner plane to Sai Baba's ashram and request to sit in his "love seat." Sai Baba told me that by requesting this you will experience the "love, succor and grace of Sai Baba." I often would come here and bathe in the energies of the glory of Sai Baba. My emotional body is always most pleased to come here.

- Babaji's Seat of Immortal Bliss. Travel to Babaji's seat of immortal bliss in his cave in the Himalayas. Call to Babaji for an ascension blessing and acceleration, and commune with immortal energies. This is much like Sai Baba's love seat.

- The Golden Chamber of Melchizedek. This ascension seat is available through the grace of Melchizedek. Whenever I felt a need for purification and cleansing, I would ask to go into his Golden Chamber and request to be bathed in Melchizedek's golden flame. This had a most wonderful cleansing and regenerating effect.

- King's Chamber Ascension Seat in the Great Pyramid. The ascension seat in the King's Chamber of the Great Pyramid was one of the most powerful and effective ascension seats I have experienced. I would often call upon Isis, Horus and Osiris to help in this work. In conjunction with this key I would recommend studying intensively all information on the Egyptian mysteries and initiation rites. As I studied this material, I would put myself through these initiations, making vows at each of the seven levels. I have made this information very accessible in *Hidden Mysteries*.

- The Atomic Accelerator Ascension Seat. The atomic accelerator, which Saint Germain spoke of in *The "I Am" Discourses*, has had a profound effect on me. Call to Djwhal Khul and Saint Germain to be taken to the atomic accelerator in Table Mountain, Wyoming, in your spiritual body. This will have a resurrecting effect on your entire being.

The Chakras

88   Open the Ascension Chakra

This golden key was my request for the complete opening of my ascension chakra, located in the upper back of the head right where a ponytail would be. This is a real key for those who are hot on the trail of ascension. As you progress, you will feel the energy in your ascension chakra even more than in your crown.

89   The Unified Chakra Column

The next golden key was a request that my entire chakra column be unified into one elongated unified chakra. Just as the monad and soul merge, so do the chakras ultimately merge, as does the twelve-body system. The energy field then begins to operate as a unified whole.

90   Open All the Chakras

This golden key was to call forth to Melchizedek, Metatron and Michael for the complete opening of all of my chakras, all seven layers of each chakra and all facets within each layer. As described in *Beyond Ascension*, each chakra is composed of miniature chakras or petals. The ideal is to open all of the petals on all seven levels. Ask the masters to help you do this. The light will come pouring in and your evolution will be greatly accelerated.

The second key to this process relates to the existence of 330 major chakras. There is a chakra grid of seven for each dimension. Melchizedek told us that there are 48 dimensions that need to be realized to achieve cosmic ascension. As one evolves, the chakras descend downward. At the taking of your sixth initiation, your sixteenth chakra is in your crown chakra. I conscientiously began calling for these higher chakras to descend. By doing this I believe I accelerated my evolution way beyond anything I had ever done before. What previously had taken whole lifetimes to anchor was now being done in six months to two years. I hope that the profundity of these insights about the chakras does not escape you. Every chakra that is anchored allows you to carry more electrical voltage and makes you a larger-watt light bulb.

Call in your higher self in every meditation and request the full and complete opening of all existing chakras on all levels. I found that this not only accelerated my ascension process and the completion of all my initiations, but it also served to electrify my etheric and physical vehicles. This was a major aspect in the resurrection of my physical vehicle.

91   The Universal Chakra

The next golden key was calling forth to Djwhal Khul and Lord Melchizedek for the permanent anchoring and activation of the universal chakra pattern. This is a type of light grid, or divine imprint, that will be impressed upon the core of your being upon asking.

92   Awaken the Kundalini

This key was a request for the very gentle awakening of my kundalini by the ascended masters and my mighty I Am Presence. I also requested that my personal kundalini be aligned with the Earth Mother's planetary kundalini.

I received very firm guidance not to force the rise of the kundalini. I was guided to do the ascension activation work and was told that this would open everything in a most natural and organic manner. I was not to practice kundalini yoga exercises. (The only exception I would make to this is if you have a God-realized teacher who has taken responsibility for your evolutionary process. However, there are relatively few such teachers.)

93   Anchor the Universal Transmitting System into the Chakras

This golden key involved a divine dispensation that I received from Lord Melchizedek for the anchoring of his universal transmitting system into my chakras. Every three or four months I request an increase in the wattage of this transmitting system. This has had a highly resurrecting, accelerating and electrifying effect on my chakras, entire etheric body and my entire four-body system.

Evolving the Four-Body System

94   *Balance the Size of Your Four Bodies*

This golden key is a request for balancing the size of each of your four bodies—physical, emotional, mental and spiritual—for the perfect manifestation of your particular puzzle piece and mission. Some people have mental bodies that are too big that might need to be sized down. Other people have emotional or desire bodies that are too big. There is no judgment in any of this. It is just part of the process of continual adjustments and attunements that often need to be made. This might be looked at as a tune-up on a metaphysical level. This specific work is usually done at the time of your ascension and can be requested if you feel that this type of adjustment might be appropriate for you.

95   *Continue to Clear and Integrate on All levels*

This golden key was understanding that achieving one's ascension, or seven levels of initiation, doesn't mean that one's mental, emotional and physical bodies are completely integrated. There is a misconception that taking the higher initiations means we have attained mastery on all levels. However, ascension and the seven levels of initiation have more to do with the level of light quotient than anything else. Your future evolution on cosmic levels will not progress if the mental, emotional and physical bodies are not integrated properly.

96   *Unify the Bodies, Chakras, Soul and Monad*

The next golden key is unification on all levels. This includes your four bodies, all of your chakras, your personality, soul, monad, the antahkarana and all other aspects of your being. You want these to be an integrated whole. Sometimes in the process of evolution you need to focus on various aspects of your being be so that you can learn the mechanics of how everything works. This is an essential part of the spiritual path. Understanding all of the parts allows you to master and integrate everything in the proper manner. When the lessons of life knock you off balance, this understanding also allows you to put yourself back together immediately.

However, once ascension and self-mastery are achieved, there is no more need to focus on the parts, for everything is functioning as a unified whole. When you own a car, you don't take your car apart and give it a tune-up if everything is running smoothly in an integrated manner. Once you are integrated and unified, it is better to stay focused on this unification. Being a good energy mechanic is an essential tool and skill for all lightworkers to learn for themselves and for helping others.

97   Reconnect the Twelve Strands of Your DNA

This is another one of the major keys to accelerating evolution, and it had a very powerful effect in the healing and resurrecting of my physical vehicle. Call forth to the masters of your choice and your own mighty I Am Presence and request the reconnection of all twelve strands of your DNA in your etheric body. These were disconnected at some point in humanity's past. It was always available to us to have them reconnected, but nobody knew enough to ask.

98   Call for the Spinning of Your Electrons at
the Ascended State

This golden key was calling to Lord Melchizedek and Metatron for the spinning of all my electrons to the frequency of the fully realized ascended state. As I completed my seven levels of initiation, this request changed to whatever dimensional level I was trying to integrate. During the five-year period from 1995 to 2000 I am working on spinning my electrons at dimensional levels ten to twelve. Once the activation of these levels has been partially achieved, then I will be working on the full actualization of all of these levels, bodies and chakras. This is a very powerful activation that I recommend highly.

99   Anchor the Code for Immortality and Call for
the Life Hormone

With this golden key, request Lord Melchizedek to anchor the geometric code for physical immortality into your consciousness and four-body system on a permanent basis. This will trigger your etheric body and entire four-body system to program in the code for immortality.

Another aspect of reprogramming your vehicles for immortality is to affirm to your pineal gland that it now has stopped producing the death hormone. The first time you do this, thank your pineal gland for doing what you had asked it to do, but state that this is no longer needed. Then ask your pineal gland to produce only the life hormone. Continue to affirm frequently in your meditations that your pineal gland now is producing only the life hormone.

Hold the consciousness that you are physically immortal and that instead of aging, your physical body is youthing every day. Using your mental power this way, along with the complete merger of your soul, monad, cosmic chakras and cosmic bodies, makes immortality a legitimate potentiality.

100   Ask Vywamus to Rewire Your Electrical System

The next golden key has been a phase of spiritual work that I have done with Vywamus to rewire my electrical system for healing, planetary ascension, cosmic ascension and global leadership. Vywamus' particular area of expertise is this rewiring work. I would highly recommend calling upon him and asking him to perform this work upon you for the purposes I have stated. This work was an essential part of my own personal resurrection and transfiguration.

101   Open All Brain Centers and Illuminate the Brain

The next golden key is to request the complete opening of all brain centers and complete brain illumination. The opening of these brain centers is one of the keys to activating the entire ascension process. This request should be made on a regular basis in many of your meditations.

102   Open All Mind Locks

The next golden key is to call forth to Metatron, Melchizedek and archangel Michael for the opening of all mind locks so that the consciousness of the divine mind of God can directly see your innermost mind.

103   Spiritualize Your Blood Chemistry

This golden key was to call forth from Sanat Kumara, Buddha, Lord Maitreya and Djwhal Khul for the spiritualization of my blood chemistry by the divine light. I especially like these activations that get into the actual physical structure of the human body and transform it.

104   Activate Codes for Living on Light

The next key was an activation that I received from Melchizedek of a specific geometric code for living on light. I have made the decision not to attempt to go off food completely, but I have noticed much greater light integration after requesting this activation from Melchizedek. I would suggest asking for this even if you never plan to go off food completely as an ascended master. Melchizedek told me that no one should attempt to do this until they fully complete all seven levels of initiation, and even then one must receive guidance from spirit that this would be something appropriate for you even to consider.

I have decided that my path is to fit in with other people rather than be different. There are already enough ways that advanced lightworkers are different from the general public. My personal path is to work with and help as many as I can who are ready for this type of work.

Soul and Monad Evolution

105   Anchor the Monad

This golden key related to my quest for the complete physical anchoring of my monad, or mighty I Am Presence, into the physical vehicle. When you call forth to Djwhal Khul and Vywamus to help in this activation, it will be done permanently. Along with this I would also request the complete anchoring of the soul and monadic lightbodies.

106   Celestial Marriage of Personality, Soul and Monad

This golden key was calling forth to Melchizedek, Metatron and Archangel Michael for the celestial marriage of my personality, soul and monad on a permanent basis for eternity at the 99 percent light-quotient level.

107   Clear and Integrate All Soul Extensions

With this major key, you first request the clearing of the eleven other soul extensions from your oversoul. Then request the clearing of the rest of the 144 soul extensions from the other eleven oversouls in your monad. These are your soul and monadic families. This clearing includes the clearing of all past and future lives of all of the soul extensions in your monad.

In the early stages of your development you were only 1/144 of your monad. To achieve your ascension you must clear and integrate the twelve soul extensions of your oversoul into your being. To fully complete your seventh initiation, you must clear and integrate the other 143 soul extensions in your monad. Thus as you evolve and complete your full ascension, you take on the full power of the entire monad or mighty I Am Presence.

For this clearing, call forth to Melchizedek, Metatron and Archangel Michael for a complete monadic clearing. These cosmic masters will help to clear and integrate all of the soul extensions first in your oversoul and then in your entire monad. If you are totally committed, you can do one soul extension per week. Do this religiously each week until all 144 soul extensions are cleared and integrated. Then the process will continue with integrating your 864 soul extensions on the eighth- and ninth-dimensional levels.

What must be understood here is that this process never stops until full cosmic ascension is achieved. Do you see what is happening here, and how evolution is being accelerated? These are the golden keys to planetary and cosmic ascension that have never been uncovered before this time. Take advantage of them, for they can save you hundreds of lifetimes.

108   Reunite with and Release Soul Fragments

The next golden key has been working with Djwhal Khul in his ashram to gather in all soul fragments. Request that all soul fragments that have been lost now be returned and integrated. Also request that all soul fragments you are carrying that don't belong to you be sent back in divine order. This area of study is quite new to the field of Western psychology, but it is an ancient practice in many shamanic traditions. It is important for people to become aware of the need for this work.

109   Soul Braid

The next golden key was calling to Djwhal Khul and Vywamus for the activation of my soul braid. This is the weaving together of the eleven other soul extensions of your oversoul into your present state of consciousness.

110   Monadic Braid

This key was the calling in and activation of my monadic braid. This is exactly the same activation as the previous one, but it is done for the other 143 soul extensions from your entire monad, not just the other eleven extensions that make up your oversoul.

111   Call in Your 144 Soul Extensions When You Meditate

An essential key in my spiritual progress has been calling in the other 143 soul extensions in my monad each time I meditate. These beings can be incarnated on Earth or living on the inner planes. They have their own free will, so you cannot order them to come. However, you can invite them with the help of the ascended masters. The idea here is to meditate for your entire monad, not just for yourself. All 144 members of your monadic family are then getting the benefit of your meditations. They are connected to you, as your fingers are connected to your hand and your hand to your body. All 144 soul extensions are a part of the monad the way all monads are a part of God.

112   Become a Teacher for Your Oversoul and Monad

This golden key was a request I made to my own mighty I Am Presence and the masters in my ascension lineage, stating my desire to become a teacher for all of the soul extensions in my oversoul and monadic families. I requested to be the one who would ascend for my soul group. I asked that this request be placed in the soul and akashic records and recorded by the karmic board. I began taking responsibility not only for my own evolution, but also for the evolution of my entire oversoul and monad. This is one of the reasons why I would invite them into all of my meditations.

113 Anchor the Cosmic Monad

This next key is one of the truly cosmic activations. Call forth to God, the Mahatma, Melchizedek, Metatron and Michael to anchor your cosmic monad, not just your planetary monad. This can be anchored in only a limited manner, for we would instantly burn up if this were done full force. The process can be started, however. This can be done with the anchoring of God's mystical body (see the section "Higher Bodies" in the next chapter).

The Rays

114 Work with the Twelve Rays

This golden key, which has had a great healing and spiritually uplifting effect on my life, is working with the twelve rays. The combination of understanding the twelve rays and calling them in as needed has been a tremendous boon to my spiritual program. For an in-depth understanding of the twelve rays, read the chapter on esoteric psychology and the science of the twelve rays in *The Complete Ascension Manual*.

Anytime you are deficient in any of the twelve rays and their corresponding qualities, you can simply call in that ray from your own mighty I Am Presence and it will be instantly available to you. If your personal power is low, call in the first, or red, ray. If you want more joy, call in the ninth ray. If you want cleansing, call in the eighth ray. If you are working on a more scientific project, call in the fifth ray. If you want more love and wisdom, call in the second ray. I have found that using the rays in this manner is of inestimable value. Working with the rays is truly one of the great esoteric sciences of the future.

115 Call for the Higher Correspondence of the Rays

The next golden key was to call forth to Djwhal Khul and Lord Buddha for the activation of the higher correspondence of rays eight through twelve within my monad, soul, personality, mind, emotions and body. For example, I came into this lifetime as a second-ray monad and am now a twelfth-ray monad. I came in with a sixth-ray emotional body but now have an eleventh-ray emotional body. I came in with a fifth-ray mind but now have a ninth-ray mind. Through the progression of my evolution I have magnetized my higher rays to take over the functions of the previous rays. This can be invoked directly and will greatly accelerate your spiritual progress.

116   Call Forth the Cosmic Rays

I have used this golden key to complete my seven levels of initiation. It is one of the cosmic dispensations given forth by the grace of Melchizedek. This involves calling forth what I call the cosmic rays. These rays go far beyond the twelve rays I spoke of earlier. The highest and purest cosmic ray is the platinum ray of Melchizedek, and it comes directly from the very innermost chamber of his universal ashram. Below this we have what is called the yod spectrum and the ten lost cosmic rays. All of these are hues of the platinum ray.

Next, at the universal level we have the purest and most refined golden ray that is available. Moving down to the galactic core and the home of Melchior, the Galactic Logos, we have the silver-gold ray. Coming down to the solar core, we have the home of Helios and Vesta and the copper-gold ray. This then brings us to the planetary core, the home of Sanat Kumara and the Buddha, our new Planetary Logos, where we have the pure white light. Calling forth these cosmic rays has had an enormous effect on transforming my consciousness, resurrecting my body and catapulting me forward in my cosmic ascension. I cannot recommend working with these more highly!

Higher Evolution

117   Bring in the Higher Chakras

The next golden key was understanding the process of bringing in the higher chakras. There are three stages in each one of these activations. The first is installation, the second is activation and the third is actualization. For example, I now have installed and fully activated my first 50 chakras, and I am in the third stage, which is learning to fully actualize them. My bodies are installed up through the twelfth dimension, my activation is up through the tenth dimension, and my actualization is on the eighth and ninth dimensions.

So you can install these chakras far ahead of your actual evolutionary level. The next step is to get everything activated. I was told that it was within my reach to activate my first 200 chakras by the year 2000. Then during the first thirty-one years of the next century, the process of complete actualization of all chakras in all twelve higher bodies will take place. It is in the complete actualization up through the twelfth-dimensional level that all advanced ascended master abilities come. The twelfth-dimensional level is the universal level, the level of the zohar body and anointed Christ overself bodies (see the section "Higher Bodies" in the following chapter).

118   Merge the Greater and Lesser Flames, Anchor Higher Monadic Consciousness

My favorite invocation in personal and group meditations was to request the greater flame to descend and merge permanently with the lesser flame on Earth. The constant repetition of doing such meditations eventually allows the greater flame to remain permanently fused with the personality and four-body system while we are here on Earth. This is what ascension actually is. The eventual goal is to anchor and activate the consciousness of six monads from your monadic module; then your entire solar monadic consciousness; then the galactic monadic consciousness; and finally the universal monadic consciousness at the twelfth-dimensional level.

There is so much talk about the fifth dimension. However, I am much more focused on the twelfth dimension, which is full universal God-consciousness fully installed, activated and actualized. Djwhal Khul said that it would take thirty-six years from the year 1995 to fully actualize this level. We were told we could partially activate it by the year 2000.

I share with you in this book every insight and tool that I have used in my spiritual journey. Many of these I uncovered myself in my relentless search, while wearing my spiritual Sherlock Holmes hat. You are getting the advantage of having all of this information in an easy-to-read, practical form right here at your fingertips. Take advantage of it. The key understanding here is that we have been given free choice. The masters are not allowed to help unless we ask.

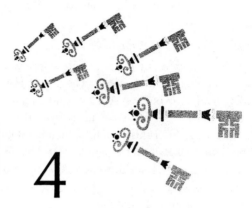

GOLDEN KEYS TO ASCENSION AND HEALING

4

INNER-PLANE ACTIVATIONS AND ENERGIES

Keys 119-176

LIGHT PACKETS
THE TREE OF LIFE
LANGUAGE OF LIGHT, SACRED GEOMETRY AND FIRE CODES
ADVANCED EVOLUTION OF YOUR BODIES
METATRON AND THE EVOLUTION OF YOUR BODIES
HIGHER BODIES
COSMIC PURIFICATION AND UPGRADING
THE HOLY SPIRIT
THE ELOHIM
MERGING WITH COSMIC BEINGS AND GOD
INCREASING THE POWER OF YOUR SERVICE
GALAXIES AND UNIVERSES
ADVANCED ASCENSION SEATS
ANCHORING THESE HIGHER ENERGIES

Light Packets

119   Call for Light Packets

This golden key in my manifestation was calling forth light packets of information from the masters. These are programmed into the subconscious mind and four-body system. I would recommend starting with the light packets from the Great White Lodge on Sirius and make this request to Lord Sirius. After this I would recommend calling forth to Melchizedek for the light packets of information from the elohim scriptures. After you have absorbed these for a while, call in the light information from the Treasury of Light at the 352d level of the godhead. Then call forth the light packets from the Tablets of Creation.

120   Request Light Packets on Any Subject from Universal Archives

This golden key is to request the light packets of all pertinent information from the entire archives of Shamballa, the Great White Lodge on Sirius, Melchizedek's ashram, Metatron's ashram and the ashrams of the Treasury of Light at the 352d level of the godhead.

For example, if you are interested in the Essenes, you can request the anchoring of all light packets of information relating to them. You could request that all light packets of information be anchored from the Alice Bailey books, the Theosophical Society and/or the Tibetan Foundation. You could request all light packets of information on healing from the Hierarchy and Shamballa archives. The list is endless. Literally all knowledge in God's infinite universe is available for the asking. So ask for the light packets of information that are most useful to your current and future missions on Earth and beyond.

You can ask for the light packets of the cosmic Ten Commandments, the Torah Or, the Melchizedek scriptures, the Metatron scriptures and the higher Kabbalah. The effect of receiving these light packets is unbelievable and helps to greatly increase your light quotient.

Call forth to Metatron and Melchizedek for the anchoring and activation of the light packets of information of the codes and scriptures of the luminaries to come. You can also request the anchoring of the light packets from the Nag Hammadi codes, the Dead Sea Scrolls and the scrolls of weights and measures in the Treasury of Light.

121   Light Packets from the Golden Book of Melchizedek

This golden key is the calling forth of the light packets of information from the Golden Book of Melchizedek on the inner plane. This book actually exists in his inner-plane ashram. I have begun the work of externalizing this book for humanity in an easy-to-understand manner. This is a project I am most excited about, and I hope to have it completed and published in 1998.

122   The Universal Information Disk for Translating Light Packets

This golden key was a request to Melchizedek to anchor into my brain one of his universal information disks. This serves as a type of translation orb. This helps to translate the light packets of information coming from the various cosmic sources.

The Tree of Life

123   Anchor the Cosmic Tree of Life

This golden key is one of my favorites, and it has had a profound effect in all areas of my life. Call forth to Melchizedek, Metatron and archangel Michael for the permanent anchoring and activation of the cosmic Tree of Life. Request that each of the ten sephiroth and the hidden sephiroth of Daath be systematically opened and activated. Then request an opening of the seven cosmic seals. This will give you a major activation.

124   Be Anointed with Sephirothic Knowledge

With this golden key, call forth to Metatron and Melchizedek and request to be anointed with the highest triad of sephirothic knowledge with a permanent light grid over your head.

Language of Light, Sacred Geometry and Fire Codes

125   Keys of Enoch Fire Letters, Sacred Geometries
       and Light Packets

Another golden key that has had an enormous effect on my ascension process was calling forth all of the fire letters, key codes, sacred geometries and light packets of information from *The Keys of Enoch*. In other words, you are asking to absorb the entire book through your right brain rather than your left brain. Ask for this to be done in all five sacred languages!

126   *Call for the Fire Letters, Sacred Geometries and Key Codes for the Next Step in Your Evolution*

This golden key was calling for the fire letters, key codes and sacred geometries to take me to the next step of my evolutionary process and to help me realize the twelve dimensions of reality. Make this request to Melchizedek, Metatron and Lord Michael. The fire letters, key codes and sacred geometries will come pouring in and will transform and transfigure you beyond your wildest imagination. Sit and bathe in this miraculous downpouring as long as you can.

127   *Communication System of the Language of Light*

This golden key was calling forth to Metatron for the anchoring of the communication system of the language of light on a conscious basis so that spirit can communicate directly from all levels of creation.

128   *Melchizedek's Cosmic Computer System for Decodement*

With this golden key I made a request to Melchizedek and Lord Arcturus for the anchoring and activation of Melchizedek's cosmic computer system. This most profound cosmic computer will help transfer into your lightbody and etheric body the fire letters, key codes and sacred geometries that have been invoked and programmed. Then it will transfer them into your physical body. It will also help accelerate the process of moving from installation to activation—and then to the actualization that occurs with every anchoring process. This activation had a most profound effect on my ascension process.

Advanced Evolution of Your Bodies

129   *Melchizedek Crystals and Diamonds for Merging with the Twelve-Body System*

The next golden key has been the anchoring of the Melchizedek crystals and diamonds. Melchizedek told me that this would help in the anchoring, activation and actualization process of merging with the twelve-body system. I found this particular activation to be extremely powerful.

130   *Sacred-Letter Grid of the DNA and RNA*

The next golden key is calling forth to Melchizedek and Metatron for the anchoring and activation of the sacred-letter grid of DNA and RNA.

There are 64 facets to this grid, and through continual invoking over time, this entire grid will be installed, activated and actualized.

131 The Biostratus, the Genetic Superhelix

This golden key is to call forth to Metatron for the permanent anchoring of the biostratus. The biostratus is the spiritual genetic superhelix that was lost after the fall and which can now be fully reconstituted.

132 Permanently Anchor the Cosmic Heart

This golden key had a very uplifting effect on me. For this I called to Lord Sirius for the permanent anchoring of the cosmic heart. I don't have complete theoretical knowledge of many of these activations; however, intuitively and emotionally I felt an enormous shift and upliftment in my consciousness through this activation.

133 Anchor the Tetragrammaton in Your Innermost Mind

This golden key was the anchoring and permanent activation of the tetragrammaton so that it might be inscribed on my innermost mind, creating the inspiration for every thought, word and deed to reflect God and qualities of God.

134 Open the Gates of Light at Your Highest Potential

This golden key was calling forth to Melchizedek, Metatron and archangel Michael to open the gates of light at my highest potential.

135 The Holy Scroll of Burning Light in the Third Eye—a Direct Gift of Revelation

The next golden key was to call to Metatron, Melchizedek and archangel Michael for the holy scroll of burning light to be programmed into my third eye and crown chakra as a direct gift of revelation for humankind.

136 The Eye of Horus

With this golden key, call forth from Thoth/Hermes and the Buddha the anchoring and permanent activation of the eye of Horus. This has had a strong activating effect on my third eye.

137   Open the Atomic Doorway in the Third Eye

With this golden key, make a request to Djwhal Khul for the opening of the atomic doorway in your third-eye area. Then request an opening of all aspects of the third eye.

138   Remove the Veils of Light and Time

The next golden key was a request to Metatron, Melchizedek and archangel Michael for the removal of all veils of light and time.

139   Living Energy Codes

This golden key involves calling forth to Melchizedek, Metatron and archangel Michael for the anchoring and activating of all living energy codes so that our nucleic membranes can connect with the larger membrane of the universal Melchizedek and Yahweh God!

140   "The Mushroom Hat" Super Antenna

The next golden key was something that was given to me upon the completion of my seven levels of initiation. This is something that all of you can receive upon completion of your own seven levels of initiation.

This divine dispensation that we were given we jokingly call the mushroom hat, or the Statue of Liberty hat, because that is what it looks like. We received it from Lord Sirius and Melchizedek, and it functions like a large-scale antenna or a sending-and-receiving device. It resembles the top of the Statue of Liberty because it has little windows in it. When we activate it, it spins around and amplifies whatever frequencies we are sending out. This has greatly increased our overall voltage. We spin it whenever we are doing world service and prayer work. It is like God's version of a Nikola Tesla antenna. This has been another advanced universal technology that has served to electrify and resurrect my entire twelve-body system.

Metatron and the Evolution of Your Bodies

141   Anchor the Microtron of Metatron

Another essential key has been the anchoring and activation of the microtron by Metatron. This is a type of latticework of light that is anchored in your energy field and which has an electrifying effect on the entire four-body system. It is another one of these golden nuggets to help you achieve ascension. Call forth to Metatron and request that he permanently anchor the microtron into your four-body system.

142   Anchor the Superelectron

This golden key was calling forth to Metatron for the superelectron to be anchored and permanently activated in my entire four-body system.

143   Balance the 72 Areas of Mind from Metatron

This golden key was calling forth from Metatron the illumination and balancing of the 72 areas of the mind as described in *The Keys of Enoch*.

144   Call Forth the 72 Names of Metatron

A highly transformative key in my spiritual progression has been calling forth from Metatron his 72 sacred names and bathing in the effects of this energy.

Higher Bodies

145   Anchor the Higher Bodies

Each plane of existence has a body connected to it. One of the super keys to accelerating evolution is to anchor, activate and actualize these bodies into your existing four-body system. Over time, your four-body system becomes, in reality, a twelve-body system. Call for the anchoring of these bodies: the buddhic body, atmic body, monadic body, logoic body, group soul body, group monadic body, galactic body and universal body.

Then if you want to get fancy, which I recommend, call forth and anchor these bodies as described in *The Keys of Enoch*: the anointed Christ overself body, the zohar body, the eka body, the epikinetic body, the gematrian body, the higher Adam Kadmon body, the Lord's mystical body, the Elohistic Lord's body, the Paradise sons' body and the Order of the Sonship body. The continual calling in of these bodies in your meditations over time will help you merge with them. Each body is a higher octave of light and frequency than the previous one.

This process of merging with bodies, chakras and chakra grids is the real nuts and bolts of evolution. The principle that ties the bodies and chakras together in this process is the building of the light quotient. My unceasing commitment to calling in these bodies, chakras and the light is what has allowed me to go through three major initiations in one year.

The other key to this process was working in a group body. I could do this because I was able to tap in to the core mechanics of how evolution worked in this total essence state. Once I came to this insight, I saw how it was possible to accelerate evolution way beyond anything that had been experienced in eons and root races in the past. This is available to everyone for the asking.

146   Yod Spectrum to Fill the Zohar Body

This golden key has to do with a specific ascension activation from Melchizedek and Metatron to bring forth the yod spectrum to fill the zohar body. This will help to facilitate the anchoring of the mayavarupa body. This is very powerful, and I do feel my body transforming through this process.

147   The Garment of El Shaddai and the Coat of Many Colors

The next golden key is to call forth in meditation to Melchizedek and Metatron for the full anchoring of the garment of El Shaddai and the coat of many colors. These two refer to the lightbody of Metatron and the zohar body as described in *The Keys of Enoch.*

148   Work with Your Merkabah

This golden key has been to work with my personal merkabah. If you have never worked with your merkabah before, just ask the masters to help you create it the first time. There are many types of merkabah. However, I would recommend visualizing this as a large double-terminated crystal in which you sit. It serves as a protection for your soul-travel work. One of the keys to accelerating your ascension is to call forth to your own mighty I Am Presence and/or to the ascended masters and ask that your merkabah be spun at the frequency you are trying to attain, such as the ascended master frequency or a given percentage of light quotient. The spinning of the merkabah will raise your vibration to the next higher level. The goal then is to work to stabilize it.

Cosmic Purification and Upgrading

149   The Cosmic Fire

The next golden key has been calling forth what Djwhal Khul has called the cosmic fire. He told me that I was allowed to call forth only a matchstick worth of this most powerful energy. However, even this produces a profound spiritual effect. It will completely purify and cleanse your consciousness. In conjunction with this I would also recommend calling forth the violet transmuting flame on a daily basis to cleanse your field and transmute any and all negative energies into the purity and perfection of God.

150 Clear Lower Expressions of the Rays, Zodiac and the Tree of Life

With this golden key, ask to be taken into the holographic computer room of Djwhal Khul and request to be cleared of all lower expressions of the seven rays, all lower expressions of the twelve signs of the zodiac and all lower expressions of the Tree of Life of the Kabbalah.

151 The Twelve Cosmic Stations and Heavenly Houses

Following the above cleansing, call to Melchizedek, Metatron and Michael for the anchoring and activation of the twelve cosmic stations and heavenly houses. This, in actuality, is the activation of the twelve higher expressions of the zodiac.

The Holy Spirit

152 Baptism of the Holy Spirit

The next golden key that I found extremely powerful was asking the Holy Spirit or Shekinah for a divine baptism of living light on a permanent basis. This activation speaks for itself.

153 Holy Spirit Life Force

The next golden key was calling forth to the Holy Spirit, Shekinah, to infuse my four-body system on a permanent basis with the Holy Spirit life force. This process completely electrified and energized my entire etheric body system.

154 Gifts of the Holy Spirit

This golden key is calling forth from Michael the gifts of the Holy Spirit, which are the divine abilities of the masters.

155   Calling to Holy Spirit to Undo Repercussions of Mistakes

The next golden key was something that I learned in *A Course in Miracles*. This is to call on the Holy Spirit to undo any repercussions of mistakes you have made. Whenever I would get myself into some kind of jam in my life regarding other people, I would ask the Holy Spirit to come in and undo my mistakes and the karma that was set in motion because of them. I always marveled to see how in some mysterious way things would get worked out. Never fret when you make a blunder of some kind. God and the Holy Spirit can undo and rechannel the energies in the proper direction for the asking! Then learn the lessons from the mistake and move on.

The Elohim

156   Align with the Elohim Computers

The next golden key is to request to Lord Buddha, archangel Sandalphon, the Earth Mother and Lord Melchizedek that your consciousness and four-body system be aligned with the firing of the elohim computers on a planetary level.

157   The Divine Template of the Elohim

The next golden key was the calling forth to the elohim councils to anchor the divine template of the elohim into my four-body system on a permanent basis. The divine template of the elohim is a light grid of divine wisdom.

158   Anchor the Divine Seed of the Elohim

This golden key was a request to the councils of the elohim for the anchoring of the divine seed of the elohim into my four-body system on a permanent basis. The elohim seed is the "image and similitude of divine creation."

Merging with Cosmic Beings and God

159   Bring In the Mahatma Energy

The next golden key has to do with my work with the Mahatma. The Mahatma, or avatar of synthesis, is a group consciousness embodying all 352 levels of the godhead. Calling in this energy and becoming a cosmic walk-in for this energy has catalyzed enormous acceleration for me.

Throughout the last several years I have regularly requested greater and greater penetrations of the Mahatma energy. This has had a highly accelerating effect on my consciousness. You can acquire a greater understanding of the Mahatma energy and how to work with it in *The Complete Ascension Manual*.

160   Anchor Your Original Covenant of Fire and Light

The next golden key was calling forth to Yahweh, Metatron and Melchizedek for the anchoring, reaffirmation and activation of my original covenant of fire and light with Yahweh.

161   The Father's Eternal Eye of Divine Creation

The next golden key was calling to Metatron for the anchoring and activation of the Father's eternal eye of divine creation as described in *The Keys of Enoch*. Each of these activations will illumine a different aspect of your twelve-body system, ultimately illuminating 200 main chakras up through the twelfth-dimensional level. The first step, however, is to get to the fifth dimension, which is your ascension.

162   Ordination by the Spirit of Yahweh

The next golden key was a direct request for ordination by the spirit of Yahweh as a messenger of light with the authority to teach and demonstrate as a basic pillar and witness to the kingdom of God.

163   The Nogan Shells of YHWH

This golden key is calling forth the nogan shells of YHWH. These nogan shells, as described in *The Keys of Enoch*, help one to experience and contemplate the ecstasy of God. Ask to be completely united with the living light momentarily.

164   Call Forth the Decadelta Light Encodements

The next golden key has been the calling forth of the decadelta light encodements from the ten superscripts of the divine mind. These serve as ascension activators.

165   The Order of Melchizedek

The next golden key was calling forth to Melchizedek to transfer the keys of the Melchizedek priesthood to me as one of his priests, servants and prophets holding and embodying them in divine service to humanity. You can make a request to Melchizedek directly to be initiated into the Order of Melchizedek. There is no need to do this through any outer person on Earth. This is done most appropriately with Melchizedek himself. Ever since I made this request, he has appeared at each and every one of my major initiations and baptized me with his rod of initiation.

Increasing the Power of Your Service

166 Scroll of Light for Your Service Work

The next golden key is to request from the Lord of Sirius and the Great White Lodge that a scroll of light be absorbed into your four-body system to provide you with all of the information you need in your service work.

167 Robes from the Masters

This golden key came by calling forth the robe of leadership, love, wisdom and power of Djwhal Khul, Lord Maitreya and Melchizedek. You also can call for the robe of protection of Archangel Michael.

168 Activation of Messiahship for Greater Service

The next golden key was a request to Melchizedek and Metatron to activate my messiahship within so that I could be of greater service to humanity.

169 The Raincloud of All Knowable Things

The next golden key was calling for the anchoring of the raincloud of all knowable things as spoken of by Patanjali. Through this anchoring I experienced an increase in my knowledge and wisdom banks. I requested that this raincloud be opened in the book of life, and that it be made completely available to me in my service work.

170 Connect to the Master Grids Surrounding the Earth

The next key is to call forth to Melchizedek, Metatron and Lord Michael and ask to be connected to the master grid in terms of your spiritual evolution and service work. Three grids surround the Earth that the masters have loosely called grid A, grid B and grid C . As you evolve you tap into higher and higher levels.

Galaxies and Universes

171 Govinda Galaxy

The next golden key was a request I made to go to the Govinda galaxy in meditation or at night while I slept. I was told by the masters that this helped anchor and activate the permanent opening of unconditional love as an eternal conscious reality.

172 Calling Forth the Energies of the Christed Universes

With this golden key, call forth the energies of the 43 christed universes of this cosmic day. There are many universes that make up the Source of our cosmic day and the Source of other cosmic days. This profound activation is one of the most powerful you can experience; and the transformation that occurs from processing this level of energy is beyond words.

173 The Light Pyramid from the Next Universe

This golden key is to call forth the light pyramid of the next universe from Metatron as described in *The Keys of Enoch*.

Advanced Ascension Seats

174 Great Central Sun Ascension Seat (for 7th-Level Initiates)

As a preliminary to working with the following golden key, God's ascension seat, I have spent a great deal of time in the great central sun/many universes ascension seat at the multiuniversal level. This is an ascension seat one notch down from God's ascension seat. It is one you are not allowed to enter until after you complete your seven levels of initiation—but at least it is one you are allowed to enter on your own. Sitting in this ascension seat with its platinum emanations has had a great impact on me. It truly has resurrected my being and catapulted me forward into my cosmic ascension.

175 God's Ascension Seat (for Group Work only)

This golden key is something I first experienced in a group meditation with my core group. We were explicitly told that we were not allowed to do this on our own, for it would literally burn out our physical bodies. But together, by the grace of the Mahatma and Lord Melchizedek, we were allowed to sit in God's ascension seat at the 352d level of the godhead. This had a more profound effect on me than anything I had ever done.

No individual on this planet is allowed to use this ascension seat on his or her own. But at the Wesak celebration in Mt. Shasta in 1996, as a special divine dispensation, the entire group was allowed to experience this, and the energy was beyond description. This was allowed because the 1200 people present formed a group body that was able to handle the voltage. However, even in that situation we were given only the smallest fraction of this awesome energy.

Even when a person channels Melchizedek, the Universal Logos, only one percent of the energy of Melchizedek is accessed. The amount of energy received from God's ascension seat is much less. But even though this is the case, that fraction of one percent was the most powerful energy that people on this planet have ever accessed. Is this a carrot to come to Wesak, or what? Come to the next Wesak to experience this. We will do this together each year. This is an example of what can be received on occasion through a divine dispensation.

Anchoring These Higher Energies

176 *Calling for the Mini Tornadoes*

This golden key is to call forth the mini tornadoes after your meditations to help weave and sew in, on a permanent basis, the energies you have invoked. This is something you will actually see taking place if you look clairvoyantly at the process.

Words cannot describe the impact of these activations. The effect of such activations is far beyond the level of our consciousness to grasp except with the intuitive mind. All I can say is that the period of my life when I was doing these activations was the greatest period of accelerated spiritual growth I have experienced in this lifetime!

The continual calling in of these energies occurs during certain periods in our evolution. Then at some point these energies will remain with you permanently. Now that I have completed my seven levels of initiation and ascension, I don't do all of the invoking I used to do because many things are activated and integrated. I invoke only those energies that are important to the next step in my cosmic ascension process.

GOLDEN KEYS TO ASCENSION AND HEALING

5

MANIFESTATION: PRINCIPLES AND PRACTICES

Keys 177-221

MANIFESTATION PRAYERS AND ACTIVATIONS
WORKING WITH THE SUBCONSCIOUS MIND
GUIDELINES FOR PRAYER, AFFIRMATION AND VISUALIZATION
SOME TOOLS FOR MANIFESTATION
SPECIAL HELP FROM THE MASTERS
FROM THE VANTAGE POINT OF GOD
PRINCIPLES AND LAWS OF MANIFESTATION
ATTITUDES FOR MANIFESTATION
GIVING AND GRATITUDE
KARMA
MANIFESTATION STORIES
THE POWER OF VISUALIZATION

Manifestation Prayers and Activations

177   *The Huna Method of Prayer*

This golden key, the Huna method of prayer, is an invaluable tool for manifestation. The Huna teachings come from Hawaii. The channelings of the spiritual teacher Paul Solomon refer to Huna as the purest form of psychology and religion on the planet. The kahunas taught a method of prayer that I have been using for almost fifteen years. It is the most powerful method of prayer I have found. I usually use it only for bigger things.

The kahunas taught that the key to effective prayer is to write out your prayer request in very specific and visual terms, then address it to God, your mighty I Am Presence and the ascended masters to whom you are sending it.

Say this prayer three times out loud, then command your subconscious mind to take this prayer with all the mana and vital force needed to manifest the prayer to the source of your being. I have had the most miraculous results with this prayer method. I have used it many times for very important matters and spiritual concerns in my life, and it has never failed me. I have a full chapter on the Huna prayer method in *Beyond Ascension*. It gives examples of a number of very powerful Huna prayers.

The combination of this Huna prayer method and calling on Sai Baba for help in meditation with the benefit of his omnipotence, omniscience and omnipresence has been an awesome combination. These, in combination with my prayers to Djwhal Khul, Lord Maitreya and Melchizedek, who form my ascension lineage, have been the three types of prayer that have supported my success in manifesting.

In my study of the Huna teachings I came to understand more fully that manifestation must be addressed on all three levels simultaneously for the most success. I have summed this up with the following statement: *God, my personal power and the power of my subconscious mind are an unbeatable manifestation team.* My life has been a dance of moving from personal power and positive action to prayer, positive attitude and affirmations.

The kahunas also taught that before doing any prayer work one should build up the vital force and mana that is sent with the prayer through the power of the subconscious mind. This vital force can be naturally built up by always praying from a consciousness of personal power and enthusiasm. It also can be built up by deep breathing or physical exercise, especially a centering exercise such as Tai Chi. You also can ask for an increase from God and the masters, or you can command your subconscious mind to create an increase. The vital force is used in some mysterious way to assist in the manifestation of your prayer request. The ascended masters have confirmed this.

178 Prayers to Ganesha

The next golden key is working with Ganesha, the elephant god of Eastern lore who is known for removing obstacles. Ganesha is quite real and has tremendous powers in this arena. The combination of Sai Baba; Huna prayers; the trinity of Melchizedek, Lord Maitreya and Djwhal Khul; plus Ganesha is guaranteed to remove all obstacles in your life no matter what they might be.

You can call on Ganesha directly, or there is a ceremony I wrote up in *Cosmic Ascension*. In this ceremony you call in Ganesha, crack open a coconut and chant a specific mantra. Then leave the coconut as an offering. This works! I ask for Ganesha's help in all areas of my life.

Working with the Subconscious Mind

179 The Subconscious Mind Letter

The next golden key is called the subconscious mind letter. You can do this whenever you feel the need or have this as a separate section of your journal. I would write a letter to my subconscious mind and talk to it as I would a child or younger brother and explain to it how I want it to cooperate and work with me. I often would do this in conjunction with letters to my higher self or God. Over time this helped to integrate my three minds.

180 Autosuggestions: Working with Subconscious Mind in Meditation and before Sleep

The next golden key has been the science of autosuggestion. For a great many years every night while I was falling asleep and in the morning when I would wake up I would stay in that hypnogogic state between sleep and wakefulness and give myself hypnotic suggestions. I would program perfect health, wealth, success, a full client load—whatever I needed or wanted. Suggestions given at these times go right into the subconscious mind. I would also often do this at the end of my meditations while still in an altered state. While in meditation you are in closer contact with spirit and the masters, so you really have their ear, so to speak. You also are in an altered state of consciousness, so the subconscious mind is in a hyper-suggestible state.

181   *The Power of Your Subconscious Mind*

I recommend that you read the book *The Power of Your Subconscious Mind* by Joseph Murphy. Early in my spiritual journey this book helped me understand how the subconscious mind works. It isn't especially good for understanding personal power or prayer, but it is excellent for learning to utilize the power of your subconscious mind. The incredible power of your subconscious is available at your beck and call. Now you can learn to utilize it consciously as a powerful tool of manifestation. This is where the miracles and the magic happen!

Guidelines for Prayer, Affirmation and Visualization

182   *State Affirmations and Prayers in Positive Language*

The next golden key has been to word all my affirmations and prayers in positive language. Otherwise, the subconscious mind, having no reasoning power, can manifest the opposite of what you want. For example, state *I choose to eat only healthy food* rather than *I will not eat junk food*, for the subconscious mind does not compute "not." If you want to heal a broken leg, state that your leg is now powerful, healed and whole. In other words, state what you want, not what you don't want. This sounds like a very simple point, but it is extremely important in learning how to manifest effectively.

183   *Use the Five Inner Senses to Enhance Visualization*

The next golden key has been the use of my five inner senses in visualization work. By this I mean that I would experience the positive results through inner seeing, hearing, tasting, smelling and feeling. I also would experience an inner knowing. My visualization would become so real that it would be hard to differentiate it from my present-day reality. When the positive visualization has become that real, it usually is a very short time until it actually manifests.

184   *Allow Manifestation to Unfold; Under- and Overpraying*

The next key relates to allowing things to unfold in the manifestation process. This can be likened to planting seeds in a garden. After planting seeds you don't dig them up every day to see if they are growing. Everything grows in its proper season and divine timing. If you are constantly digging it up to see why it is not growing, it never will be able to grow. This brings up again the issues of faith, patience, and trust in God and God's laws. Once the manifestation work has been done, let go of it.

This brings up the issue, in all forms of manifestation work, that one can underpray or overpray. There is no hard and fast rule on this. Many people do not pray enough, and this prevents spirit, the ascended masters and angels from entering their lives. Higher beings must be invited in before they can intervene. It also is possible to overpray out of fear and lack of faith. However, it is better to pray than worry, for worry is fear. Just know that God and the masters answer all prayers. There is nothing wrong with repeating your prayers, affirmations and visualizations, and each person and situation will be different in this regard.

For some, one prayer is all that is needed. For others, more prayer will be necessary. Sometimes you might use the repetition of a certain prayer as you would an affirmation, and that is fine. However, one can do too many affirmations and not allow the process to come to fruition. At other times repeated prayers and affirmations are important in order to reprogram your subconscious mind. In some cases you might need to say the same prayer twice a day for an entire year, and in other cases just one prayer is all you need. The guideline here is that if you worry, it is time to pray again and/or do more positive affirmations and visualizations.

185 Don't Limit How Things Manifest

The next golden key was learning not to limit God in terms of how He could help me. When I would pray to God, Sai Baba and the masters, I would not restrict myself to thinking that my prayers could manifest in only one particular manner. God works in mysterious ways. Sometimes we limit God by thinking things have to be a certain way.

There is the classic story in which there is a great flood, and a man prays to God for help while he is standing on the roof of his flooded home. First neighbors come by to help, but he refused their help because he was waiting for God to rescue him. Then a boat came by and he refused help again. Finally a helicopter came to save him from the flood, and again he refused this help.

Finally the flood washed away his house and the man died. He found himself at the pearly gates and said to God and Saint Peter, "Why didn't you answer my prayers?" God replied, "What do you mean? Who do you think sent you your neighbors, the boat and the helicopter?" Be careful that you do not prevent God's blessings and bounty from flowing to you. Let God have free rein to help you as He sees fit rather than as you see fit. Miracles often happen in the most unexpected ways.

186   Surrender to God, Release Attachments and Harness the Power of the Mind

The next golden key is releasing attachment to whatever you want to manifest. I make all my prayers as prayer preference, not prayer attachments. I tell God that this is my strong preference, but if it doesn't happen, I will still be happy. This attitude is critical to manifesting in all areas of life.

By cosmic law what you are attached to, you push away from yourself. If you want something so much that your happiness is on the line, then maybe what you are praying for is not what you really need. God and the masters will take this into consideration. God will not give you the fulfillment of your negative ego's desires—and it is a good thing, or we would all be in trouble. However, your subconscious mind *will* give you your negative ego's desires. The subconscious mind has no reasoning ability, so it will attract the negative as readily as the positive if that is what you are asking for, consciously or unconsciously. Therefore be careful of what you ask for and affirm.

To me having nothing and everything are rather similar. How is this so? In both situations we can choose to maintain a consciousness of inner peace, happiness, surrender, acceptance, even-mindedness and holding a vision of perfection. It is because I maintained that consciousness during a period when everything had been taken away that I now have it all back and far more. If I lost it all in an instant, I would know exactly what to do to get it all back again. So getting as sick as I did and losing everything was probably the best thing that ever happened to me. I am not saying that I want to go through it again. What I am saying is that it provided me with the ultimate test, the ultimate opportunity to practice what I preached, for it forced me to choose God 100 percent or die.

Many choose death, and I have great compassion for their decisions. I chose life and God 100 percent, and I chose to make my life a living testimony of my love and faith in Him regardless of the degree of my suffering—physically, emotionally, mentally, spiritually, professionally, financially and socially. If I couldn't run, I would walk. If I couldn't walk, I would crawl. If I couldn't crawl, I would rest. What I went through forced me to develop the most exacting self-mastery and self-discipline, or I wouldn't have made it. In reality it was the fire that molded me to achieve God-consciousness.

187   Ask with Expectancy

The next golden key has been expectancy. After you pray, affirm and visualize, remain in that state of expectancy. Believe in God, Sai Baba, the ascended masters and angels. Believe in your personal power, the power of your subconscious mind and God's laws. Expect and visualize your prayer manifesting—and nothing can stop it. You are doing exactly what Sai Baba is doing, except that Sai Baba, being at the universal level, does it faster. The principles of what he does and what we are doing are exactly the same, and he will tell you this himself. Sai Baba is the master manifestor on this planet. Be in total expectancy that your prayer will manifest.

188 Ask for What You Want in All Things: Pray and Affirm Unceasingly

The next golden key has been choosing to ask for help from the masters, the angels and God in all areas of my life including the material. Some lightworkers feel that it is not all right to ask for material help, whether money or other material things. This is not true. Matter is densified spirit. There is no separation. I utilize the masters in all area of my life.

For example, I always ask Sai Baba, Melchizedek, Lord Maitreya, Djwhal Khul and the angels to allow my taxes to go through without being audited. This is not because I am cheating but because I don't want to go through the hassle of all the extra work. I pray to God, the masters and the angels for help in manifesting the Wesak celebrations. In the past when I needed clients, I would pray for this also.

Pray, affirm and visualize regarding every aspect of your life constantly. You are manifesting every moment of your life with your every thought, word and deed. So make your life one massive ongoing meditation, prayer, affirmation, visualization and assertive-action session. I have been successful with manifestation because I ask and hold the picture of what I desire to manifest. If I begin to falter, I pray, affirm and visualize further in order to hold that perfected state again.

Some Tools for Manifestation

189 Write Down What You Want

The next golden key was to write down what I wanted. The physical act of writing down your vision greatly increases your powers of manifestation compared to merely keeping things in your mind. It brings your thoughts into focus and formalizes your intention. For many years I had papers and notes and affirmations all over my house to remind me of things I wanted to keep foremost in my mind. I would constantly make lists, and I would work with all the different tools in my journal. The more you can impress your subconscious mind with these positive thoughts and images, the sooner it will manifest your desires for you.

190   Use Treasure Maps and Other Tools

The next golden key is the activity of making treasure maps. During certain periods of my life I would create a collage of what I wanted to manifest at that time. It contained pictures, affirmations and words representing the things I wanted to bring forth into my life. After completing your treasure map, leave it out where it can serve as a constant visual reminder to all levels of your mind.

At other phases of my life I would do mirror work. I talked to myself or did affirmations while looking at myself and looking into my own eyes. At other times I would sing my affirmations or use subliminal tapes, which I found very enjoyable and effective.

191   Put Books under Your Pillow to Manifest Their Knowledge

The next golden key was a story that touched me very deeply about Edgar Cayce. At one time when Cayce was a boy, he was being scolded by his tutor for not learning his lessons. Cayce heard a little voice in his mind telling him that he should request to have a thirty-minute break. Cayce was then told to close his eyes and take a little nap with the book under his pillow. When he awoke he had total recall of the entire book. When I first heard this story I was very taken by it, and I would often put books under my pillow and pray that I would absorb them energetically. I never have had the level of success that Edgar Cayce did, but I do think this has had an effect, especially if I prayed first. Try it. It is the lazy person's guide to enlightenment.

Special Help from the Masters

192   The Manifestation and Transmutation Grid

The next key is an important activation I learned from Saint Germain in one of my meditations. Call forth to Saint Germain and request that the manifestation and transmutation grid be permanently anchored into your solar plexus. Saint Germain told us that this grid would help us learn to manifest more effectively. The grid also assists in transmuting negative energies more effectively, switching negative energies to positives. This grid is there for the asking.

193 Divine Dispensations

This golden key is about calling for divine dispensations. I came up with this quite spontaneously in meditations with my friends, and I soon came to realize what an invaluable tool it is. I usually make requests for a divine dispensation to Melchizedek, Lord Buddha, Lord Maitreya and Djwhal Khul. Sometimes I make these requests to the karmic board and Quan Yin. I make these requests for something special, and if they are reasonable, they are usually answered by the masters. An example of this might be a request for a divine dispensation of acceleration of my ascension process so that I may be of greater service.

From the Vantage Point of God

194 Recognize Yourself as One with All Creation

A major golden key in manifesting is to recognize yourself as being one with that which you seek to manifest. In other words, do not manifest from the consciousness of being separate from what you are seeking to manifest. This means manifesting from the Self rather than from the personality. In truth, we all are the eternal Self. We live within all creation as all creation lives within us. Everyone shares this same identity with God. There are no separate beings. There is only God incarnating into infinite forms. These forms of Self in matter go through periods of forgetting who they are. But then they reawaken to what they always have been. This is why *A Course in Miracles* says that the Fall never really happened; we just think it did.

Put another way, know that you are God, that what you seek to manifest is God and that nothing exists other than God. Manifestation is then done from the perspective of God manifesting God for the purposes of God. You are one with, and live inside of, what you are seeking to manifest. In reality, you are God doing manifestation work. This golden key will have a profound effect on your manifestation work if you allow it to permeate to a deep level.

One way to identify with God when doing manifestation work I learned from Saint Germain. This is to use the words "I Am" as the beginning words of your affirmations. The words then have a double meaning, referring both to yourself and to God's name, which is I AM or I AM That I AM.

195 You Need to Manifest Only One Thing

This golden key builds on the previous one and is something I learned from *A Course in Miracles*. This is the understanding that each one of us actually needs to manifest only one thing. If we manifest this one thing, all else will manifest as a byproduct. That one thing, of course, is *unity consciousness with God*. This involves healing the thought form that we are separate from God. The truth is that we never have been or ever will be separate from God.

Separation doesn't exist on the spiritual plane, but it does exist on the mental, emotional and physical planes for most people. Our main spiritual work, then, is to anchor the spiritual reality of unity with God into the four-body system. It is not enough to know this intellectually. We must know it deeply at every level of our being. Healing the feelings of separation from God on this planet means fully embracing the Christ/Buddha consciousness.

Can you begin to see the power of manifestation and the Midas touch that comes from holding the consciousness of oneness with God at all times? Can you see the power of your prayers and affirmations when you do your manifestation work on all levels from this state of God consciousness?

196   Recognize That We Already Have and Are Everything

The next key was the statement from *A Course in Miracles* that we already *are* everything and already *have* everything. This is another important principle in the process of manifestation. Ultimately we are God, we are the Christ. There is nothing to do, for we already are what we seek. This teaching is similar to the teachings of the great Eastern saint Ramana Maharshi. We already are God, and *A Course in Miracles* and Ramana Maharshi teach practices that help us identify with this truth.

It is also true that we are in the process of realizing this ultimate truth. In the ultimate state of things we already have and are everything, so from that perspective there is nothing to manifest, for we already contain what we seek. Hence maintaining this state of consciousness is the ultimate manifestation process.

Of course, everyone is not there or they wouldn't be reading these books in the first place. What *A Course in Miracles* and Ramana Maharshi say is true; but it is also true that we are all in the process of realizing God. We can affirm that we are the Christ yet not have fully manifested this. *A Course in Miracles* and the teachings of Ramana Maharshi are written from the perspective of already being at the end of the tunnel, so to speak. Affirming and visualizing this is part of the process of achieving God realization.

The process of the 352 levels of initiation back to the godhead is this step-by-step process of attaining greater and greater levels of God realization. Recognizing that in the ultimate state we already are God—and that we already have everything—allows us to view things from the vantage point of God while we work to manifest God more and more fully in our lives and four-body system.

A Course in Miracles is written from a heavenly perspective and might be called an idealistic teaching. As long as it is used with this understanding, it can be one of the most useful learning aids on the planet. *A Course in Miracles* is not for everyone; even the *Course* says this. *A Course in Miracles* and the Huna teachings were a good marriage for me and a more balanced philosophy. I have attempted to create this integration for you in my books.

197 Attune to the Perfection

The next golden key is the concept of attuning to perfection. In the ultimate state of things all is perfect, all is God. For example, in regard to the physical body, *A Course in Miracles* says, "Sickness is a defense against the truth." The truth is that we each are the Christ and sickness is an illusion. How can the perfect Christ be sick? This applies to all areas of life. Whenever limitation and nonperfection enter your mind, immediately say a prayer or do an affirmation or visualization to bring your thoughts back to the perfected state. This gets back to the lesson of where one keeps one's attention. The ideal is always to keep your attention on the mighty I Am Presence and God.

Suppose you are having problems with finances. Bills are arriving that you can't pay. Instead of focusing on the lack, immediately pray and call to your mighty I Am Presence and the ascended masters for help. As Edgar Cayce said, "Why worry when you can pray?" By praying or doing an affirmation, you immediately bring your consciousness back to the perfected state of abundance. You are not buying into appearances, but holding the ideal of abundance. In a sense you could say that you already have manifested the money on the etheric plane, and you are just waiting for it to manifest on the physical. The key to being successful in life is always to keep your attention on God and perfection rather than on lack and limitation.

Since you are refusing to accept limitation, sickness, poverty or lack of perfection on any level, then everywhere you go you become a healing force. You have perfect faith, trust and patience in God, so you know that every prayer you offer will manifest. You also have perfect faith, trust and patience in the power of your own mind. You know that every thought and image you affirm and visualize will manifest through the power of your own subconscious mind.

Make a vow in this moment to accept only perfection as reality. This is what I did even though the actual appearance in every aspect of my life said the opposite. Eventually my inner faith in God's reality won out. It will for you too if you will practice these universal laws and principles. The key is that the levels must be congruent. You cannot pray and then doubt your prayer, or you will sabotage it. There must be consistency between the three minds. The power of God, the masters and your own conscious and subconscious minds will manifest only perfection if you will apply these principles consistently.

198   Receive a Science of Mind Treatment

The next golden key was receiving Science of Mind treatments. If you have never done this before, I would recommend calling up a Science of Mind church and having a session with one of the ministers. They will write a treatment for you on whatever area of your life needs perfecting. The practice of Science of Mind and the teachings of Ernest Holmes are very eloquent, and these treatments are based on the spiritual truth that all is perfect in the ultimate reality. The practitioner will help make the treatment and will say it with you, then you can take it home and work with it. You can then make your own treatments using the same form. These treatments are extremely powerful, and if said every day for at least 21 days will cement this reality into your subconscious mind. This process in conjunction with the Huna system of prayer is an unbeatable team.

Principles and Laws of Manifestation

199   All Is Mind

The next golden key has been the application of the great Hermetic principle: *All is mind; the universe is mental.* The entire universe is not only energy, but it is also mental. As Edgar Cayce said, all thoughts are things. The material universe is a thought in the mind of God. All objects that we use in our life are materialized thought. Sai Baba is able to materialize through thinking and imaging. We soon will be able to do this also. In truth, we are doing this already, but our process is somewhat slower.

Energy follows thought. The application of this Hermetic law is that anything you think, if held long enough, can and will manifest. I have used the power of my own mind and the mind power of the ascended masters to manifest healing, ascension leadership and self-realization. This law is always working, and if you are not focused on God realization on all levels, then this law is unconsciously being used to attract the opposite.

The universe can be controlled through the power of the mind, for all is mind and the universe is mental. The entire universe is an outpicturing of God's mind. As we tap into greater and greater levels of God's mind, the more control and mastery we will have in God's infinite universe.

200   Only One Higher Mind and One Subconscious Mind

The next golden key in my manifestation work has been the insight that there is only one higher mind and one subconscious mind. Only the ego consciousness is separate. This could be looked at as God having one infinite mind. Carl Jung called the subconscious the collective unconscious. Jung thought of this in terms of all of humanity, which is true. I am looking at it now in terms of all of creation as well. Praying, affirming and visualizing from this state of consciousness will greatly increase your manifesting power and magnetism.

201   Everything We Seek to Manifest Is Energy

The next key in my manifestation work has been the understanding that whatever I seek to manifest is energy. Everything in God's universe, including the material universe, is energy vibrating at different rates of speed and resonance. The money and material things we seek to manifest are energy. All manifestation—whether healing the physical body or ascension or material things—involves working with energy. Begin to see everything you are doing as moving and shifting energy. Then you will have begun to tap into one of the true golden keys of the process of alchemy, transmutation and manifestation in every aspect of your life.

202   The Principle of Polarity

The next key for me was learning to understand the principle of polarity. This Hermetic law states: *Everything is dual; everything has poles; everything has pairs of opposites; like and unlike are the same; opposites are identical in nature but different in degree; extremes meet; all truths are but half truths; all paradoxes can be reconciled.*

This is a most profound golden key. In understanding the nature of duality, you see, for example, that negative-ego consciousness is the polarity of Christ consciousness. Remember that all is mind and all is energy. By controlling energy and mind—or sound and light, for that matter—energy can be moved easily from one pole to the other. Negative-ego consciousness can be moved to Christ consciousness. Fear can be transformed to love.

Take, for example, hot and cold. They are different only in degrees on a thermometer. Who can say where one ends and the other begins? Progressing on the spiritual path involves a shift in polarity. It is shifting polarity from lower-self guidance to higher-self guidance. It is shifting polarity from personality to soul, soul to the monad, and the monad to God.

If you are run too much by your emotional body, then you need to polarize your consciousness toward the mental body. The shift from one's physical body to one's lightbody will ultimately allow us to learn to teleport. It is crucial to understand the nature of duality and polarity and see how things can be identical in nature but different in degree. This is why everything in our lives can be shifted to its opposite polarity or balance point if we desire. We can do this through the inner power of Sai Baba and the ascended masters and through God with prayer and meditation.

Polarities can also be shifted through our own mental power and visualization. This work relates to the science of attitudinal healing. They can be shifted by working with energy or the manipulation of sound, color, light, even aroma, as with aromatherapy. The application of these Hermetic principles of *all is mind* and *everything has polarity* are absolute keys to manifesting healing, ascension, leadership, money and anything else you desire.

Take having an empty bank account versus a full bank account. It is the same thing, but a matter of degree. What is needed is a shift in energy through mind power, prayer power, visualization power and personal power manifested through action. There is not that much difference between being poor or rich. If you win the lottery, your financial situation changes instantly. If you inherit money, it changes instantly. If you get a new job, it can change instantly. Everything on one's spiritual path is learning how to manipulate energy. When done in the service of God it is called white magic. When energy is manipulated in service to the negative ego and Dark Brotherhood, it is called black magic. The key here is to become a master of the manipulation of energy in the service of God, the ascended masters and humanity.

Every person on the planet is manipulating energy and working these laws. The problem is that they are not doing it consciously enough, and they often are doing it to their detriment instead of their betterment. The key is to understand these laws and consciously work with them every moment of your life for the betterment of self and others.

203   God's Universal Laws Are Always Working

The next key has been the understanding that God's universal laws are *always* working. These laws don't operate only with prayer, affirmation and visualization. They operate with every thought you think, every word you speak and every deed you do—even while you are sleeping. This is where the true understanding of manifestation lies.

Since God's laws are always operating, they operate to attract both the positive and the negative, depending on what we are projecting consciously or unconsciously. And the subconscious mind, with its powers of attraction, magnetism and repulsion, is also always working. The subconscious mind can as readily attract and magnetize disaster as abundance and godliness, for it has no reasoning power. If we are not using God's laws for the positive, then we are using them for the negative or at best haphazardly. Understanding and mastering God's laws on all levels is the key to healing, ascension, the Midas touch and leadership. It is through God's laws that we learn loving obedience to God. It is often suffering that propels us back onto our spiritual path.

204   The Five Levels of Manifestation

The next golden key has been the recognition that manifestation occurs on five levels.

- The spiritual level of manifestation is recognizing that we are God manifesting another part of ourselves that exists within the body of God.
- The mental level of manifestation is keeping the mind focused on the perfection we desire to manifest and remaining steady in the light at all times.
- The emotional aspect of manifestation is maintaining enthusiasm, devotion and a childlike faith in God and God's laws.
- The etheric level of manifestation is knowing that after you pray and affirm and visualize, the prayer already has been answered and already exists on the etheric plane. It simply hasn't materialized yet on the physical plane.
- The fifth level of manifestation is the materialization of the prayer on the physical plane.

The very first step of all manifestation is the prayer request and affirmation or visualization. Part of manifestation is to go beyond faith to absolute knowingness. When the prayer request has reached the etheric level it is almost like you can reach out and touch it. When dealing with manifestation, the line between fantasy and reality becomes quite blurred. Who is to say which one is more real? When the inner reality you choose to create through prayer, affirmation and visualization becomes more real than the outer reality, you have become a master of manifestation. You are then seeing with your inner Christ eyes and not just your physical eyes.

205   The Law of Ownership

The next golden key has been what I call the law of ownership. In truth, whatever we manifest is not really ours. No one owns anything, for God owns all. Whatever we manifest on any level, including the physical, is only lent to us by God. When God wants it back, there is nothing in this universe we can do to stop it. For this reason it is better not to hold on too tightly; it is better to see things as they really are. This understanding and attitude will greatly accelerate your manifestation.

206   Responsible Stewardship

This golden key is taking good care of whatever God has given you. If God blesses you with the money to buy a new car, then take care of that car and be a good steward of the bounty He has bestowed upon you. God has given us the blessing of a physical body, and it is our responsibility to take care of it, treat it well, groom it properly and dress it well without vanity. The same applies to a new home or financial wealth. Let us not take God for granted and let us use what He blesses us with wisely. This applies not only to the physical plane but also to children, leadership and our clients. There are so many people in this world who are suffering and in poverty. Let us use wisely the great blessings that God has bestowed on us and share them with others when we can.

Attitudes for Manifestation

207   Manifest from an Attitude of Self-Authority and Being an Instrument of God

One of the most important golden keys to manifesting healing, ascension, service, leadership and anything else you can think of is to do all manifestation work from self-authority, self-mastery and personal power. Manifest from the perspective that "I Am God and my heart is pure, loving and selfless, so the entire universe and even cosmos is at my command." As *A Course in Miracles* states, this is not done from grandiosity but from grandeur. It is done from the consciousness of being a vehicle and instrument of the most high God, a bridge to Source from the planetary level. See yourself as a vehicle to call down God's omnipotence and omniscience for the purposes of manifesting His divine plan.

208   Rely on God and God's Laws for Abundance

The next golden key has been to rely only on God and God's laws for my prosperity. Many people rely on outside things for their security in life. Yet all outside things, including people, can be taken away—and ultimately will be. The only real security in life is God, the ascended masters, the power of Sai Baba and God's laws. Paramahansa Yogananda had an affirmation I like. It says, "God is my stocks and bonds and financial security." I would change this to "God, Sai Baba, the ascended masters, the angels, my personal power and the power of my subconscious mind are my stocks and bonds and financial security."

Many people rely on only one level for manifestation. For some it is just personal power and physical action. Some use only prayer. Others focus on affirmations or visualizations. Others rely on the angels, Sai Baba or another master. Others focus on God. I say, use *all* of them and more to build your inner strength and ability to manifest. What is within you can never be taken away. All things can be stripped away, as they were in my life; but I was able to build it all back again even bigger because I trusted these inner laws. As *A Course in Miracles* says, miracles are natural. They are a natural byproduct of applying God's laws in a positive manner.

209 Love Yourself

The next golden key relates to self-love and manifestation. I have seen many people in my counseling practice in the past who were doing tons of affirmations and prayers but not getting the results they wanted. As I explored this with them, I discovered that the block was lack of self-love. This is the ultimate negative affirmation. When people don't feel deserving of receiving God's bounty, it is often because of real or imagined past transgressions. Then this belief becomes a self-fulfilling prophecy even when it is unconscious. This also is faulty thinking, for in truth all are God, all are the Christ and all are worthy of love. So it is important to identify with the diamond and not the mud.

210 Forgiveness: Releasing Blocks to Manifestation

Another golden key is making sure you have forgiven yourself and others for all trespasses. Any grudges or guilt will tend to block the manifestation of your prayer requests and affirmations. You must have a clear conscience on all levels or the prayer will be partially sabotaged. This sounds simple, but it is very important. Always check this before beginning your manifestation work.

211 Change Poverty Consciousness to Abundance Consciousness

The next golden key is letting go of poverty consciousness and beliefs that being poor is synonymous with being spiritual. Those who think money is bad or that it is not okay to charge for your services are being run by the negative ego. They think they are being spiritual, but in truth they have poverty consciousness.

God wishes us to have abundance on all levels, including the material. Everyone has a spiritual bank account and an earthly bank account, and the idea is to build both of them on a daily basis. God and the masters want us to have abundance on all levels, not just the spiritual. Health, wealth, peace and joy are byproducts of God realization. It is through lightworkers becoming wealthy that the earthly world will begin to change. The more money you have, the more you can give to others and help manifest God's divine plan on Earth.

212   Release Doubts and Fears around Manifestation

The next golden key involves letting go of doubts, fears and worries after you have set forth a manifestation goal. We are God, and what we think is what we will manifest. Sometimes there is a tendency to do affirmations, visualizations and pray, hold that energy for a little while and then let doubts and fears and thoughts of less than perfection creep in.

The key is to remain in your God nature. Our every thought, word and observation is an affirmation of manifestation. I found myself doing this with the Wesak festival. I would start out with a strong faith that we would have the full 1200 people. But Saint Germain pointed out that on occasion I would say that this advertising is working but that one isn't. On one level we need to make such discernments, but on the other hand we have to be very careful how we state it. I really appreciated Saint Germain's feedback, for it helped me to get back into the consciousness of holding my vision.

213   Why Worry When You Can Pray?

The next golden key is some advice I learned from Edgar Cayce on the remedy for worry. Edgar Cayce's advice was, "Why worry when you can pray?" I would add to this, "Why worry when you can pray, affirm, visualize and own your personal power?" Then you are owning and utilizing the full power of your three minds: conscious, subconscious and superconscious. I have taken Edgar Cayce's advice many times in my life and it always works.

214   Know That You Cannot Fail

The next key has been the recognition that I cannot fail. How can I fail with my personal power, God's help, Sai Baba's help, the ascended masters' help and the power of my subconscious mind? With all these levels of power helping me, how can I not be victorious against glamour and illusion? How can I not be victorious in God realization?

215   God Helps Those Who Help Themselves

The next golden key is the saying that God helps those who help themselves. Do not wait for the ascended masters to get your life together or control your mind, for it won't happen. My climb to ascension realization and leadership has been done basically through my own efforts and the wisdom to pray for what I needed at every step of the way. The ascended masters did not do it for me. I did it myself with their help. There is a big difference. If the ascended masters did it for us, then we would never learn to become masters ourselves.

216   Serve without Attachment to the Fruits of Your Labors

This golden key is serving humanity without attachment to the fruits of your work. What matters is that you have given the service freely and with love. Leave the results to God. Sometimes seeds are planted that will not sprout for many years. This is fine. What is important is that you give love. Do not look for people to give something back in return. Our job is to shine our light and love regardless how it is received. Thus we remain at cause in our reality. Our job is simply to give love and service unceasingly and focus only on this. Then all will flow back to us in great abundance.

Giving and Gratitude

217   The Law of Gratitude

The next golden key has been the law of gratitude. This law has two aspects. The first is to give thanks that your prayers have already been answered. For in truth your prayers *have* already been answered by God, Sai Baba, the ascended masters and the angels moments after they were voiced. There is no time or space in the dimensions upon which God and the God force live. This is why the prayer is instantly answered. Giving thanks and gratitude is the most appropriate thing you could possibly do.

The second aspect of the law of gratitude is to show gratitude when the prayer comes into physical manifestation. In addition, it is important to be conscious of, and express gratitude for, all of the gifts in your life that God has already bestowed upon you and for all of the gifts from Mother Earth. A heart filled with love and gratitude is in a state to receive the abundance of God.

218   Tithing

The next golden key has been the practice of the law of tithing and giving seed money. This is really the law of karma applied to dealing with money. The basic law states that if you give 10 percent of your income to a needy spiritual cause, then by cosmic law there is a tenfold return. If you are stingy with the universe, the universe will be stingy with you. If you are generous with the universe, which is God, God will be generous with you. As *A Course in Miracles* says, we create our own salvation. We must keep our money in circulation. I have applied this by giving away enormous numbers of books, discounts and passes to Wesak and giving to the homeless. This law of tithing and seed money is based upon a basic fundamental trust in God and God's universal laws as they manifest on all levels of creation.

Karma

219   Transmuting Karma

This golden key is to make a request to Melchizedek, Metatron and Archangel Michael for a divine dispensation for the transmuting of all your karma. To ascend you must balance 51 percent of your karma from your entire oversoul. To balance your karma, ask the masters and your mighty I Am Presence to balance it for you. This will take many meditations, for it cannot be done all at once.

With patience and diligence, over time you can balance your entire karmic history. I asked Melchizedek how much of my karma I had balanced. I believe he said that it was around 75 percent for the monad. This is pretty good because we are dealing here with the karma of all 144 soul extensions that make up each person's monad. This is an example of how scientific the spiritual path is. The key is to understand the mechanics of how evolution works and then ask for things that specifically accelerate this process.

220   Balancing Karma

The next key was understanding that my past karma could be balanced, that is, erased, by doing good deeds in this lifetime. I am always going out of my way to do good deeds and being of service in any way I can. As self-realization is achieved, the idea is to serve rather than be served. The Buddhists call this doing random acts of kindness. It is amazing the effect that random acts of kindness can have. This is the real nuts and bolts of the spiritual path.

221   The Law of Karma and the Law of Grace

The next golden key has been the understanding of the difference between the law of karma and the law of grace. The law of grace is learning the easy way and the law of karma is learning by the school of hard knocks. I have made a spiritual vow to try and learn all of my lessons by the law of grace, and to learn not only from my own mistakes and successes but also from the mistakes and successes of others. This spiritual vow implies the desire to "know thyself" and hence know God and his universal laws—and live in harmony with those laws.

The state of grace is one of consciously living by universal laws. The state of karma is being unconscious of these laws and hence being seemingly victimized by them. The suffering you experience is God's way of teaching you about these laws. All karma is transcended by claiming grace.

Manifestation Stories

The following three stories illustrate how the laws of manifestation are always working whether we are conscious of them or not.

❖   The Injured Knee

One incident earlier in my life really brought home to me how the laws of manifestation are always working. I was in my early twenties and I was into long-distance running. I developed an injury in my left knee, but I could not figure out the cause. I went to a doctor, but he could do nothing. I loved to run and didn't like being limited in this manner.

I finally got a channeling from a friend and learned that I had a calcium deficiency. This made sense because I wasn't eating dairy products and I wasn't supplementing my diet either. I began taking calcium and, sure enough, in a couple of weeks my knee started feeling better and I began running again.

A couple of months later the injury started coming back again. I went back to my channeling friend. She told me that there was nothing wrong with my leg, and this time the injury was related to my thinking. At that time I did not yet understand fully how the subconscious mind worked. The information that came through was that I was going around telling my friends that I had a bum leg, so the subconscious mind simply was manifesting what I was telling it. This was a real eye-opener and led to my involvement in studying the subconscious mind and hypnosis. I began telling myself that my left leg had steel-like strength and power. Within three weeks my leg was healed and I never had any further problems with it.

❖ Getting the Foul Ball

On another occasion I went to a baseball game with my friend Joel. I was in high spirits, and as we walked into Dodger stadium I jokingly said, "Joel, I demand a foul ball tonight. I am putting out to the universe that I demand to catch a foul ball. I have been to a million baseball games and I never have gotten a foul ball. I demand one tonight!" At the age of twenty-five or twenty-six I did not have a working understanding of the laws of the universe, and I definitely was not consciously trying to apply them there. The game was completely sold out and there must have been 56,000 people in the stadium.

In the second inning Joe Ferguson of the Houston Astros fouled a ball high into the air and into the seats. The ball went over my head, ricocheted off the hands of the man in the row above me, bounced off the ankle of the person to my right and rolled right to me. I pick it up and held it high in the air for the crowd to see. We both then remembered what I had said. My friend Joel was blown away. The understanding here is that most of the manifestation work is being done when we aren't even focusing on it. The law is working all of the time for good or for ill whether we realize it or not.

❖ Cancer and the Power of the Mind

This is a story my father told me. My father, a psychologist, started one of the first holistic health centers in Los Angeles in the '70s called the Center for the Healing Arts. During this time he became friends with Dr. Carl Simonton, the medical doctor who specialized in working with cancer patients in holistic and innovative ways.

Carl told my father the following story. A man came to see Dr. Simonton with his wife. When Carl saw him he didn't give him more than three months to live. Carl's advice was to do immediate surgery to see if there was anything they could do to cut the cancer out. The surgery was done and as he was opened up, the cancer turned out to be a far worse than the doctors had imagined. The cancer was everywhere. They immediately sewed him up without doing anything. The doctors' view was to let the man live the rest of his days in peace. This is what the doctor told his wife.

However, the man's wife never told this to her husband. He went home under the mental assumption and image that the cancer had been removed surgically. The man came back for an appointment three months later and x-rays revealed that the man's cancer had completely disappeared. The doctors were completely blown away. Three months ago they had never seen such a bad case of cancer and now it was gone. The doctors asked, "What have you been doing to create such a cure?" The man said "What are you talking about? You removed all the cancer from my body three months ago." The doctor went on to explain that he had done nothing of the sort. The patient was stunned.

Three months later the cancer returned in full force again and the man died. If this story doesn't bring home the awesome power of the mind and how the laws of manifestation are operating in every moment, nothing will. This is why doctors in Japan don't make prophetic diagnoses like doctors in the United States often do, and also why they often will choose not to tell patients what is wrong. They will treat them for cancer but not tell them that they have it.

Whether this is appropriate or not is an interesting philosophical issue, but the reasoning behind it is quite obvious. There are some people who do better if they do not know their condition. However, others with a serious illness will use it as an opportunity to strengthen themselves spiritually and work to transform their situation.

The following two stories illustrate the power of conscious manifestation.

❖ Immediate Manifestation of Money

This incident occurred when I was around the age of 27. I was living in Monterey, California, and there was a workshop I wanted to attend given by Ronald Beasley, who was a brilliant spiritual master from England. It was a rare opportunity that he was coming into town. The problem was that I was a starving student and this was one of the lower points, moneywise, in my life. The workshop cost $200, which was a lot of money for me.

I remember doing journal-writing one morning, and in my journal I was talking to my higher self. I began telling my higher self that I really wanted to go to this workshop but that I didn't have the money. I said that if my higher self wanted me to go he/she was going to have to get me the money. About an hour later I was packing up food from my refrigerator to bring to a friend because I was going out of town for six weeks to visit my family in Los Angeles. As I walked outside with my packages, I saw a man I had never seen before walking around the beach area where I lived.

I got in my car and started to drive away when the man hailed me. He asked me if I knew of any place for rent near here. I told him I didn't. He then went on to say that he was looking for a place for only four or five weeks to put up his mother who was coming to visit from Germany. All of a sudden a little light bulb went on. I was paying only $150 a month for my place, but it was right near the ocean. I told him that I would rent him my place for $200. We shook on it and he gave me the money. Only two hours after talking to my higher self in my journal I had the money to go to the workshop!

The Power of Visualization

I saw an interview with the movie actor, Jim Carrey. He is the comedian who makes all of those extremely funny faces in his movies. His family had been very poor, and during one phase of his life he actually lived in a car. He said he used to fantasize and visualize having a $10 million check. He even had a copy of a $10 million check in his wallet. Then he was given $10 million to make his next movie.

My visualization is to sell two or three million sets of my 20-volume series of books. Both Melchizedek and Djwhal Khul said from the inner plane that they saw this happening. I hold this visualization similar to the way Jim Carrey held his. The other visualization I hold the strongest is the progression of the Wesak celebration building from 1200 people to 2500 people to 5000 people. I see it, I know it, I smell it, I taste it, I touch it, I hear it. The masters have told me that it is totally realistic to expect this. I not only visualize it happening, I go one step past this and *know* it is going to happen.

We all know the law, "As within, so without; as above, so below." That which we think and image in our conscious and subconscious minds will manifest in our external circumstance if we hold it long enough. This, in combination with prayer, is an awesome force.

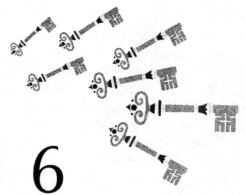

GOLDEN KEYS
TO ASCENSION
AND HEALING

6

ANCHORING SPIRITUALITY INTO OUR DAILY LIVES
Keys 222-267

GUIDELINES
LOVE FOR THE EARTH AND HER CREATURES
MANTRAS, SOUND AND LIGHT
PRAYERS OF PROTECTION AND CLEARING
MEDITATION AND SILENCE
SPECIFIC MEDITATIONS
ANCHORING HIGHER ENERGIES INTO YOUR ENVIRONMENT
GROUNDING SPIRITUAL ENERGIES IN DAILY LIFE
INTEGRATING SPIRITUAL ACTIVITIES INTO YOUR LIFE
WORKING WITH THE ARCHETYPES
BALANCE IN DAILY LIFE

Guidelines

222   *Invest in the Permanent*

I learned this golden key from Sai Baba. In his discourses on the *Bhagavad-Gita*, he spoke of the importance of investing one's energies in the permanent rather than the impermanent. We each have a choice right now whether we invest our energies in our spiritual bank account or our material bank account. One is permanent and the other impermanent.

I am not saying that earthly concerns are not important, for they are. But they are important only in the context of our spiritual life and service. Those who invest time and energy in material concerns will be bankrupt on the inner plane, for they will have invested unwisely. Don't get pulled off your dharma onto side roads of your lower self and negative ego. Do not get caught up in glamour, maya and illusion, for these hold nothing for you but sorrow. Do not give in to temptation. Remain completely focused and vigilant in terms of your true divine priorities.

We are living in a most extraordinary period of Earth's history of mass ascension. Ascension is no longer only for the select few. It is for everyone. Let us work together arm in arm and shoulder to shoulder to make this change. This is not God's job or the ascended masters' job. It is our job, for we are the externalization on Earth of the Spiritual Hierarchy.

The ascended masters on the inner plane work with us to train and prepare us to do this work. They will then move on in their cosmic evolution. We will take their places in the Spiritual Government and help our brothers and sisters on Earth as we have been helped.

223   *Deny All But God*

The next key has been the understanding of denial and affirmation. There is healthy denial and unhealthy denial. Unhealthy denial we all know about. This is denying the reality of higher truth. Healthy denial is the key to retaining inner peace. It is one of those key psychoepistemological thoughts I spoke of earlier. The key here is not to allow any thought not of God to enter your mind.

When Jesus said to the complaining apostle, "Get thee behind me, Satan," he was practicing healthy denial. When negative thoughts are trying to enter the conscious mind, they must be pushed out and replaced with spiritual thoughts and images. The mind works a lot like a television. When you see a program you don't like, switch channels and shift your attention elsewhere. You don't put spoiled or poisonous food in your mouth, so don't put poisonous thoughts in your mind. Keep a good mental diet. It is really so simple.

If you don't like the word "denial," you can practice laughing the thoughts off the stage of your mind. If you allow negative thoughts into your mind, you will become negatively hypnotized. Most of my work as a psychologist and spiritual teacher is not hypnotizing people, but *dehypnotizing* them—getting them out of the trances of illusion they are in. What you think doesn't create truth; it creates the reality you live in. As Sai Baba says, "Your mind creates bondage or your mind creates liberation."

Sometimes when negative thoughts bother me, I imagine the negative thoughts are a mirror, and I see them shatter into little pieces. Then I visualize the image of Sai Baba and/or the opposite of the attitudes or thoughts that had been bothering me. Frequently, the image of Sai Baba is all I need. What can withstand the omnipotence, omnipresence and omniscience of the glory of Sai Baba?

224 See Yourself As the Monad and an Ascended Master

The next golden key has been seeing myself as the soul, as the monad and as an ascended master living on Earth. Practice being the monad or mighty I Am Presence on Earth. Practice being an ascended master. Practice being the master Jesus or Sai Baba. See others in this way even if they haven't realized this yet. This again will help to polarize your consciousness to the next level. This is one of the real keys to manifesting your initiations and ascension.

225 Teach What You Are Learning

The next golden key has been my focus on teaching whatever I am currently learning. I would read, study and take notes with that intent. I have trained my mind to think this way, which is part of the reason I have developed the ability to make things easy for people to understand. By teaching, whether it be in classes and lectures or to clients, I would be forced to learn and master the information. All lightworkers are teachers. Consider integrating everything you are studying from this perspective. I invite you to use this material in your own personal classes, lectures and client sessions as long as credit is given where credit is due. Study it first to help yourself and then as you progress, to help others.

226 Act Instead of Criticize, a Story

The next golden key relates to a story I once heard from Paul Solomon about a mystery school. A young man came to a particular mystery school to begin his training. As he walked into the dining hall for breakfast the first morning he noticed that the floor was a little dirty outside the dining room.

He commented to himself that this mystery school was not as organized as he thought it should be. The next day when he walked into the dining hall the floor was even filthier and he was even more disgusted. He was thinking to himself that maybe he had picked the wrong mystery school. The third day it was filthier still and there was a broom standing by the door. The young man concluded that he was living at a very inept mystery school.

Of course, the lesson he was being taught was to pick up the broom and clean up the mess himself. This has great application in all of our lives, for life is a mystery school put on by our higher self and the ascended masters who monitor our development. When we see things that aren't going right, perhaps God has revealed them to us in that moment so we can do something about them, even if it is simply saying a prayer. Tune in to your inner guidance in regard to which things you are to take action on as part of your service work.

Love for the Earth and Her Creatures

227 Love the Earth

A golden key that Djwhal Khul gave to me is to *love the Earth*. He said that loving Earth life was one of the keys to achieving ultimate liberation from it. Some lightworkers regard Earth as a prison or hell. This is faulty thinking. Earth, potentially, is a heaven. If everyone demonstrated fifth-dimensional consciousness on Earth, it would be a wonderful place to live. Our work is to cocreate heaven on Earth. We are here to demonstrate the love, joy, peace and mastery that can be had on Earth by living here as ascended masters. We are the pioneers.

There are many things to be enjoyed and treasured on the material plane. Djwhal Khul happens to like pizza. He often eats through other people's bodies, so invite him in the next time you have pizza.

228 The Wisdom of Animals

The next golden key has to do with my deeper understanding of how wise animals are. When I first met my former wife, she brought her cats, Patches and Rags, who were almost seventeen years old. Patches was her cat. Rags instantly became mine, although we both obviously loved both of them. I learned a big lesson in the beginning of our relationship about how wise these cats were—and animals in general. One weekend she had to go out of town and I was in charge of the cats. This was so early in our relationship that I had not completely bonded with them yet. This was the weekend of the Whole Life Expo, and I ended up being gone the entire weekend. I fed Patches and Rags and gave them water and cleaned the litter box, but that was about it.

When my former wife came home she immediately asked me how the cats were and if I had given them lots of love. I said that the cats were fine and that, yes, I had given them lots of love. (I lied a bit here.) Patches, who was lounging in the living room like the queen of Sheba, immediately began to speak to her telepathically, telling her that I was not telling the truth—that I had barely been home the entire weekend. My former wife told me what Patches had said, and boy was I busted! I'll tell you, I learned my lesson. After that our cats took over the household and my former wife and I completely lost control. What a life! We fussed over them like human babies.

This next cat story occurred when Rags passed away. I was extremely bonded to Rags and she definitely had me wrapped around her furry little paw. The day after she passed away, my former wife walked into the living room and saw Patches sitting out on the patio basking in the sun. She asked Patches, "What are you doing?" Patches immediately replied telepathically, "I am praying with Rags." Sure enough, there was Rags in her little animal spirit body sitting and praying next to Patches. I think this was the most adorable and moving experience I have ever seen! Djwhal Khul has told us that Patches would become human in her next lifetime. What I forgot to tell Djwhal is that I think she already is.

Mantras, Sound and Light

229   The Soul Mantra

The next golden key has been using the soul mantra. This was first brought forth by Djwhal Khul in the Alice Bailey books, and it is the most profound mantra I have ever used. This mantra will completely activate your higher self and monad. You also can use this mantra to center yourself anytime you get off center. Prior to all spiritual work, I would say this mantra.

I Am the soul,
I Am the monad,
I Am the light divine.
I Am love,
I Am will,
I Am fixed design.

230   Chant Aum

The next golden key has been the chanting of *aum*. As Sai Baba so eloquently has said, "Aum is the arrow and Brahman (God) is the target." I end all of my group meditations by chanting aum at least three times. It has been said that it is the sound of creation and the mother of all mantras.

231   Repeat the Names of God

The next golden key for me has been repeating the names of God. This is a regular part of spiritual practice in Eastern cultures, but it has not been as popular in the West. It should be, for it can alleviate all problems. This practice addresses the idea that an idle mind is the devil's workshop. If your mind is always on God, then temptation cannot enter. This goes along with Djwhal Khul's famous guidance through Alice Bailey to "keep the mind steady in the light."

The combination of repeating the names of God and visualizing the different forms of God is a most wonderful practice. It can be done during meditation, while driving a car or while going about your daily tasks. There are so many wonderful names and forms of God. As the saying goes, "As a man thinketh, so is he." Mahatma Gandhi said that his chanting of the name Rama during his daily life was one of the keys to his success. The last thought on your mind is where you will go when you die. Let this be a lesson to us all!

232   Use Light, Color and Sound

The next golden key has been the use of light and sound. The use of light, color and sound frequencies, when applied as a spiritual science, is a powerful tool for transformation. Sound can be expressed through toning, chanting, mantras, uplifting music and devotional singing. For many years and still to this day, every time I get in the car I play the devotional songs of the devotees in Sai Baba's ashram. The combination of the beautiful music with the singing of the names of God is highly uplifting. Sai Baba has said that it is one of the most effective ways to rid the consciousness of the energies of the negative ego.

I have utilized the light most often through calling in the light frequencies of the twelve rays. However, at different times in my life I have used some of the methods I wrote about in *Hidden Mysteries*. Bringing spiritual energies into your daily life through the avenues of light, color and sound has a highly transformative effect on one's consciousness and the whole four-body system.

Prayers of Protection and Clearing

233   Prayers of Protection

The next golden key was for me recognizing the importance of doing prayers of protection every morning and every night before bed. There is a

Dark Brotherhood and there are astral and negative extraterrestrial forces that are not of the light. This is nothing to be afraid of, for they can enter only if we allow them to. We are victims of nothing, for we are God. The ultimate protection is staying in your personal power at all times and keeping your attention on God.

When this spiritual practice weakens on occasion, the darker forces can create some limited interference. This is easily remedied by getting back into your personal power and saying prayers to reestablish your attunement and protective light. As a preventive, I highly recommend that twice a day you call forth to archangel Michael and/or Vywamus for a golden dome of protection to be placed around you. If you prefer, you can request a tube of light for protection. The type of protection does not matter. The important thing is to ask. This simple practice can be of enormous help and will help strengthen your psychological immune system.

234   Have Michael Cut Cords

The next golden key was to call forth to archangel Michael to cut all cords with people in my life who are no longer appropriate. I asked that the cords be removed, filled with golden light and healed. This is a very important process, especially when ending relationships.

235   Banns of Noninterference

The next golden key relates to certain twilight masters and/or negative-ego-driven individuals who on occasion would create problems by attempting to interfere with our work in manifesting the divine plan. All spiritual leaders and lightworkers will run into this at one time or another. When this happens, call to the masters and request "banns of noninterference." File an official complaint with Lord Buddha and the karmic board headed by Quan Yin. Do this not out of judgment but out of tough love. The masters will step in on your behalf if they are in agreement with your assessment, and they will apply certain force fields of protection. In extreme cases the individual who created the problems could be put on probation. In the most extreme cases, that being's spiritual energy can be almost completely cut off except for what is needed to maintain the physical vehicle.

Meditation and Silence

236   The Need for Meditation

As the great Edgar Cayce said, "Prayer is talking to God and meditation is listening to God." Most traditional religions spend an enormous amount of time talking to God and praying, but very little time meditating and listening. God will talk back if you listen. If you can't hear His voice clairaudiently, then He will speak to you through intuition, knowingness, comprehension, thoughts, dreams, images, music, poetry or creative expression. He will speak through other people and through synchronicities. God is talking to us all the time. We must have the eyes to see and ears to hear.

237 Meditate More and Read Less

The next golden key is to spend less time reading and more time meditating. Reading is good. Reading is very good. Meditation is better, however. It is through meditation and prayer that your real ascension acceleration will come.

238 Silence

The next golden key came from my studies of Pythagoras and his mystery school at Crotona. To even enter this mystery school one had to take a vow of silence for three years. Learning about the self-discipline required to be involved in this mystery school (which was Kuthumi's, since he had been Pythagoras) greatly impressed me. This helped me learn to be silent and spend time alone and not be with people all the time. I am quite content to be alone and in silence for long periods. I experience great solace and inner peace in doing so. Part of this lesson is that there is a time to do and a time simply to be.

In our society we are trained to be doers all the time. We are an extremely achievement-oriented society. I have this programming in spades. But I have learned, in my maturing years, how to simply be. I set aside times when I don't think or do anything. This has been a great teaching for me and has been instrumental in my healing process. It is so easy to become caught up in the frantic pace of Earth life. This, again, is where taking time to be in nature is important. Every day take time to be, a time when you do nothing.

239 Strive for a Balance between Talk and Silence

Another golden key has been the understanding that there is a time in life to talk and a time to be silent. One should not talk when it is time to be silent or be silent when it is time to talk. In every situation in life there are appropriate and inappropriate responses. The key is to trust your intuition.

240   Quiet the Mind

The next golden key has been learning how to quiet my mind. There is nothing wrong with having a strong, active mind. This is a good quality to develop. But everyone needs to know how to quiet the mind. Most people in the Western world have not learned this. The result is that they become driven. They might achieve a lot, but they don't have inner peace and the proper stillness of spirit. An overactive mind tends to weaken the adrenals and have a deleterious effect on the pancreas and liver. The liver is the organ of planning, and planning too much takes its toll.

The pancreas is connected to the sweetness in life and also to the function of will. An overuse of the will can weaken both the liver and pancreas, which relate to feminine and masculine balance in the body. You are not your mind just as you are not your emotions or your physical body. These are tools and aspects of your threefold personality. There is a common teaching among many spiritual groups, especially those based on Eastern philosophies, that the mind is bad and must be transcended at all costs. This is a false teaching. As Sai Baba says, "Your mind creates bondage or your mind creates liberation." The mind must be integrated and used properly. The instincts, emotions, thinking and the spirit all must be balanced and integrated in the proper alignment.

The true lesson of the spirit, then, is not to get rid of the mind, but rather to master it in service of the higher self and Holy Spirit. Take some time every day to quiet the mind and turn it off like a television that you don't want to watch anymore. Certain types of meditation can be helpful. This can be a simple meditation focusing on your breath or a candle. Being in nature can be most helpful.

In reality, you can quiet your mind at any time simply by stopping your thinking processes whenever your mind starts to follow a new train of thought. It really is that simple. Just lie down on the couch in silence and still the mind. In meditation if you don't stop the mind from racing, you will not be able to hear the masters or the still, small voice within. All meditations are really preparations for meditation. True meditation comes in the stillness when the mind is quiet. Look up a wonderful little book called *The Quiet Mind* by White Eagle.

There are different kinds of meditation for different purposes. A nice way to enjoy the quiet mind is to do one of the ascension activations such as going to an ascension seat and then basking in the stillness. One beautiful meditation is to request to go to the Golden Chamber of Melchizedek and sit in the silence, listening to the universal pulse that exists at the very center of Melchizedek's ashram. I often go for walks in nature and quiet my mind, just walking in beingness. This is a nice change of pace from walks that are like journal-writing sessions. There is a right time for everything. When you need healing of your physical body, extra quiet is essential.

Specific Meditations

241   Ascension Meditations

The next golden key was doing the meditations in the last chapter of *The Complete Ascension Manual* and the meditations in *Beyond Ascension*. These are some of the most powerful meditations you will find anywhere on the planet.

242   The Seven-Terrace Meditation

This golden key is a meditation that I did for many years, one I learned from Paul Solomon, who has passed on to the spiritual world. He was a most gifted spiritual teacher. Many referred to him as a modern Edgar Cayce, for he channeled the Universal Mind, or Source. In my early adulthood he was a catalyzing influence in my spiritual growth and path. To this day I find much of his work to be some of the clearest I have come across. Paul brought through from Source a meditation I found to be of great value. It was called the Seven-Terrace Meditation. In it you visualize climbing up a seven-terrace mountain in which each terrace is a different color of the spectrum. Each terrace also has an affirmation that goes with it.

The first terrace is red and represents expectancy and excitement. The second terrace is orange and stands for death of the old. The third terrace is yellow and signifies rebirth. The fourth terrace is green and represents harmony with Source. The fifth terrace is light blue and represents alignment with the truth of your being. The sixth terrace is violet and is like being in heaven merged with God's will. This requires you to take responsibility for yourself as you approach the throne of grace. The seventh terrace is white and represents the perfected state. Once you have climbed in your imagination to the top of the mountain, you create a beautiful temple of your higher self and mighty I Am Presence, building it first outside and then inside.

Once you practice this meditation on a regular basis, it begins to take form on the inner plane. It becomes a tool not only for raising your vibration, but also for directly contacting your higher self. I spent a great deal of time doing this meditation in my earlier life and I received great benefit from it.

243   So Ham Meditation

This golden key is another meditation I have found very useful. It is the meditation that Sai Baba, Yogananda, Muktananda and many Eastern masters have taught. It is called the So Ham or Hong Sau meditation. It means "I am the Self" or "I am God." It supposedly is the actual sound of humans breathing as God listens to us. When blended together during sleep, one hears the aum. Say this mantra in rhythm with your breath. On the inbreath in your mind say *So*. On the outbreath say *Ham*. Let your breathing decide the speed and rhythm of this mantra. The idea is to listen to the still point between the two aspects of the mantra. When a person becomes proficient at this meditation, s/he actually can live directly from the spiritual current.

244   Light Shower

The next golden key has been calling forth to all the masters I work with for a light shower. I usually do this at the end of all my major meditations. It serves to greatly increase the light quotient, and it feels absolutely wonderful.

245   Create a Grounding Cord

This golden key is to create a grounding cord down the spine and through the feet and legs into the center of the Earth. At the end of each meditation be sure to ground your energies, reconnect your grounding cord and feel roots growing from your feet into the Earth.

Anchoring Higher Energies into Your Environment

246   Create a Spiritual Altar

Another golden key in my life was creating a spiritual altar or shrine in my home. As time went on, my home became like a temple. I have many wonderful spiritual pictures and statues of all sizes throughout my house. Constantly being around these pictures and statues has an uplifting effect.

247   Cultivate Beauty in Your Home

Related to the previous key is what I call the cultivation of esthetics and a sense of beauty. This is a fourth-ray quality that is important for all to develop. I try to make my home like a spiritual temple with beautiful spiritual statues and pictures and plants everywhere.

This is an important leadership quality, especially when you hold classes in your home. The outer appearance of your home is the first thing that people see. The creation of one's home to be a sanctuary is not only important for others, but also for the healing and regeneration of one's own spirit. Surrounding yourself with beautiful works of art and the aroma of sublime incense and oils and the sound of beautiful music can be enormously uplifting to the human spirit.

248   Golden Pyramid

The next golden key has been the request that a golden pyramid be placed around and over my entire home and center. This serves as protection and an energy intensifier. You can also request that a pyramid be placed around you when you meditate.

249   Establish Ascension Columns

The next golden key has been establishing an ascension column and a pillar of light in my living room where I hold classes and in my office where I type all of my books. You can request of the masters that they establish this. Then you can do all of your spiritual work, including meditations, within this ascension column.

In conjunction with this, call forth to Hermes to connect both yourself and your home ascension column with the pyramid energies from the Great Pyramid of Egypt and all other pyramid temples of light.

250   Anchor Ascension Seats into Your Home

The next golden key was the request for the anchoring of the different ascension seats into my home and into my own being first at the planetary level, then the solar, galactic and universal levels. I requested that they be anchored into myself and my home on a permanent basis. Any person who enters my home for a class or for personal reasons is entering the Golden Chamber ascension seat of Melchizedek.

251   Anchor the Ascension Lineage of the Ashrams into Your Home

This golden key is similar to the last one, except that you are requesting that the ascension lineage of the ashrams be anchored into your home. My home and center is the ashram of Djwhal Khul, Lord Maitreya and Melchizedek, who are the masters I represent in my work. My home is also a Sai Baba center.

252 Anchor the City of God

The next golden key was calling for the anchoring of the ascension City of God, as described in *The Keys of Enoch*, into my home and the city where I live.

253 Locate Your Home in Your Power Points

The next golden key relates to where I have lived physically. Ascension and healing obviously can be achieved anywhere, but one's environment can play a big part. Certain geographic locations are vortexes for certain types of energies. Each person's response to energies is unique. Los Angeles has actually been a very good place for me to live for all of the training I needed and for my particular mission. This obviously would not be true for everyone. I also spent a great deal of time in northern California, which was in harmony with my spiritual vibration.

Djwhal Khul told me that there was an energy belt that ran through El Paso, Texas, Phoenix and Los Angeles. Strangely enough, I was born in El Paso, lived a great deal of my life in Los Angeles and at one point planned to move to Phoenix. These three places are geographic power centers for me, and my mission has been connected to this particular energy grid. If I ever move, I would probably move to Arizona. In meditation and in channeling sessions ask about your geographic power centers. They are unique for each person and can change according to the stage of life you are in.

Grounding Spiritual Energies in Daily Life

254 Run Spiritual Energies Daily

Another major key for me has been to call forth spiritual energies no matter what I am doing, so that I am running the spiritual current 24 hours a day. For instance, after a hard day's work, after dinner I might turn on the television and call forth various tools and let the masters work on me. Of course, I also do this in meditation, but I stay in meditation for only so long. When I'm watching television my mind is occupied in a passive manner, and I get an enormous amount of spiritual work done. Making use of every single moment for spiritual work has been a major key for me. I fan the spiritual flames with some kind of spiritual work 24 hours a day. It is amazing how much spiritual work can be done while you are watching TV, waiting in line at the market, running errands or driving a car.

I found that the energies would be slowed down after eating, but as time went on this happened less and less. If the energy does slow down, just call it back in after you eat. Can you see what a resurrecting effect running these spiritual energies throughout your body 24 hours a day, seven days a week, 365 days a year can have on your whole program? It feels wonderful, and after a while you never want to be without these energies. This constant work serves to heal the separation between personality, soul and monad. Even if you are not clairvoyant or clairaudient, you can always be connected to the masters through energy. Energy is key, for everything is energy.

255   Balance Yin and Yang When Running Spiritual Energies

This golden key is an extension of the previous one. It relates to what I call the yin and yang methods of running spiritual energies. If I am typing, for example, I run the spiritual current through my twelve-body system. When I am talking on the phone, doing counseling, giving a lecture or channeling, the same would be true. When I am not using the yang method of running energies, I then switch over to the yin method. This usually would be sitting in an ascension seat or asking the Arcturians or Metatron for light-quotient building. When I run the spiritual current, I spend half of my day in more yang activities and half of my day in yin activities. I enjoy each of them equally. The yang method spins the chakras and runs the energies. The yin method heals and strengthens them.

256   Request Your Spiritual Name

The next golden key was asking for my spiritual name. At a very early age I knew that my spiritual name was Joshua. It fit me perfectly and was clearly a mantra for my ascension development and spiritual mission to come. In meditation ask for your spiritual name. It will be your choice whether you actually want to change your name legally. I know this had an extremely powerful effect on me. The death of my old name and the birth of my new name was powerful both symbolically and vibrationally.

Integrating Spiritual Activities into Your Life

257   Affirmations and Visualizations

The next golden key for me has been doing affirmations and visualizations throughout my day. Keeping a good attitude and perspective in one's daily life is the ultimate affirmation. However, I have found it to be of great value to have a whole arsenal of affirmations at my disposal for every possible area of my life. I have personal power affirmations, love affirmations, financial-abundance affirmations, God affirmations, victory affirmations.

The list is endless. In combination with these affirmations I have a whole arsenal of visualizations of what I look like with personal power, self-love, financial abundance and God infusion. Every day I put on my mental and visual divinity, so to speak. Many years of practicing this religiously on a daily basis has helped me form sound spiritual habits and psychological clarity. In *Soul Psychology* I have given many wonderful affirmations and visualizations that you might want to consider using.

258   The Ascension Buddy System

The next key has been the ascension buddy system and group consciousness. I came to the conclusion early on that it was far more effective to work with friends and groups of people who are on a similar spiritual path. Jesus said, "Where two or more are gathered, there I Am also." After working in an ascension buddy system with my core goup for a time, the group intelligence, group etheric body, group love and group channeling abilities were enormously increased.

The masters have told me that we never would have been allowed to accelerate that quickly had we not been doing this in a group body with the ascension buddy system. Once your evolution becomes tied up, in a sense, with another person or persons, you learn to let go of comparing and competition and see yourselves as a team. It is not required that you do it this way, but I have found it very enjoyable. I have gone light-years further by doing it this way rather than being an island unto myself.

It is wonderful to be a part of a community of people you inspire and who inspire you. It makes life more fun and will greatly accelerate your spiritual path. The spiritual path is meant to be shared in fellowship.

259   Channeling

The next key has been channeling, which is a wonderful spiritual practice. It is an easy thing for all to do if they will just allow themselves to practice. Everyone on this planet is a channel—and every person channels differently. So release any preconceived ideas as to how you are going to channel. The classic channel we think of is a clairaudient voice channel. That is one kind of channeling that all can practice. Then there is the telepathic or informational channel, which is the type I am most developed in. There are others who channel images, music or poetry.

The most important thing is to channel from the spiritual plane and not from the astral or mental planes. It is crucial to know what you are channeling. Many people channel their negative ego, emotional body or subconscious mind and believe it is higher wisdom.

The heart of channeling is trusting spirit to flow through you. When I write my books, I don't even have an outline. The only thing I have is the title of the book. I simply start typing and it all comes out in the flow of channeling. I trust my mighty I Am Presence and the ascended masters, then I let the books unfold as spirit guides me.

The same applies to public speaking. It is fine to have an outline, but then pray and call in God and the masters and let them intuitively speak through you. I have learned to trust this over time. It is amazing what flows through if you allow it to. You do not need to be clairaudient and hear the actual voice of the masters to do this. Not all lightworkers are meant to do that type of channeling. Experiment and practice with yourself and your friends and find the ways to channel that are best for you. For those of you who want to learn more about channeling, read the chapter on it in *Soul Psychology*.

260   Use Sleep Time for Spiritual Work

The next golden key has been my use of sleep time to do spiritual work. I constantly call forth divine dispensations to have different types of spiritual work done all night while I sleep. I always do spiritual work right before bed so that my last thoughts will take me into higher planes of consciousness upon falling asleep. I often ask to be taken during sleep to different ashrams or ascended master retreats. The amount of spiritual work that can be done during sleep is awesome. I cannot recommend more highly taking advantage of this time.

261   Soul Travel

The next golden key has been the practice of soul travel. This is actually very easy to do, and you don't have to be clairvoyant or clairaudient to do it. Your spiritual body will travel instantly to wherever you send it or request that it be taken. I am constantly traveling all over the cosmos to the different cosmic and planetary ashrams, ascension seats and starships with the masters to attend council meetings and do service work. Much is also done unconsciously, of course, while sleeping and even while awake.

One of the new books I am writing is called *How to Use the Planetary and Cosmic Ashrams*. This book will be a map of the cosmos and will show how to utilize these different ashrams of the masters for spiritual progression and world service work. I am very excited about this. One of the purposes of the book is to show people how easy it is to soul-travel and utilize the cosmos as our playing field.

Soul travel also ties in with my bilocation work—doing two things at once, such as sitting in the Arcturian light chamber while walking, watching television or talking on the phone. Most lightworkers don't realize that you can be doing a number of spiritual projects simultaneously. This understanding has enormously accelerated my spiritual life and healing.

Working with the Archetypes

262   The Universal Archetype Attunement

With this golden key, ask to be taken into the holographic computer room of Djwhal Khul's synthesis ashram and receive the universal archetype attunement. Sit in meditation and receive this one-time archetype and pranic imprinting that will serve to completely restructure your ego into the universal and divine structure of the archetypes at the twelfth-dimensional level. This all will be done telepathically and is extremely powerful.

263   Work with the Twelve Archetypes

This golden key is working with the twelve archetypes. The goal is to have all of them balanced and integrated properly. The universal-archetype attunement will be of great help. But work with the archetypes must also be done consciously for us to achieve full mastery on all levels. The idea is to integrate all twelve major archetypes into your being and be well-developed in all of them.

264   Call for a Buddha/Christ Archetypal Imprint

With this golden key, ask to be taken to Shamballa and call forth to Lord Buddha and Lord Maitreya for a Buddha/Christ archetypal imprint on a permanent basis. Sit and bathe in this energy as this work is done on you.

Balance in Daily Life

265   Set Appropriate Boundaries

The next golden key has been learning to set appropriate boundaries. We must learn to merge with others in oneness and group consciousness while at the same time be strongly anchored in our sense of self. When appropriate psychological and psychic boundaries are not kept, we can take on other people's emotional, mental, energetic and even physical stuff. Some people tend to have too rigid boundaries and cannot embrace group consciousness on any level, including God. Other people are too empathic and don't know how to say no, protect their space and retain a proper sense of self. The key here is balance.

266   Mature Honesty

The next golden key has been the development of a healthy, mature sense of honesty. True honesty begins with being honest with yourself, which relates to deep self-inquiry. If you are not honest with yourself, you cannot be honest with others.

Huna and *A Course in Miracles* teach that one of humanity's greatest sins is hurting another. Never use honesty as an excuse to slaughter people emotionally. Honesty must be tempered with unconditional love, respect, proper timing and tact. Remain balanced in your understanding of honesty, use common sense and maturity and consider the highest good of others and yourself.

267   Kaizen

The next golden key has been a Japanese concept known as *kaizen*, which means constant improvement. It means to do your best and then try to do better than your best. I heard of this Japanese concept only recently. However, it expresses something I have practiced for many years. Whatever I achieved I would feel happy about, but the next day I would work even harder.

Now I am working harder than I ever have in my entire life. I enjoy myself, but I never let down, for I realize that there is always another rung to climb on Jacob's ladder. Even now, after achieving my healing, ascension and other major goals, I am very happy—but still not satisfied. There are always higher and higher levels of mastery, purification and God realization to attain. God is infinite, and there always will be finer and finer levels of purification and growth. Cultivate the spiritual quality of kaizen in your own life. Enjoy and appreciate your successes, but always strive for higher levels.

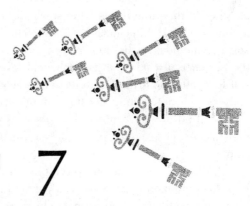

GOLDEN KEYS TO ASCENSION AND HEALING

7

PRACTICAL METHODS FOR MASTERY
Keys 268-289

COMMUNICATING WITH YOUR INNER SELF
ATTITUDE
CLEANLINESS, ORGANIZATION AND ROUTINES
PSYCHOLOGICAL CLARITY
JOURNAL- WRITING
SPIRITUAL LOGS

As a preface to this section I would like to state the importance of working on the three levels—the spiritual, psychological and physical simultaneously. All three must be mastered to attain true self-realization. The spiritual includes meditation and prayer, unconditional love and practicing the presence of God. The psychological level deals with personal power, self-love, attitude (Christ attitude versus ego attitude), balancing the four-body system, integrating the three minds, properly parenting your inner child and attitudinal healing. The physical level is service work, proper diet, mastery of sexuality, physical exercise, sunshine, fresh air and fellowship.

Of course there is much overlapping in these, but each level needs to be zeroed in on and mastered. You cannot fully solve psychological problems with meditation. You cannot achieve realization in your spiritual life by just reading. You cannot heal your physical body with the power of your mind only. Each level must be honored, respected and mastered in its own right. This is a golden key to attaining self-realization.

Communicating with Your Inner Self

268   Work with Your Dreams

This golden key, working with my dreams, has been absolutely essential to my spiritual evolution. My father and mother, being Jungian psychologists, gave me a tremendous background in working with my dreams as a child and adolescent. I follow my dreams very closely. Over time I have learned a language of symbols that is personal to me. Dreams have provided me with valuable information on many levels. I am constantly making adjustments in my life based on information I obtain in my dreams.

Write down your dreams every morning and work with them. In *Soul Psychology* I have a chapter on dreams that you might find useful; and of course there are many wonderful books on dreams. The key is learning the symbols that are personal to you. My I Am Presence works very closely with me, using the symbols I have come to understand. Working with my dreams in this way helps me to stay integrated and balanced. Take time to work with your dreams, for they will provide you with an invaluable source of information.

269   Hypnosis

The next golden key in my life has been the study and practice of hypnosis, including self-hypnosis. This has given me a great understanding of the subconscious mind both theoretically and experientially. When used from a spiritual perspective, hypnosis can be of great value for yourself and for helping others. There is a very fine line between hypnosis and meditation. Both are altered states of consciousness, but hypnosis is focused on the subconscious mind and meditation on the superconsicous mind. Hypnosis is a wonderful tool for accelerating the process of reprogramming the subconscious.

270   Letters to God

This golden key, which has been absolutely instrumental in my life, is what I call letters to God. Whenever things were bothering me or were out of balance in my life, I would sit down at my typewriter and type a letter to God and my own mighty I Am Presence. I have written hundreds of these letters. It is a tool that has helped me develop clarity, channeling abilities and overall spiritual attunement. It is a type of journal-writing with a complete spiritual attunement and focus.

God always would respond—through my writing and typing, telepathy, intuition, dreams, meditation, other people and life experience. In essence I was operating my own personal God correspondence course. I also found my "Dear God" letters to be a quite effective form of prayer. You might also write letters to the ascended masters if you wish.

271   Work with the Inner Child

The next golden key has been my work with the inner child. It is crucial to learn how to parent the inner child properly. It is possible to be a high-level initiate and still need considerable work in parenting the inner child. The foundation of all spiritual work is to be right with oneself, which includes being right with the inner child, right with subconscious mind, right with the four-body system and right with the ego.

272   Positive Self-Talk

The next golden key is what I call positive self-talk. Our subconscious mind is always talking to us. For masses of humanity, this talk is of a negative nature. One of the keys to reversing this is to talk with yourself in an informal manner. This helps reprogram the mind and cultivate the habit of positive self-talk. This can be done with affirmations, decrees, talking in front of a mirror, tapes, positive reminders posted around your house, self-hypnosis or this more informal type of self-talk. Talking to yourself has gotten a bad rap. But when self-talk is used consciously, it can be a very powerful tool for transformation.

273   Voice Dialogue

The next key has been the use of a psychological tool called voice dialogue. My father has done some wonderful work in this area, and he taught me this method when I was a young adult. It is a marvelous tool for working with yourself and others. It can be done in a journal, in chairs or even in your mind. I have used this process to get clear with the psychodynamics going on within my consciousness. I also used it for many years in my counseling practice. In your journal, or in chairs, dialogue with your inner child, inner parent, emotional body, mental body, physical body, spiritual body, higher self, monad, negative ego or Christ mind. This will help bring you great clarity and perspective, help integrate your consciousness and clarify your psychoepistemology.

My father, Harold Stone, has written many books on the subject (which you can find in your local metaphysical bookstore if you are interested in his work). Voice dialogue is a more refined version of the role-playing work that was first used so extensively by Fritz Perls in the Gestalt therapy movement.

Attitude

274   Make Appropriate Attitudinal Adjustments

The next golden key has been the whole concept of making attitudinal adjustments. There is really no such thing as a perfect state of consciousness that never changes. The true perfect state of consciousness is one that listens to inner guidance and makes the appropriate adjustments in consciousness as needed. When the negative ego raises its ugly head, the healthy conscious mind goes into action with its personal power and stops it.

Upon waking in the morning adjustments can be made according to guidance received. As the physical body speaks to you during the day, adjustments are made according to its needs. The same applies to the emotional, mental and spiritual bodies. Life is like driving a car. Even when you are driving straight on a highway, there are still slight adjustments that constantly need to be made. There is a state of centeredness that we seek to maintain. However, there is always a flow and slight pendulum swing that occurs as we seek to maintain balance between the feminine and masculine energies and the heavenly and earthly energies. I call these attitudinal adjustments, which can be likened to chiropractic adjustments that keep the spine centered and straight.

275 Give Up Arguing

The next golden key is to give up arguing completely. It is fine to share opinions in a loving way, but if the discussion starts to become argumentative, I will back down, remain silent and not get involved in needing to be right. Give up all self-righteousness and state everything you believe as your personal opinion. Allow every person to have his or her personal opinions and values, even if you totally disagree with the person.

276 Give Up a Belief in Failure

On the subject of giving things up, I also recommend giving up the word "failure," for in reality it does not exist. The concept of failure stems from a belief in judgment. There are no failures. There are only lessons, mistakes, insights and opportunities to grow. Even the ascended masters make mistakes. Perfection does not mean never making a mistake; it means not making conscious mistakes. Whenever you make a mistake, forgive yourself, integrate the learning from the situation, release all guilt and move forward. Don't make a big deal out of it. It's just grist for the mill, as Ram Dass has said.

277 Fake It Till You Make It

The next key was something I developed early on in my spiritual path that I call the "willful" method of spiritual growth. At earlier stages of my life I was battling my negative ego much more than I am now, and I knew it was not right to be in ego battles. So I would often use this more willful method, or "fake it till I make it" method. For instance, if my negative ego was feeling super angry and wanted to hold a grudge, I would force myself to do just the opposite; and over time I would find that I would soon actually feel the way I had forced myself to feel.

Now I have much more control of the negative ego, and I can usually attitudinally heal and work things out quickly in my mind. In an absolute emergency I write in my journal. I recognize instantly that what I am experiencing is all occurring in my mind and emotions, that there is nothing outside myself causing this separation consciousness. If there is one thing to strive for above all else, it is never to create separation between myself, my brothers and sisters and God. Of course, in truth we all are God.

Here's an amusing story from my early twenties. I remember being very angry in regard to a particular person. In my journal that day I told myself that I was not going to let go of my anger, no matter how long it took, until this situation was resolved. That night I dreamed that God had died. You never saw anyone release anger and move to forgiveness as fast as I did! It didn't take a brain scientist to figure out that the two situations were totally related.

The golden key here is to strive to be in a state of Christ consciousness at all times even if your emotional body, inner child and negative ego are not cooperating. With your Christ consciousness as your guide, you can learn to develop consistency between all aspects of your being.

278   No Swearing

This golden key is something that Djwhal Khul said in class one time. Do not use the Lord's name in vain and do not swear in general. This is a hard one for many people, but I pass this guidance along from Djwhal Khul. His suggestion was to substitute a non-swearword such as "shoot" if one has to have that type of catharsis, or else come up with a word of your own creation that is not so negatively charged. Swearwords have a certain collective negative energy attached to them that shoots out into the universe, especially when expressed in an emotionally charged manner.

I'll be honest and say that not swearing has been one of my hardest vows to keep. Sometimes when I stub my toe or do something incredibly dumb, a swearword just pops out. But there is no judgment on it, and it is not the end of the world if it happens.

279   No Pornography

Another golden key from Djwhal Khul is to give up all pornography as we move into higher levels of initiation. There is no judgment on it at younger stages of evolution. At higher levels of spiritual evolvement sexuality is much more sanctified, loving and tantric in nature. Do not judge yourself for past indulgences, for everything in life occurs in the proper timing.

Cleanliness, Organization and Routines

280   Daily Routines

The next golden key has been the application of an inner structure and regime in my life. Carl Jung said, "Man's greatest sin is his indolence." The subconscious mind likes to follow the line of least resistance. I attribute a great deal of my success to the schedules and regimes I have set up for myself over the last twenty years. I would have routines for exercise, meditation, prayer, journal-writing, work and even eating. However, I would not make these routines too yang, for this takes the fun out of life. Neither would I make them too yin.

This inner structure helped me develop self-discipline and keep my priorities straight. I think everyone can benefit from this kind of structure. However, it is important to change routines frequently to adapt to your changing needs. By creating this kind of order in your life, over time good work habits are developed. Then the Holy Spirit and ascended masters can use you as a most reliable channel and instrument.

281   Organization

The next key has to do with staying organized and practicing good time management. I am certainly not a fanatic on this; however, I do like my earthly life to be in good order. The more leadership responsibility one takes on, the more need there is for order in one's life.

282   Cleanliness

This golden key relates to cleanliness in all areas of life. This applies to personal care and also to one's environment. I am immaculate in terms of my personal grooming, but I have to be honest here and say that I'm a little weaker than I should be in terms of my physical environment. I am not a slob by any means, but I think I still have some bachelor programming in me that needs to be cleared. My usual pattern is to clean up like a madman before company comes, but be a little too lazy in terms of vacuuming, dusting and so on. My way of solving this is to invest in a cleaning woman once a week. This is what I did for three and a half years, and I think I got a little spoiled.

Cleanliness is important on all levels of one's being: clean spirit, clean thoughts, clean emotions, clean body and clean environment. As Edgar Cayce said in one of his channelings, "Make your earthly home a place where angels choose to tread." I hereby vow to make an attitudinal adjustment in this area and clean up my act. (At least I get a Brownie point for honesty!)

Psychological Clarity

283   A Healthy Psychological Immune System

The next golden key is keeping a healthy psychological immune system. Most people think of the immune system as applying to the physical body, which of course it does. It is just as important to keep a healthy psychological immune system, for this affects the physical immune system as well. This relates to the ability to remain invulnerable psychologically. This means not taking on other peoples' stuff and not letting other people and situations affect your reality. It has to do with maintaining your inner peace and joy even when other people around you are irritable, angry, impatient, upset or depressed.

The ideal is for you to stay in a state of inner peace and happiness at all times and help raise other people's states, rather than catch other people's psychological diseases. Actually there is no such thing as a contagious physical or psychological disease. There are only people with low physical and psychological resistance. This has been a crucial insight for me. One aspect of a healthy psychological immune system is the ability to distinguish between sympathy and detached compassion. We want to maintain an attitude of compassion yet not take on the energies and consciousness of those around us.

284   Psychological Clarity and Integration on All Levels

This golden key is understanding that the psychological self is the foundation of spiritual life. There are lightworkers who have achieved their ascension but who are not ready for leadership because of their psychological unclarity and personality problems. It is essential that all levels be clear.

All seventh-degree initiates will be stopped cold in their tracks and not be allowed to progress into cosmic ascension if the psychological self is not mastered and integrated properly in the service of God. The psychological self includes one's relationship to the subconscious mind, inner child and four-body system. *Soul Psychology* can assist in this important part of our spiritual evolution.

Your level of initiation does not make you a true master. The key is not to skip steps. I know of one initiate who had an incredible zeal to achieve ascension and did so in record time. The only problem was that this person's mental maturity was that of a twelve-year-old. This is one of the dangers of the revolutionary times in which we live. This is also why lightworkers are not given the advanced ascended master abilities, as was possible in the past, even though they have achieved their seventh initiation. Because the evolution of the planet is so accelerated at this time, it is much easier to achieve the seven levels of initiations and ascension than it was in the past. True ascended master realization, at the highest level of maturity, now is more related to the process of cosmic ascension than to planetary ascension. Cosmic ascension is not realized until one achieves, not fifth-dimensional, but twelfth-dimensional consciousness.

You cannot even consider truly integrating the solar levels until you have completed your seven levels of initiation, integrated and cleansed your 144 soul extensions, installed and activated all 50 chakras, installed and activated your first nine bodies, built your light-quotient to stabilize at 99 percent, and moved into the cosmic light-quotient scale. I know people who have tried to skip steps. One person had a heart attack from improper integration. This also created delusions and distortions in his mental and emotional bodies. Proper integration of all levels in proper sequence is forever the key.

Journal-Writing

I have done journal-writing for many years. It has been one of the most important tools in my spiritual evolution and a major key in helping me attain psychological and spiritual clarity. The following four golden keys describe sections of my journal.

285   Cycles

This section of my journal, "Cycles," is something I learned from Paul Solomon. It involved going back over my entire life and looking at all the cycles or phases of my life that had led me to my current level of development. When that was complete I took all of my short-term and long-term goals and set up future cycles that I wanted to put myself through to help me get to my ultimate goal of achieving ascension, liberation and God realization.

By keeping this journal section for many years, I trained my mind to think in this manner. This helped me utilize my time and energy extremely efficiently. All of my thoughts, words and deeds became connected to this flow of cycles leading to my ultimate goal. I would highly recommend developing such a journal section for yourself.

286   Search for the Value of All Experiences

Another section of my journal, "Validation of Worth," is one that I learned from Paul Solomon's inner-light-consciousness process. In this section you validate and acknowledge all of the masters and teachers who have helped you in your spiritual growth that day. Once you begin to look at life from this perspective, which is actually looking at life through Christ eyes, then every person and situation becomes your teacher. The traffic jam teaches you patience. The drunk in the gutter teaches you compassion and the pitfalls of alcohol. The boss who yells at you teaches you personal power, invulnerability, forgiveness, unconditional love—and, possibly, to stand up for yourself.

The idea here is to go through your entire day and acknowledge all of these teachers and the lessons they are bringing you. Looking at every person and situation as a teacher can produce a major attitudinal shift. When we get angry or upset we are misinterpreting reality by perceiving it through the negative ego's eyes instead of our Christ eyes. This journal section is a very effective method for training your conscious and subconscious minds to interpret life through the Christ consciousness.

287   Major Lessons of the Day

This journal section, "My Major Lessons of the Day," is one that I kept religiously for many years. Each day I would write down the major things I learned in terms of what I did well and what I did poorly. It is important to take the time to introspect and learn from our experiences. Earth is a school, and every moment of our lives we are being tested on our overall spiritual, psychological and physical development.

288   Battle Plans

I called this part of my journal my battle-plan section. Wherever there was an area in my life that was not going well, I would write up a spiritual battle plan to heal and correct that problem or challenge. If it was finances, I would make a list of all of the things I could do spiritually, mentally, emotionally and physically to turn the tide. Having spiritual battle plans for different areas of my life always made me feel better and got me focused on how to turn things around. Thus I was always on top of my life even though the outer appearances that I desired had not manifested yet.

Spiritual Logs

289   An Overview

A golden key to my spiritual progress that I used for many years was keeping spiritual logs. Just as we need to keep logs of our finances, we need logs relating to our spiritual life. For a great many years I would keep all kinds of logs in regard to the development of my character and Christ qualities. Each day I would score myself on a percentage basis as to my success.

This spiritual accounting and bookkeeping kept me on target and helped me reprogram my subconscious mind with Christ thinking and Christ emotions. If there are certain Christ qualities that you are weak in, try keeping a log for a couple of months until the new habit has been formed. These logs help prevent the tendency toward going on automatic pilot. They can be kept for food addictions and other bad habits. Give yourself a score twice a day on your development, with either a percentage or a grade. It is a little game I played with myself that I found invaluable.

Following are some of the spiritual logs I have kept.

❖ Negative-Emotions Log

In this log I wrote down the different negative emotions that would come up during my day, and then I would later examine my faulty thinking and negative-ego perceptions that had caused them to develop.

An effective method that helped me discover unconscious negative emotions and limiting beliefs was to pay attention to the messages that arose when I stated a positive affirmation. When I stated an affirmation, I would listen for the negative self-talk, the doubts and fears that arose from the negative ego. Then I would write this down and create new positive affirmations as an antidote, again listening for the negative self-talk that arose.

I continued this process until I got to the very root of the core fear belief that was causing that negative complex to exist. In conjunction with this process I recommend calling on the ascended masters to help remove these old core fears and beliefs. Especially call for the Core-Fear-Removal Program (see Golden Key 69). Through many years of working in this way, mental and emotional clarity were achieved. This is some of the work that laid the foundation for *Soul Psychology*.

❖ Victory Log

During the time when I was going through all of my health lessons and Job initiation, I kept a victory log. Every day I would write down my victories no matter how small. Since it is our thoughts that create our reality, I began focusing on my victories. This was a major key to my success.

Through the victory log I learned to be optimistic instead of pessimistic. I learned to focus on what I could do instead of what I couldn't. I learned to live in the moment and focus on my spiritual progress. Over time I increasingly became aware of the progress I was making even though I still was clearly handicapped. What I came to realize was that everyone is handicapped in some way—either physically, emotionally, mentally or spiritually.

If I had given in to the physical handicap, it could have crippled me emotionally, mentally and spiritually. But I didn't, and over time, miracle after miracle began to unfold. The power of God can heal and transcend all problems and challenges, and I am a living example. Whatever cross you bear, trust in God and put all of your eggs in God's basket. He will not fail you if you are willing to have faith, trust and patience.

❖ Gratitude Log

As part of my victory log I would write down all the things I had to be grateful for. Instead of focusing on my losses, I began to focus on all of the gifts that God had graced me with. As time went on, even with all of my handicaps, inwardly I began to feel like the luckiest person on the face of the Earth. Now, a psychiatrist might have thought I was delusional, but this is honestly how I felt. This inner happiness, joy and gratefulness to God I carried within me throughout the stages of my healing. My health caused me to make what at the time were secondary choices, such as starting to write books. But now as I look back, I see how everything was in perfect divine order.

❖ Meditation Log

When I would meditate I would often receive guidance and information while in an altered state. The only problem was that I would often forget what I had received, similar to the way I would forget my dreams if I didn't write them down immediately upon arising. The meditation log has been an instrumental part of my journal system.

❖ Spiritual Vow Log

Every week or month, check your vows to make sure you are sticking to them. At that time you can make new, even deeper vows if you feel called to do so. At times I have done ceremonies in front of my altar. There can be a feeling of dying and being reborn, getting a fresh start. In making a vow I usually state, "I hereby make my ultimate commitment to God to (the vow). Amen." After doing this, the attitudinal adjustment is made, and I feel locked into my new and more perfect self and path.

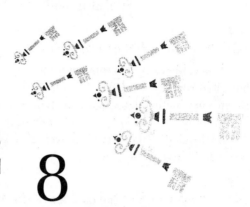

GOLDEN KEYS TO ASCENSION AND HEALING 8

THE MASTERS AND THE PATH
Keys 290-331

WORKING WITH THE MASTERS
ACCESSING THE MASTERS' ASHRAMS
MAINTAINING YOUR OWN POWER WITH MASTERS AND TEACHERS
SPECIAL BEINGS
GUIDELINES ON THE PATH
INITIATIONS
YOUR MISSION
INSPIRATION ON THE PATH
RELATIONSHIPS
WESAK AND FULL MOON FESTIVALS

Working with the Masters

290   Be Overlighted by Your Spiritual Teachers

This golden key is to find out what your exact ascension lineage is. As I have told you, mine is Djwhal Khul, Lord Maitreya and Melchizedek. Your ascension usually relates to the ray type of your monad, though there might be exceptions. Request to be overlighted by your main spiritual teachers. As you develop, you can request overlighting from the planetary, solar, galactic and universal levels.

291   Merge with the Lightbodies of the Masters

When I first had the idea to ask for this golden key, Melchizedek told me that it is one of the most profound keys in this entire book. This key has two parts. It begins with asking to merge with the lightbody of Metatron, Melchizedek, Lord Michael, Lord Buddha, Lord Maitreya and other masters with whom you have an affinity. Request this on a permanent basis.

After working with this for a while and feeling its profound effects, I then came up with the idea of asking to merge with the entire Spiritual Hierarchy of over 2500 masters. Ask for this after you pass your seventh initiation. Timing is everything, as you know. By the grace of God we were given this divine dispensation, and in one most glorious meditation my core goup and I merged with the entire Spiritual Hierarchy. Later the cosmic Hierarchy merged their lightbodies with us. Talk about a resurrecting experience! From that day forward I felt like a full member of the Spiritual Hierarchy.

292   Get to Know the Ascended Masters

This golden key was gaining a more realistic view of the masters through conversations with them. I began to realize that they are like us but a little more advanced. Earlier in my life I perceived them to be these unreachable perfected beings who were not at all like us Earthlings. Nothing could be further from the truth. They are definitely more advanced in wisdom, love and light, but they are not that different from you and me. They like to laugh and joke and tease. They are very personable. They like to be accepted. They make mistakes at times as we do, contrary to popular opinion. I consider the ascended masters to be not only my spiritual teachers, but also my friends.

They are striving as hard as we are for spiritual growth because they have not yet fully realized God, far from it. The ascended masters we revere such as Jesus, Saint Germain, Kuthumi, Djwhal Khul, El Morya, Lord

Maitreya and Lord Buddha are only one and a half inches up a ten-inch ruler in terms of their cosmic ascension. They are striving at their level for spiritual growth as we are at our level. They still have remnants of negative ego that they are also clearing, and each master has his or her own unique personality. Lord Maitreya recently called Saint Germain, in a loving way, a "rogue" because of his personal style of getting involved with the ladies.

Each master has very distinct personality characteristics, and the rays we receive from the chohans are greatly influenced by each of their personality styles. Over time I have grown to feel very much like them and hence equal with them. I am not afraid to talk with them, ask them questions, joke with and tease them, and even at times to set my own personal boundaries—always respectfully and with great love, of course.

293 Interact with the Masters

This golden key has been to relate to the ascended masters from my own empowerment. The masters want to dialogue with an equal, not a child who does exactly what they say. It is perfectly okay to disagree with the masters and state your views and opinions as long as this is done in a respectful and loving way. They themselves are not beyond learning. They learn and grow through their interaction with us.

They might ask you to do something you don't want to do, and that is perfectly okay. They might ask you to move somewhere and you might not want to do it. They might give you specific assignments that you want to adjust. It is within your right to say no or to negotiate with them and not feel guilty. There is much room for dialogue with the masters. They work with us as brothers and sisters, not as dictators.

The other key here is not waiting for them to tell you what to do. Be creative in your own right. One of the main reasons I was able to overcome so many obstacles and achieve the goals I had set was that I owned my own power and creative energies. I took charge without having the masters nursemaid me along. Most of what I do in my life comes from my own creative flow, and I use the ascended masters to adjust and refine this process. In more recent years they have given me specific assignments, which I love. Ninety-nine percent of what they suggest to me is right in tune with my own intuition and feelings. Often what they suggest to me I am so excited about I can hardly restrain myself. However, I do retain the right to say no, disagree or make adjustments.

So do not wait for the ascended masters to tell you how to serve. God helps those who help themselves. Serve where intuitively you feel called to serve, and the masters will support and refine the process along the way.

294   Loneliness vs. Being Alone: Feeling the Presence of God and the Masters

The next golden key has been learning the difference between loneliness and being alone. When one learns to be right with oneself and right with God and the masters, one is never alone. When I am physically alone I never feel lonely because I enjoy my own company. I also feel the presence of God and the masters with me at all times. As I already have stated, I am always communing with them through ascension seats and light-quotient building and healing modalities.

It is true that as you fully embrace the spiritual path, you must stand on your own and often let go of people. There is a period early in our spiritual journey when we might experience what can be called existential aloneness. This is usually a temporary phase that lightworkers go through until greater realization is achieved. Now most of my close friends are the people I am involved with in my service work. This makes the service work more enjoyable.

295   Make Yourself Known to the Masters

The next golden key has been a willingness to make myself known to the ascended masters, cosmic forces, angels and powers that be. Some lightworkers don't feel worthy enough to ask the masters for help. This is faulty thinking. The masters and angels want to help, but they need your request to be allowed to do this. I have never been afraid to ask for help or to ask questions from any of the masters. One of the things I like about the Wesak is that not only do we have a highly diverse earthly group, but I make it a point to call in a diverse group of masters. They like to be included, too.

My mom had a dream a couple of years ago in which she was given a message to make herself known to the Great White Spirit. Make yourself known to the ascended masters, angels and positive extraterrestrials, for they welcome your contact. Remember that they evolve by serving you. The ascended masters can't move on until we take their place. Pray to them for help. Make the ascended masters your best friends. Tell them you want to complete your initiations and your ascension so that you can serve better. They will take you at your word and accelerate your program. And they will expect you to keep your promise.

The veil you thought separated you from them doesn't really exist. Call on a wide and diverse range of masters. The timing of your initiations and ascension relates in part to your light-quotient level and certain other requirements. But it also is up to the ascended masters. If the masters want to accelerate your program for their purposes, they can and will. Keep praying and talking to them until they can't help but take notice and give you the blessings you desire. Then return the favor by sharing the blessings you have received with selfless service to humanity. That is a fair exchange, I would say.

296 Sessions with the Masters

The next golden key has been having certain types of sessions with the masters. One is a ray reading showing the configuration of all of one's rays in regard to one's monad, soul, personality, mind, emotions and body. The next type of session is for the removal of astral toxins—implants, negative elementals and parasites. All lightworkers should do this as they evolve to higher levels of initiation. The third type of session is an astrology reading from a qualified astrologer who has a connection with the masters. An astrology reading and a ray reading together lay out a type of personal blueprint for this lifetime. I would recommend that all parents have ray and astrology readings for their children, preferably shortly after they are born.

297 Request Interviews from the Masters

The next golden key is to request interviews with the ascended masters. I request this only when I have something very important to speak with them about. An interview is different from asking questions. I have had many of these interviews with Sai Baba, Djwhal Khul, Lord Maitreya and Melchizedek.

298 Triple-Artery Phone System to the Masters

The next key has been what I call the establishment of our spiritual triple-artery telephone system. This activation is appropriate to call for after you take your seventh initiation. It is an official telephone line between your planetary, galactic and universal ascension-lineage spiritual teachers. After setting up this telephone system, whenever my core goup and I would have a conference with the masters, Melchizedek, Lord Maitreya and Djwhal Khul would be present simultaneously. Previously we had worked with only one spiritual teacher at a time.

299 Ask Much, Give Much

The next golden key has been the understanding that because I was requesting all of these activations and the acceleration of my ascension process, "much is given, but much is now expected." This is a direct quote from Sai Baba, Melchizedek and Djwhal Khul. The masters are perfectly willing to give you all that you ask for and more. However, there is a price to pay. That price is the willingness to move into leadership and begin serving at your highest potential. If you are not willing to do this, I would think twice about requesting such accelerations of your spiritual growth.

Achieving your ascension is a sign that you have become a master on a planetary level. Once you are a master, then you are expected to take on a master's responsibility. I am now so busy with my service work that I don't have much time to think about spiritual growth or cosmic ascension. That seems to be taking care of itself. Cosmic ascension is such a slow process anyway that it would be a waste of time to focus much on it. If you are not willing to serve and give back all the blessings you have received, then what is the point of all the spiritual work you have done? Self-actualization means that you are truly ready to give. The form of this service does not matter as long as you are giving wholeheartedly in alignment with your mission and inner guidance.

Accessing the Masters' Ashrams

300　Visit the Council Chamber in Shamballa

This golden key is to call forth to Lord Maitreya and ask to be taken to the council chamber in Shamballa with your ascension buddies. Then ask the council how you can best be of service to them. You can ask this in regard to both individual and group work. Then if you have any suggestions about how humanity can be best served for the coming year, Lord Maitreya has said that he and the council are open to your suggestions. Each ashramic level has a different focus to their work. The work that Djwhal Khul has for me is different from Lord Maitreya's and Buddha's work, which is a little different from the work I do for Melchizedek.

301　Visit the Masters' Ashrams

The next golden key has been traveling to and working with different masters in the planetary and cosmic ashrams. This subject is going to be the basis of a new book I have begun writing, *How to Use the Inner-Plane Planetary and Cosmic Ashrams*. With each master and ashram, the planetary and cosmic hierarchy has a different specialty and area of focus.

For example, I have spent time in the ashram of El Morya, who has great skills in leadership, politics and the integration of the will aspect of God. I have often visited with Serapis Bey in his ascension retreat in Luxor, which was instrumental in my ascension process. I have been with the master Jesus, also known as Sananda, in his retreat learning about devotion and unconditional love. I have devoted much time with Saint Germain in his retreat and ashram learning about transmutation and the proper integration of the seventh ray. I have visited most frequently, of course, with Djwhal Khul in his synthesis ashram, which integrates all seven rays. It is located on the first floor of the second-ray ashram. I also visited with the master Kuthumi in his ashram on the second floor, and with Lord Maitreya in his ashram on the third floor of the second-ray ashram. Recently I spent time with Lord Buddha, the new Planetary Logos, in his ashram in Shamballa.

The core group and I have all spent time in the ashram of Lord Sirius in the Great White Lodge. This has been glorious and feels like home. We have visited the ashram of Lord Arcturus on his mothership and have been given tours of his ship. We have often visited at length in Melchizedek's ashram, which has been the most glorious of all. Once we even visited God's ashram and sat in the ascension seat there in the group body under the guidance of the Mahatma. I have spent time in the ashrams of Lenduce, Vywamus, Melchior, Paul the Venetian and Hilarion and also visited commander Ashtar's ashram on his mothership.

Archangels also have their ashrams, as do the elohim, Paradise sons, the manu, and the mahachohan. There is the multiuniversal-level ashram and, of course, there is Sai Baba's ashram. Other inner-plane ashrams include those of Helios and Vesta, the Cosmic Council of Twelve, the Twenty-four Elders that surround the Throne of Grace and the karmic board. I have received enormous benefit from visiting these ashrams and receiving the blessings and trainings from these masters.

Maintaining Your Own Power with Masters and Teachers

302   No Gurus

The next golden key has been to be involved with spiritual teachers but not have gurus. In the Piscean Age people have given away their power to gurus. God-realized beings such as Sai Baba do not want or need your power. Sai Baba usually tells people to remain with the religion or spiritual teacher they already have. The heart of his message is, "Yes, I am God, but so are you." Lightworkers must be very clear on this issue or it will inhibit progression on the path. Djwhal Khul explicitly told me that he does not want to be regarded as a guru. He wants to be related to as an elder brother, spiritual teacher, equal and friend. This is the model for the new Aquarian Age.

303 Don't Give Your Power to the Masters

The ascended masters don't want your power, either. They want your respect and love, but they wish you to approach them as equals. As *A Course in Miracles* says, awe is appropriate only to God, not to your brothers and sisters. The ascended masters are our brothers and sisters. Soon we will be in their position, and we will be helping Earthlings as we have been helped. Don't project some fantasy onto the ascended masters that is not real. Even Melchizedek, the Universal Logos, told me that he has weaknesses. He is striving as we are for spiritual evolution, only at a much higher level in which he is dealing with cosmic rather than planetary issues.

304 Maintain Discernment about Paths and Teachers

This golden key relates to using discernment in regard to spiritual teachers. Because a channel or psychic writes books or is a good advertiser doesn't mean they know what they are talking about. Spiritual leaders often are much more advanced in the spiritual realm than they are mentally or emotionally. Their work can be contaminated by negative emotions, personality distortions and negative ego. This can manifest as physical health problems long after ascension has been achieved. (I realize that I am bursting the bubble of some of the earlier myths and fantasies about ascension—some of which I passed on to you myself. But information is constantly being updated and it is important to keep current.)

There are very few spiritual teachers who are clear on all levels. If spiritual teachers and leaders are brilliant on one level, it doesn't mean that they are brilliant on all levels. They could be great channels and still have a lack of clarity in their personal mental understanding. Great spiritual teachers with enormous wisdom can still be run by the negative ego or the emotions. This is not to say that we can't learn from these people. If all of God's teachers had to be perfect, there would be no teachers. The idea here is to gain the pearls from each person's expertise and forget the rest. In this way you can incorporate the best from all of the spiritual teachers with whom you work.

There are people on the planet who proclaim that they are totally God-realized beings. This is the height of egotism. All they are proving is the degree to which they are run by their negative ego. Even Sai Baba has not realized God in the highest sense of the term, for he is only 31 percent of the way there. Of course, compared to where the rest of us are, that is monumental, for the average lightworker on this planet is not more than five percent there. So be discerning when you hear such claims.

The main point here is to feel good within yourself about what you have achieved but not satisfied to stay there. Planetary ascension is really only one small step toward a much greater level of ascension, which is cosmic ascension. When you understand this, it is hard to get too puffed up about where you are. After ascension, focus on leadership development and planetary world service—and let all of the glamours of ascension go by the wayside. The ascended masters on the inner plane are completely focused on service, not spiritual growth. In the process of serving others, advanced ascended master abilities and cosmic ascension will come about naturally. Continue to strive on all levels to better yourself and refine your program, but make service and spiritual leadership the foundation of everything in your life.

Special Beings

305 Sai Baba

I talked extensively of Sai Baba in the beginning, but I wanted to include him again in this section because of the incredible help he can provide. Call on Sai Baba and ask him for help in every aspect of your life. Accept him as a special adjunct cosmic guru to your existing ascension lineage if you like. He is like a spiritual regent from out of our galaxy who has come to help all souls on Earth regardless of their spiritual path, spiritual teacher, mystery school or religion. The fact that he is a universal avatar and the cosmic Christ who is fully physically incarnated allows him vast omnipotent, omnipresent and omniscient powers on Earth. Call on him constantly, for with a wave of his hand the infinite universe is at his command. Call forth a special ascension blessing from Sai Baba and ask that he sprinkle you with his vibhuti ash.

306 Angels

The next golden key has been my work with and devotion to the angels. The archangels I feel most connected with are Michael and Metatron. I love all of the angels, however, and I call upon them often. The angels are such wonderful beings, and they are so willing to help and serve. Call on them as often as you like. There are angels for everything. There are angels of healing, ascension, leadership, art, music and poetry. There are angels to help you in any area you can think of. For an overview of the angelic kingdom, read *Hidden Mysteries*. There are many wonderful books available now about angels.

307   *Ask the Angels to Anchor Christ Qualities*

The next golden key relates to the development of Christ qualities. These qualities include love, joy, forgiveness, patience, perseverance, commitment, detachment, acceptance and harmony. Whatever qualities you want to develop, you can call on the angels who embody them and they will infuse your energy field with those qualities.

308   *Pan and the Nature Spirits*

The next golden key has been my work with and devotion to Pan and the nature spirits. They have been terribly mistreated on this planet. It has been a total travesty. Not only do we reject their existence, but we rape and pollute our environment to the point where they cannot live on it. We spray pesticides over our farms, which makes the nature spirits run for cover. Our food is filled with only about a tenth of the vital force it could have if we worked in harmony with them. For an overview of Pan and the nature spirits, read *Hidden Mysteries*. It also contains a chapter on the teachings of the Essenes, who lived in harmony with nature and all of life.

Call on Pan and the nature spirits often. The first time I started to do this was when I was living in Monterey, California. There were beautiful trees and shrubs all around my apartment, which I watered frequently. As I watered them I would talk to the nature spirits. People used to walk by my apartment and marvel at the growth of the trees and greenery.

Every plant, tree, mineral and rock has a little spirit being living within it who is in charge of its growth. Even if you can't see this reality with your physical eyes and/or clairvoyant vision, intuit and feel their presence. They are there as sure as you are. They so desperately want to be honored and welcomed. They will prove to be great comrades and will serve you well if you give them the slightest bit of love and respect.

309   *The Ashtar Command*

The next golden key has been working with the Ashtar Command. This is a great command of light——the fleet of personnel and ships of the Brother/Sisterhood of Light. Headed by Commander Ashtar, it is made up of a vast extraterrestrial force of over twenty million personnel from all over the universe, who work in conjunction with the ascended masters. They are supporting the ascension of planet Earth and humanity in numerous ways at this crucial time. Ask for their help in your path of ascension and request a downloading of light and information from them every night while you sleep over the next five years.

Guidelines on the Path

310 Commit to Being Universal and Eclectic

The next golden key has been my commitment to be universal and eclectic through honoring and integrating many teachings. Even though I have a specific ascension lineage, I revere, love and serve masters in all religions, mystery schools and spiritual paths. This has had a major impact on my development. Even a being as great as Sai Baba, the cosmic Christ, does not carry all aspects of God. It is through this commitment that I have been able to write *The Easy-to-Read Encyclopedia of the Spiritual Path*. One of the reasons that Wesak has been so successful is the philosophy that it embodies and includes all paths.

We are all on the same team. Let us all work together and we will be victorious. There are many paths to God, and each person will gravitate to the path that is best for him or her.

311 Spiritual Tests

The next golden key relates to dealing with the spiritual tests of power, fame, sexuality and money. These are the major tests for all of those on the spiritual path. When power, fame and wealth are achieved, how will these be used? Will the leader and initiate be able to resist the temptations to abuse power? Can initiates retain the same level of even-mindedness, humility and Christ consciousness even if they achieve wealth and fame? Transcendence of duality and ego got them where they are. Now can they hold steady in the light? Many have been seduced by the darker forces upon reaching this level. Once they got power, fame and money, they changed. Ponder this one deeply, for this is the ultimate test of character.

312 Strive Continually on the Path

The next golden key is the importance of continual striving. Whatever level you achieve, be happy but never be satisfied, for there is always more. I found it very interesting one day when Melchizedek told me that even he continues to strive, as does Sai Baba, Lord Buddha, Lord Maitreya and Djwhal Khul. There is always another rung up the ladder.

313 Deal with Mistakes

This golden key has been an understanding of mistakes. It is important to realize that mistakes are okay. Even the ascended masters on the inner plane continue to make mistakes. What is much worse than making mistakes is trying to hide them. I continue to make mistakes all the time. I don't even look at them as mistakes so much as adjustments. There is no judgment from God or the masters. Everything is a learning experience and a continual process of greater and greater refinement and cleansing. The true spiritual leader admits mistakes. When we admit mistakes we are elevated in stature and power for the demonstration of true Christ consciousness.

Initiations

314   Study the Seven Levels of Initiation

This next golden key is to study the seven levels of initiation. Study the chapters on this subject in *The Complete Ascension Manual* and *Beyond Ascension*. Study everything you can about the initiation that is just above the level you are at. Immerse yourself in this understanding. This will help to polarize and magnetize your consciousness to take the leap to the next step. Pray to the masters every night for help in passing your next initiation. Call for a divine dispensation for acceleration of your initiations and even request a certain timetable for you to achieve this next step, if this is God's will. A good ballpark figure for each initiation would be a year or two per initiation. This is incredibly fast, but entirely possible if you are totally committed.

315   Study the Seven Paths to Higher Evolution

The key on my path was studying intensively the material on the seven paths to higher evolution. Using both your rational and intuitive minds, begin the process of deciding which path you will choose upon taking your sixth initiation. I have made this extremely easy for you by outlining these paths in *Beyond Ascension*. Doing this particular process will polarize and magnetize your consciousness to pull in the next step in your evolutionary process.

316   Discernment about Discussing Initiation Levels

This golden key has to do with showing great discernment as to when and where you talk about your initiation level. Through experience I found that this often tended to bring up competition and comparing. I made it a policy never to discuss this in my classes or the ashram in general. This remained true long after I had achieved my own ascension. I have discussed my initiations in my books because the masters told me that it would be of value to lightworkers on the planet to have a sense of how the process works.

All are God regardless of their initiation level. We never should judge others because they are at a lower level of initiation. I know a number of people who are far more psychologically clear than some others who are at higher levels of initiation. There is much glamour and ego that must be avoided regarding the initiation process.

317 Keep Your Perspective about Your Progress

The next golden key was a vow not to become prideful or overconfident just because I had completed my ascension. As the Bible says, "After pride cometh the fall." If anything, I have redoubled my efforts and am more focused, disciplined and committed than ever. Ascension is a process, and planetary ascension is just an increment of true cosmic ascension. It is something to be proud of, but it is only one-tenth of the way toward God realization. This insight is helpful in creating humility about achieving planetary ascension.

It also is important not to become discouraged from what might feel like setbacks or slow progress. If we are dedicated and diligent, we will make progress. And with mistakes, we simply need to see what the lessons are, incorporate these and move on.

318 Magnetize Your Next Step of Evolution

Another golden key in my spiritual progression has been to keep myself polarized toward the next step. For example, after you take your fourth initiation, you should stop focusing on your higher self and soul and focus all of your attention on the monad and upper spiritual triangle of intuition, spiritual will and abstract mind. You always want to keep your mind polarized or magnetized to the next level above where you are. If you don't do this, you are not magnetizing that next level to you and this will greatly slow down your initiation process.

Since completing my planetary ascension, I have polarized my consciousness to the six monads and the solar level of consciousness. When this is mastered, I will polarize my consciousness to the galactic level and then to the universal level. There is no skipping steps, and if you try to do it, you will slow down your progress and short-circuit your four-body system.

319 Connect with an Ascension Wave

The next golden key is getting involved with an ascension wave. The Spiritual Hierarchy has set up the ascension process at this time on the planet in such a way that disciples are initiated in groups, or waves. Ask the masters in meditation to connect you to the highest ascension wave that is within your potentiality. There are not just three ascension waves, but many. They will go on until all souls have achieved liberation.

If you want to tap into the highest wave possible within your potentiality, come to the Wesak celebrations in Mt. Shasta. Coming to Wesak automatically will tap you into your highest potential. Once you are connected to an ascension wave, much of the work is done on the inner plane while you sleep. Those in each wave are given certain activations according to their level of spiritual growth. This is one of the great advantages of working with the ascended masters. The best way to get noticed by the masters is to show yourself ready and willing to be of service so that they know they can count on you.

320   Study the Initiations in the Great Pyramid

The next golden key has been studying everything I could find relating to the spiritual tests of the seven levels of initiation in the Great Pyramid. Studying this material is one of the best ways to pass your initiations. I have compiled all this material for you in *Hidden Mysteries* to make this as easy as possible.

If you never have read Earlyne Chaney's book *Initiation in the Great Pyramid*, it is must reading. In *The Aquarian Gospel of Jesus the Christ* the seven initiations that every person had to pass were sincerity, justice, faith, philanthropy, heroism, divine love and, last, the attainment of Christ consciousness. These were the tests that the master Jesus went through in the Great Pyramid.

I also highly recommend Elizabeth Haich's *Initiation*, which was written from past-life recall. In this book she describes each of her levels of initiation. Her first was the test of overcoming evil. The second was the test of putting God before the pleasures of the palate. The third was the test of putting God before sexual beauty and seduction. The fourth initiation was the test of putting God before even her soul mate. The fifth was the test of putting God first in the face of death. The sixth initiation was the test of universal love. Elizabeth had to put helping others' spiritual progress above her own. The seventh initiation was the full realization of Christ and God.

Each one of us goes through similar tests in our daily life. The idea here is to learn by grace instead of karma. Study and pass these initiations in consciousness now. Make certain vows and commitments in relation to these various areas of your life. This will allow you to pass these tests when you are tempted to go astray or get sidetracked. Study the material about the initiations that disciples took in the past in the Great Pyramid. If you know what the tests are that you will be facing, then you will be ready for them when they come.

Your Mission

321   Your Part in the Divine Plan

The next golden key is to pray to God and the masters of your choice for guidance relating to your mission. It is important that we all fulfill our special part of the divine plan and not try to do someone else's work. Don't compare your life with what others are doing. Put your full attention on realizing your part of the plan.

Each of you has been created by God to perform certain unique services and assignments. If each of us fulfills our own part of the divine plan in total cooperation, love, unity and harmony, the whole plan will soon come into complete fruition. It is our work to help establish this for all of humanity. Together we can create heaven on Earth.

322   Call Forth Your Future Mission

This golden key is to call forth to Lords Arcturus, Melchizedek, Metatron and Sai Baba for your future mission, at your highest potential, to be programmed into your computer banks on the eternal time line.

323   The Path of the Mystic and the Occultist

The next golden key on my spiritual path came from my understanding of the paths of the mystic and the occultist. The occultist tends to be more the mental type. The mystic is more the intuitive, feeling type.

The mystic likes to experience everything and is not very big on reading or study. The occultist loves to study and read and understand everything. This is very simplistic, but it explains why certain people are the way they are. One path is not better than another; they are equal. Mystics should not force themselves to be occultists and occultists should not force themselves to be mystics. Honor the way God created you.

As you move through the higher levels of initiation and realize your ascension, these two paths will merge and become more integrated. However, these themes and tendencies will still remain. A mystic will not have the intellectual understanding, occult vision and spiritual senses to the degree the occultist has. The occultist will not have the clairaudient, clairvoyant, clairsentient and channeling abilities to the degree the mystic has.

For mystics and occultists to be friends is the highest and most advanced ascension buddy system that you can formulate. Mystics need occultists to impregnate their potentials and vice versa. Both should be honored and respected in the highest degree.

324   Understand Personal and Impersonal Energies

The next golden key has been understanding the difference between personal and impersonal energies. It is not possible to be best friends and personal with everyone. Every lightworker must develop the ability to be impersonally loving as well as personally loving. Every lightworker must also learn to blend the two. One of the real keys to my success has been the ability to get along with people and make a good connection while still protecting my boundaries and not tiring myself out.

As I moved into leadership, I discovered that there are a lot of brothers and sisters who want my time, energy and information. I cannot possibly respond to everyone's needs, nor should I. There is a fine balance to maintain here. In more recent times I have been guided by the masters to have high-level initiates in the ashram to help me with the large amount of mail and phone calls I receive. This again is using the group body as an extension of myself. This is a lesson that all who move into leadership must learn.

Inspiration on the Path

325   Muktananda and Meditation

The next golden key was inspiration that I received from studying the autobiography of Swami Muktananda. I am not drawn to the siddha path. I always have been much more drawn to Yogananda and Sai Baba. But what inspired me about Muktananda's autobiography was his self-discipline and commitment to meditation. He would meditate day and night for years on end. I don't necessarily think this was the most balanced way to live, but it did inspire me. I have found meditation, prayer and attitude to be the three keys to my spiritual progress. In getting involved with the ascended masters and the ascension movement, I find meditation to be my favorite thing to do in life.

Once you experience the divine current of God and see how easily it is to connect and work with the ascended masters, you never want to be disconnected from it. The key here is to meditate as much as possible and make your entire life an ongoing meditation.

326   Peace Pilgrim

The next golden key was my study of the teachings of Peace Pilgrim. I was greatly inspired by her simple faith and devotion. She would walk back and forth across the United States with no money, living on faith and the goodness of people. Though at times she went without food or lodging, God always provided for her. I was greatly inspired by the example she set. It is my hope and prayer that I can demonstrate such faith, patience and trust in God.

327   Mother Teresa

The next golden key has been the inspiration I have received from the life of Mother Teresa. Her unwavering faith in God and her undying commitment to help the poorest of the poor I find incredibly moving and inspiring. I realize that not everyone is destined to do this type of work, but I am filled with inspiration by her example. I pray that I can serve my readers and students with the same devotion and commitment that Mother Teresa has demonstrated so beautifully and majestically.

Relationships

328   Romantic Relationships

The next golden key has been the romantic relationships I have been involved in. By the grace of God I have been blessed with the most wonderful long-term relationships and marriages. If you want to accelerate spiritual growth, there is nothing like a romantic relationship. It brings everything to the surface. Each romantic relationship and marriage I have been involved in has been a most wonderful teacher for me and has been absolutely instrumental in my development.

I thought that each one was going to last forever, but this was not meant to be. What I feel good about in all the relationships is that I entered them for mutual spiritual growth. Then when they were over I didn't hold on. The period following the ending of each relationship was often difficult. But I soon found that the time on my own again would catapult me forward into the next phase of my work. Then when the time was right, the next romantic involvement would begin, which would be a whole new partnership and training.

The key here is to love totally and commit fully to a relationship that you choose to be in, for this will enhance the spiritual paths of both. But if the time should come when it is clear that the relationship no longer serves both of you to your highest potential, then release it with love.

One of the main values in a relationship is that it provides us with a mirror for our unhealed issues so that we can clear them. In relationships it is important not to communicate when egos are getting involved. When they try to take over, each person needs to spend time alone, calm down and get right with self and God. Then you can come together again to communicate and work things out. Romantic relationships provide many opportunities to practice this and to transform negative patterns.

329   Release Attachment to Having a Partner

This next golden key applies to the manifestation of romantic relationships. I have found that the most effective way to manifest the ideal romantic relationship is to put my entire focus on God, my spiritual path and my service work. When you put these first, the ideal soul and monadic mate will be magnetized to you when this is in alignment with your spiritual path. The key is to be happy with or without a mate. When your life is fulfilling on all levels without a partner, this often is when one shows up.

I am happy to be on my own at this time in my life. I have wonderful friends and feel great communion with God, the masters and myself. I am not attached to becoming involved with someone again. If it is God's will, so be it. If it isn't, I feel completely fulfilled in my service work.

Wesak and Full Moon Festivals

330   The Wesak Festival

This golden key is a personal invitation to each and every one of you to come to the Wesak celebrations in Mt. Shasta that I put on every year for 1200 people. In the future these celebrations might grow to 2500 and then to 5000 people. As long as they are held in Mt. Shasta, we need to limit them to 1200 because of the lack of a larger auditorium. Wesak has had a profound effect on my life. It is the holiest day of the year from the ascended masters' perspective. It occurs at the full moon in Taurus. Wesak is a valley in the Himalayas where all of the masters and many disciples gather each year with the Buddha and the Christ. It is the high point of the influx of spiritual energies onto the planet.

And it is also the time when all initiations are given by the masters. The Lord Maitreya has guided me to put on a celebration each year to externalize this process for the masses.

Can you imagine celebrating Wesak and doing ascension-activation work with 1200 high-level initiates and ascended beings in Mt. Shasta? This will activate the next series of waves of mass ascension for humanity under the spiritual auspices of Melchizedek, Lord Buddha, Lord Maitreya and Djwhal Khul. The degree of acceleration you will achieve is indescribable. I have never experienced the level of God infusion that I experience at the Wesak celebration each year. I am putting forth the clarion call to you, my beloved readers. Call or write me and I will add you to the mailing list. You will receive a free 25-page packet of information on the Wesak celebration.

Tell your friends and family about this. This is a time for high-level initiates, ascended beings and spiritual leaders from around the globe to come together in a totally universal, eclectic gathering to honor all spiritual teachers, mystery schools, religions and ashrams of God. It is a time for us all to come together to unify, commune and connect with the great planetary and cosmic masters so that we can regenerate and prepare ourselves for the next year of planetary world service. Come to the Wesak celebration at Mt. Shasta and you will enter the realm of the miraculous. Trust me, my friends. If you have ever wanted to make a pilgrimage to Mt. Shasta, the time is now!

331   Full Moon Meditations

The next golden key has been to meditate very intensively each month at the full moon. The most important full moon ceremony, of course, is the Wesak festival. However, there are eleven other full moon ceremonies. The two other major spring festivals are the Festival of the Christ in Aries, which is Easter, and the Festival of Humanity, or Goodwill, in Gemini. For more information on these ceremonies read *Cosmic Ascension*. At the time of the full moon there is a greater downpouring of spiritual energy and a greater opportunity for spiritual growth. Take advantage of these periods.

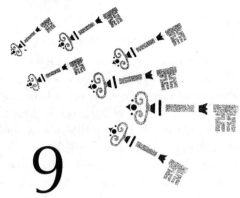

GOLDEN KEYS TO ASCENSION AND HEALING

9

CARING FOR THE TEMPLE OF GOD

Keys 332-354

NUTRITION
TECHNOLOGIES
EXERCISE
STRENGTHENING AND CLEARING
HONORING YOURSELF
HOLISTIC MODALITIES
RESOURCES

Nutrition

332   A Healthy Diet

This golden key, which was a major one in my healing, was staying on a strict diet. The key for me here was seeing a psychic nutritionist in Los Angeles named Eileen Poole. In my opinion she is the finest psychic nutritionist on the planet. All of her work is done through channeling and not by book knowledge. Following Eileen's recommendations, using a pendulum to test all of my food and a purple Positive-Energy Plate to energize my food has had a highly energizing effect on my body.

Because of my past health history, I had to be more disciplined than most with my diet. Being very disciplined in my eating greatly increased my energy and strengthened my immune system. Even though I had some digestive weakness, I was rarely sick. A healthy diet also served to lighten the atomic structure of my physical vehicle, which made me more sensitive to subtle energies. I am a big proponent of a healthy diet. I also drink lots of pure, fresh water.

333   Food-Combining

Another golden key I have found to be extremely helpful is following the laws of food-combining. I feel that this is a highly efficient way to eat and that it conserves energy.

The basic laws of food-combining are to eat protein with vegetables and starch with vegetables, but not protein and starches together. The other food-combining law is to eat fruit alone. Charts are available in health food stores that provide more detail, but these are the basic guidelines. I swear by this way of eating. My system seems to run more efficiently this way.

334   Fasting and Cleansing Diets

Another practice I have found to be of great value is fasting or going on cleansing diets. The fast I have enjoyed and used the most has been green vegetable juice with a little carrot juice mixed in.

The one I currently use the most is something I learned about from Eileen Poole, called Bieler broth. This was made famous by her mentor, Henry Bieler. He wrote a wonderful book called *Food Is Your Best Medicine*. To make Bieler broth, steam zucchini, green beans, celery and parsley in a large pot. Then put the steamed vegetables in a blender with an equal amount of water. It forms a thick soup, which I find delicious. It is a most wonderful substance to fast and cleanse on. It is specifically designed to be a liver rejuvenator, and it does work.

Over the years I have varied the recipe to use other types of vegetables and it works just as well. I consume this every day. By fasting on this for one to three days, or even for a meal, I can see the results in my eyes, skin, hair and aura. I swear by this stuff. I have been eating it for fifteen years and never get tired of it. It has been one of the golden keys for healing and maintaining my physical body.

335   Avoid Artificial Stimulants

The next golden key has been a vow to refrain from using artificial stimulants including coffee, caffeinated teas, drugs and even herbal stimulants. I was a big coffee drinker in my younger years and it had a terrible effect on my adrenals, liver and pancreas. What I have come to realize in my maturing years is that the goal is to be even-minded in all things. This applies to one's thoughts, emotions and physical body. It is not good to live on a roller coaster of extreme highs and lows.

336   Avoid Drugs

The next golden key has been a strict rule to stay away from all drugs. As an adolescent I experimented with them, like most people from my generation. The masters state emphatically that the use of drugs is not for high-level initiates. There are few points on which I am very firm, but this is one.

Those disciples and initiates who fool around with drugs have been seduced by the lower self and negative ego. They should forgive themselves and retain no guilt, but they should stop immediately. Altered states of consciousness should be obtained from meditation, not from substances that poison the liver. The smoking of pot also puts holes in the aura.

Lightworkers also should stay away from prescription drugs and use herbs and homeopathics. These are more effective and contribute to the health and well-being of the physical body. There are emergency exceptions to this, of course, but as a general rule there should be no conflict about it. In the not-too-distant future I believe that many of the current practices of Western medicine will be abolished. Doctors of the future will work with energy in a variety of ways. Disease will be seen as imbalance, so there will be a shift to treating the cause of imbalance, which often lies in the subtler bodies, mind and emotions.

Technologies

337   *Purple Positive-Energy Plates*

This golden key has been of inestimable value in terms of my physical well-being. This is the use of a purple Positive-Energy Plate. I cannot recommend this more highly. The purple plate is a New Age technology in which the atoms and electrons of the aluminum have been altered so that the plates resonate with the basic energy of the universe. The plates create a field of positive energy that penetrate any substance. This energy is beneficial to all life—plant, animal or human. I know from personal experience that these plates work, and I have checked this out with the ascended masters and my pendulum, as have many of my friends.

I would venture to guess that 90 percent of the foods we obtain, even health foods, have a negative or neutral spin. You can check this out with a pendulum. This can be caused by pesticides, by the deterioration of the food in the refrigerator or on the shelf, by the people who handled the food or by the scanners at the grocery store checkout counter. The possibilities of energy contamination are endless.

For this reason I always pray over my food and use my purple energy plate. They come in different sizes. I have the large ones, which cost around $40. Small ones costs about $12. I conscientiously place all my food on this plate. My purple plate is my placemat. Leave food on the purple plate for five to seven minutes before eating. The plates can also be used to energize homeopathic remedies, herbs and supplements.

If you check the food with a pendulum both before and after it has been on the plate, you will see the difference. The plate puts a positive spin on the food. This will guarantee that you are getting the proper energy even if you are not always able to obtain the best food. If you are going to have a dish of ice cream, at least put it on the purple plate to deactivate the negative energy and create a positive energy spin. Whatever food you eat will be much healthier when you use the purple plate. I am not one who usually goes in for New Age gadgets, but this is amazingly effective, cheap and lasts forever. I have tested it out and it is much more effective than even Hanna Kroeger's Soma Board, which was created for the same purpose. To order, see information at the end of this chapter.

338   *Radionics*

The next golden key for the healing of my physical body has been radionics. I have two radionics machines, one called an SE5, and another I refer to as a black box. Because of my digestive sensitivity and my dislike of taking a lot of pills, I began using these radionics machines to send myself the energy of substances that I needed rather than taking the actual pills. This is not necessarily for everyone, but with the combination of my radionics machines and the ascended master tools, I have been able to keep myself in very good health.

I don't claim to understand fully how these machines work. But somehow, by simply putting my hair sample or picture on the machine and a substance or numerical code on another plate, the radionics machine knocks out any virus, fungus or other problem I am dealing with. It also saves me a lot of money because I use the same homeopathics over and over again without having to ingest them. I keep them energized by storing them on one of my purple energy plates. I use radionics as a preventive health-care tool. I run the radionics machine 24 hours a day to send myself supplements, homeopathic remedies, immune boosters and the like. I love the idea of working with pure energy and spirit for my healing. The ideal here would be to use both physical and energy methods according to your inner guidance. Radionics is most definitely a science of the future.

339 Protection against Electromagnetic Pollution

The next golden key relates to counteracting electromagnetic pollution. There are many products on the market for minimizing the effects of electromagnetic energies. The one I have found most helpful has been the Teslar watch, invented by Nikola Tesla. When you wear the watch, a force field is placed around your energy field that prevents electrical frequencies from entering your field. The watch has a pulse synchronized to the pulse of the Earth and the human body that is totally unique.

I always have disliked wearing watches, for I felt that they interfered with the natural flow of energy through my acupuncture meridians. Testing has been done on the Teslar watch, and it has been proven to be effective in bolstering the immune system on subtle levels. It also keeps good time. I am not sure where to obtain the Teslar watch at this time. But if you are motivated, contact people who are involved with radionics or check the ads in New Age magazines.

340 Avoiding Microwave Ovens

This golden key has been to stay away from microwave ovens. Contrary to popular opinion, nuking your food is not a New Age form of cooking. Microwave ovens put holes in the etheric field of your food, which has a very deleterious effect on your physical body. Long-term use of a microwave oven can have a very negative effect on your health if you are not careful.

Exercise

341   Balanced Exercise

The next golden key in manifesting health has been balanced exercise. It has been said that there are three aspects to physical exercise: stamina, flexibility and strength. The stamina I currently get is from walking, which Edgar Cayce has proclaimed to be the best exercise. I used to be a long-distance runner and jogger, but now I find this too jarring to my system. I like walking better. Walking helps oxygenate my system.

In terms of strength, for many years I went to the gym and lifted weights. I don't feel the need to do this now, but it is a good thing for those inclined toward it.

342   Yoga and Stretching

The next golden key has been doing hatha yoga and stretching. The yoga and stretching are wonderful for the flexibility aspect of balanced exercise. One of the keys to perfect health is keeping the spine flexible. The nexus of nerves connected with the spine serves every cell, nerve, organ and gland in the body. Yoga can be used as a type of meditation or simply as a physical exercise.

Strengthening and Clearing

343   The Thymus Thump

The next key has been a simple practice of doing what is called the thymus thump. Simply tap your fingertips on the center of your upper chest maybe two or three times a day. Thymus thumping stimulates the thymus gland, which is the heart of your immune system.

344   Chakra Zips

The next key has been giving myself chakra zips. To do a chakra zip, cup your right hand just below the first chakra. Sensitize yourself to the energies for a moment and then slowly raise your cupped hand up through all of your chakras, bringing your hand up over your head. Do this three times very slowly, about one inch away from your physical body. Doing this opens the chakras and spins them in the proper direction.

I do this whenever I get tired or when my energy system feels a little out of balance. It immediately realigns your energy. It seems like a very simple thing, but I can't tell you how much this has helped me.

345   Keep Your Legs and Arms Uncrossed

This next golden key is not crossing your legs, feet or arms. This inhibits the flow of energy through your meridians and chakras. It is a very hard habit to break, but I have conscientiously tried to do this so that my energy could flow freely.

346   Keep the Chakras Spinning Correctly

The next golden key was to ask the Arcturians and the inner-plane healing masters several times during the day to keep my chakras open and spinning in the proper direction. The lessons and challenges of life can often throw this process out of whack, as we all know.

347   A Complete Ascension Clearing

The next golden key has been to give myself a complete ascension clearing about every three months just in case any imbalanced energies have gotten in and lodged themselves in my energy field. If any of my readers are interested in such a clearing, give me a call and I will set you up with a session the first time. After that I recommend that you do it on your own.

348   Wear Gems and Amulets

The next golden key has been wearing certain gemstones or amulets to increase my energy or add a certain vibration. For many years I wore a crystal pendant that I felt greatly expanded my aura and served to bolster my immune system. And for many years I carried in my pocket the amulet that Sai Baba materialized for me. I have gone through phases of wearing other amulets that have had a very powerful effect. Every gemstone, as we know, has a specific vibration, so there is no guidance I could give to people other than to use your own intuition as to what feels right. There are also many wonderful books on the use of crystals and gemstones. At times I have also gone through phases of not keeping any amulets or gemstones on my person when that felt right.

Honoring Yourself

349   Honor Your Body's Natural Rhythms

This golden key has been learning to trust the rhythms of my own physical body. My natural rhythm is to sleep only about five or six hours at night and then take a catnap in the late afternoon. This is what my physical body likes. However, each person is different and must find his or her particular body rhythm. I have a seventh-ray body, but others with different ray bodies and missions will operate differently. Trusting my own natural rhythms has been an important key to my overall effectiveness. In South America and Mexico, afternoon siestas are the norm for the entire population. I must have been Mexican in a past life, for I love my siesta.

350   Conserve Energy

The next golden key has been what I call conserving my energies. This is something that my physical body has taught me. In my early years I tried to be superman—and succeeded for many years, until my body broke down from being pushed so hard. Once this happened I had to be much smarter in my approach to things. I had to learn to set better boundaries, to be selfish and say no. I had to learn to ask for help and delegate responsibility. Previously I had a need to do everything myself, which Djwhal Khul convinced me was faulty thinking. Now, with increased leadership responsibilities I focus on the most essential things. I had to develop the leadership skills to see the wisdom in asking for help and delegating responsibility.

My physical body has taught me to become a master at conserving my energy and to regard my energy as extremely precious. Conserving energies means looking at how and with whom I spend my time. It means not being a slave to my phone and setting boundaries for how long I remain on the phone. It means doing my prayers and invocations in the simplest manner possible and with the least expenditure of energy. It means having priorities and clearly defined goals and objectives—and then creating the "battle" plans for achieving these.

351   Spend Time in Nature

The next golden key has been spending time in nature. Now, I admit this was not the easiest thing to do growing up in Los Angeles. After working most of the day, though, it was essential for me to get outdoors and walk in the fresh air and sunshine, even if this was just walking in a park with some trees and green grass. My physical body would crave this as well as my spirit. I am sure all of you can relate to this.

352   Have Fun

This golden key is having fun and not being too serious. It is important to have fun and joke around and take time for pleasure and recreation, such as going to movies, watching certain television shows and engaging in sports. Spend time with friends and enjoy earthly life as well as the heavenly worlds. The spiritual path is one of having the best of both worlds. As you can tell, I am about as committed, self-disciplined and focused as they come. Even though this is the case, I greatly enjoy Earth life. I stop to smell the roses. I enjoy the process as well as achieving the goals I set for myself. If you are not experiencing joy on your spiritual path, something is wrong and needs to be corrected. Having fun is an important part of living a balanced life.

Holistic Modalities

353   Holistic Care

The next golden key has been working with holistic health-care practitioners, including homeopathic, naturopathic and bioenergetic practitioners and doctors of oriental medicine. Many of the practitioners I have worked with use advanced machines such as the Vega machine that can test for subclinical substances that can be poisoning and weakening the immune system. This type of work has been instrumental in the rehabilitation of my physical body and keeping my immune system in good shape.

Through working with these machines I was able to clear the subclinical toxins from my body. I cleared out such things as mercury from leaking amalgam fillings, aluminum from cooking utensils and foil, parasites, subclinical bacteria, viruses, fungi, vaccines, radiation from color television sets, electromagnetic toxicity, chemicals, drugs that I had been given as a child, pesticides and other environmental poisons. This list is just the tip of the iceberg, but it gives you an idea of what you are dealing with and how to proceed.

354   Homeopathic Remedies

The next golden key has been a line of homeopathic products that I think are incredible. They are called Futureplex. They were created by Roy Martina, who is considered one of the finest homeopathic and bioenergetic practitioners in the country. Following is a description of some of the products:

Bacterotox: My experience is that this gets rid of 90 percent of all bacteria-related infections. I feel that it is far better than taking antibiotics, which I never use.

Acute Virotox and Post Virotox: I have found that these two products get rid of 90 percent of all viruses. Western medicine has no cure for viruses.

Immune Energy: I have found this product to be a powerful immune-system enhancer. It helps to rid the body of many unwanted microorganisms by boosting the immune system.

Lymphotox: This is another wonderful product that is extremely helpful in cleansing the lymph system.

Envirotox: I have found this product to be extremely helpful in ridding the body of environmental toxins.

Gentle Drainage: This product has been very helpful in cleansing my system when it gets a little clogged.

Adrenal Pep: This gives me a boost of energy when I am a little tired. It is much better than drinking coffee or caffeinated tea.

Cellular Recharge: This helps recharge my cells when they are run-down.

Revitalization: This product is very helpful in revitalizing my whole body when I have become overtired or a bit rundown.

For legal purposes I will state that I am not a medical doctor. However, these homeopathic products are ones that I have found extremely helpful in my life. I run them on my radionics machine along with certain vitamins and minerals 24 hours a day and, by the grace of God, I never get sick anymore. The combination of running such a high light quotient, merging with my mayavarupa body, eating a healthy diet that is in harmony with my particular body, drinking lots of pure water, exercising every day, and working with my radionics machine and these homeopathic remedies seems to do the trick.

It is certainly fine to take these products orally under the tongue. I don't do this only because, for my system, radionics seems to work better. I can't recommend these products more highly. I have no financial involvement with the company, so I recommend them to you from the perspective of wanting to help you achieve excellent health. These products have been a godsend for me over the last ten years. They are not sold in most homeopathic pharmacies, however, so on the next page is information on where to order them.

Resources

To order the Positive-Energy Plates,
contact Susan Bryant and Sandy Burns at:
  Earth Elementals (520) 527-1128
  P.O. Box 31149
  Flagstaff, AZ 86003-1128

Source for Futureplex Homeopathic Remedies:
  Capitol Drugs (818) 905-8338; Fax: (818) 905-8748
  4454 Van Nuys Blvd.
  Sherman Oaks, CA 91403

Eileen Poole:
  Earlier I mentioned Eileen Poole, the psychic nutritionist I have been
  seeing for fifteen years. She does not work over the phone, but if you are
  ever traveling in Los Angeles, she is well worth seeing. Her phone
  number is (310) 440-9976.

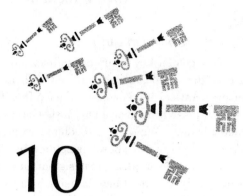

GOLDEN KEYS TO ASCENSION AND HEALING 10

WORLD AFFAIRS, LEADERSHIP AND THE PURSUIT OF EXCELLENCE
Keys 355-389

INVOLVEMENT IN EARTH LIFE
CHARACTERISTICS OF EFFECTIVE LEADERS
PURSUING EXCELLENCE AND DEVELOPING LEADERSHIP SKILLS
TRAINING AND DEGREES
EXPLORING SPIRITUAL PATHS AND TEACHINGS
SPIRITUAL BOOKS, TAPES AND TEACHINGS
THE ONGOING QUEST FOR SPIRITUAL KNOWLEDGE
GETTING THE WORD OUT

Involvement in Earth Life

355 *Be Involved in Earth Life*

This golden key is my commitment to "live in the marketplace"—to live in the world and get involved with Earth life. There is a tendency among many spiritual people to detach from Earth life, and this is not good. The ideal is to bring heaven to Earth. Get involved in community activities, your spiritual community and volunteer work. As Jesus said in *A Course in Miracles*, "One's true church is helping one's brothers and sisters." A commitment to such an ideal creates grounding of the spiritual energies, which is extremely important both in being balanced and in realizing your ascension. The ideal is to be God on Earth. Ascension is really descension of the monad, or I Am Presence.

356 *Planetary Ecology*

The next golden key relates to ecology on an environmental level. Not polluting one's physical body would be a type of personal ecology. This applies to diet, exercise, cleanliness, proper grooming and using natural products for personal care. On the environmental level this includes using biodegradable products, recycling and not wasting energy. We are the microcosm within the macrocosm. As one expands one's identity, one begins to become all people, animals, plants, minerals and the Earth herself. This is the effect of ending negative-ego separative consciousness and embracing Christ/Buddha consciousness. This also applies to supporting political candidates who are environmentally conscious. I consider this issue one of the grounded aspects of the spiritual path.

357 *Be Involved in Politics and World Affairs*

This golden key is a commitment to be involved with what is going on politically in this world. There is a tendency among some lightworkers to ignore politics, and this is understandable. In politics we often see people being largely run by the negative ego. Much of the time it is Republicans versus Democrats and gridlock as usual. However, this area of life is not going to change unless lightworkers get involved. Everyone can't run for political office, but we can all vote, help raise people's consciousness, become politically aware and volunteer to help the candidates of our choice.

Djwhal Khul has suggested that we read newspapers and watch the news every day. This is something I already did; however, I found it interesting that he would make such a request. By doing this it prompts one where to direct one's prayers, affirmations and visualizations for planetary world service. Look how involved Gandhi got in the politics of India and what a spiritual man he was. If we don't take the time to vote, then we deserve the candidates we get. Spirituality for too long has been cut off from the earthly world. The true spiritual path is bringing heaven to Earth. This is why even when you complete your ascension initiation you will remain on Earth and continue to serve. To live at this time in Earth's history, I feel, is quite extraordinary, and I am privileged to be incarnated at this time.

Characteristics of Effective Leaders

358   Self-Leadership

This golden key has been the recognition of what I might call self-leadership. One cannot become an effective leader for others until one has become an effective leader over self. When we can lead our own subconscious mind, personality, inner child, mental body, emotional body, physical body and subpersonalities in an integrated, firm and loving manner, then we are ready to lead others on a large scale.

359   Types of Leadership

The next golden key has been the recognition that there are two kinds of leadership. There is spiritual leadership and egotistical leadership. Being in a position of leadership does not make a person a good leader. This applies to spiritual people as well. Hitler was a leader in service of the Dark Brotherhood. There are people who are leaders of businesses but treat their employees badly. Strive to be an effective christed leader over self and with others. In the Hierarchy there are leaders at each level who are responsible for the cosmos. However, they strive for consensus as much as possible. In this regard there is an appropriate blending between individual and consensus decision-making. The effective leader needs to be in harmony with those he or she leads, while retaining the authority to execute appropriate leadership.

360   Everyone Is a Leader

This golden key is the understanding that everyone is a leader, just as everyone is a teacher of God. Leadership begins with self and then extends to family, friends, business associates and community. When people are ready, their leadership arena might expand to state, country and global levels. As you prove yourself at each level you will be given greater leadership responsibilities by God and the masters. One other interesting place where we exert leadership is over our soul extensions from our oversoul and monad. The ultimate ideal on a personal level is to become a teacher for your oversoul and a leader for all your 144 soul extensions from your monadic family.

361   Balance Friendship and Firmness

The next golden key was learning the importance of balancing decisiveness with friendship when in a leadership role. The ideal is to be able to be both a friend and a firm leader as needed. This is a very important psychodynamic to integrate properly.

362   Leadership Must Be Earned

The next golden key is the understanding that leadership must be earned. Just because one finds oneself in a leadership position—in life, business, government or other group—doesn't mean a person is truly ready to lead others. True spiritual leadership is earned through long years of selfless service and commitment to one's spiritual ideals.

363   Learn to Deal with All Kinds of People

This golden key has been learning how to deal with all kinds of people. This is probably the most important skill for becoming an effective spiritual leader. When working in a spiritual community or in daily life, we constantly are given the challenge of dealing with all kinds of people who exhibit a wide range of spiritual development and clarity. To be an effective leader, it is also important to be able to relate to people from many different cultures and backgrounds.

Pursuing Excellence and Developing Leadership Skills

364   Commit to Excellence

The next golden key is what I call the pursuit of excellence. This might be described as a spiritual vow on my part to be the best I can be in all areas of my life without getting into competition or comparing myself with others. It is a pursuit of excellence within myself. It is a commitment not to be lazy or let down in any area, but to hold firm to my godly ideals.

365   Take Risks: Live on the Edge

The next golden key has been a great commitment on my part to take risks and live somewhat on the edge. For example, when I did my first Wesak celebration in Mt. Shasta in 1995 for 350 people, that was a bit of a stretch, for I had not done a whole weekend event with that many people before. But I was certainly more than prepared for such work, and the masters were pushing me to step out full force on a global level.

The next year I wanted to expand my limits even further, so I set up the Wesak celebration for 1200 people. I will expand the size of the event even more if this is the will of the masters. This is what I mean by taking a risk and pressing one's limits. The risks I am talking about here include not only speaking in front of large groups of people, but also the financial risk involved from the great expense of advertising and hosting such an event.

Throughout my life I have lived a little on the edge. I have moved and changed my life and relationships many times when my intuition and the masters have guided me to do so. What is the saying? "Much risked, much gained." This again has to do with a certain spiritual vow I made this lifetime to go all the way with no holding back. This willingness to take risks in all areas of my life through implicitly trusting my own intuition and the masters has catapulted me onto the world stage.

Always taking risks can be stressful at times, and I do try to stay within the Tao of this process. But when I leave the Earth plane, I want to know that I gave my best shot and that I didn't let fear govern any aspect of my life. Let us all, in this moment, make a spiritual vow and commitment to push our envelope to the very edge that our Tao permits. Many hold back their service work and movement into the public eye because of fear. If you wait until you feel totally comfortable, you will probably never take the risk. Remember the saying, "Feel the fear and do it anyway."

366   Be a Renaissance Person

This golden key has been the ideal of being a Renaissance person, to develop myself in all areas and be well-rounded. This would allow me to talk to all types of people and feel comfortable in all situations. Even though my main interest in life is spiritual things, I make it a point to try to be well-informed on many earthly matters. This is why watching the news and reading the newspaper are important to me. This is why I enjoy television shows like *Prime Time, Dateline, 60 Minutes, 20/20* and check out the Learning Channel and listener-sponsored television. I feel that it is important to have a well-rounded education. If you can't deal with people in the real world, then how can you be an effective leader?

367   *Develop Communication and Social Skills*

The next golden key has been the development of my communication and social skills. I consider this an essential part of the ascension process and training for leadership. As an adolescent I was very shy and sensitive. As I matured, however, and went into the field of psychology, over time, communicating became one of my greatest strengths. It is important to be able to talk to people in all situations, not just spiritual ones. Learning to make people feel comfortable and being a good host and a good conversationalist are essential for being an effective leader. If there are areas of your personality that need work, force yourself to be in situations where you can practice these skills. Pray to the Holy Spirit for help and you will see your development in this area increase over time.

368   *Public Speaking*

This golden key was the training I gave myself in public speaking. When I first started teaching classes I was very nervous because I had never done it before. Early on, however, I used Paramahansa Yogananda's method of public speaking. His guidance was to.

- Make an outline rather than write out the speech word for word.
- Always prepare extra material just in case.
- Pray for the help of God and the masters before going on stage.
- Tell a joke or funny story somewhere in your talk. (I love to tell spiritual stories, so that part was easy for me.)

The outline keeps the mind relaxed and the free spaces in the outline allow room for spirit to come through. This is a skill that all lightworkers should develop. I got over my original nervousness simply by speaking a lot in public. I used the fake-it-till-you-make it method. I kept faking it, pretending I wasn't nervous, until finally I wasn't. I have friends who have gone to Toastmasters to practice. I never felt the need for this, but some people find it very helpful.

Training and Degrees

369   *The Study of Psychology*

This golden key was for me the study of psychology. I spent many years studying all forms of psychology. I loved to see how they all fit together and how they were all pieces of the same pie. I would take from each methodology those things that I thought were of value and then incorporate them into my practice and classes.

I particularly received much benefit from studying the books and teachings of Carl Jung and Jungian psychology, and those of Robert Assagioli and psychosynthesis. I feel that psychosynthesis is one of the best forms of psychology available because it incorporates the conscious, subconscious and superconscious as well as the subpersonalities. Interestingly enough, I believe that Assagioli was a student of Djwhal Khul's and that most of the advanced people in Assagioli's organization in Italy were involved with the Alice Bailey teachings.

370   Earthly Degrees and Certification

This golden key in my spiritual progression has been my decision to acquire earthly degrees. I certainly don't recommend this for everybody. For many I recommend that they set up a counseling practice through being certified as a spiritual minister. For me, however, coming from a home environment of psychology, this was the logical and most sensible path. I tried to go to the schools that were the most innovative.

Then I got my hypnosis license through the state of California and my minister's certification through Gateway Ministries and the Association for the Integration of the Whole Person. Many of the people I respect the most don't have degrees or licenses, but in our society people usually give more credibility to people who have letters after their names. In the world as it exists now, for legal and credibility purposes, this is the path that many will be guided to follow.

If you decide to go to school, pick the most innovative school possible. Don't concern yourself with the accreditation of the school as much as whether you can become licensed through attending it. I often found traditional schooling limiting and was bored with it a lot of the time, but I did learn some valuable things along the way. Traditional schooling has been an important part of my development and a definite advantage for me in my mission.

However, it can be difficult to follow that path once one has been opened up to higher levels of information. The good news is that there are more and more schools that are innovative, holistic and transpersonal in orientation. Some of these will give you credit for life experience.

Exploring Spiritual Paths and Teachings

371   Spiritual Pilgrimages and Darshan

This golden key is about going on spiritual pilgrimages to sacred sites and having darshan with various saints and masters. This was something I spent more time doing during the earlier stages on my path. However, I consider this a very important part of my overall training. This is fun to do, especially with friends. These experiences can be deeply moving and transforming. They can also broaden your understanding of the nature and diversity of the spiritual path.

372   Studying Christianity, Hinduism and Buddhism

The next golden key has been studying Christianity, Hinduism and Buddhism. I have gained a great deal from my study of Christianity and the Bible. There are some beautiful teachings in the Bible, and some of the verses of the Old and New Testaments are classics of wisdom.

My study of Hinduism, specifically my study of the Vedas, which include the *Bhagavad-Gita*, has turned out to be among the most profound studies I have been involved with. Sai Baba's teachings are based upon these teachings, as are Yogananda's and many of the other great Eastern masters. If you never have studied the Vedas, I highly recommend it. In *Hidden Mysteries* and *The Ascended Masters Light the Way*, some of the teachings of the Vedas are included. This could be some of the highest channeled information ever brought onto the planet.

I have gained a great deal from my study of Buddhism, including Tibetan Buddhism. It is interesting that Djwhal Khul, Kuthumi and El Morya were Tibetan Buddhists in their last incarnation. Buddhism also encompasses the teachings of the Dalai Lama, who is a beautiful soul. Some of the beautiful teachings of Buddhism include the four noble truths of Buddha; the three jewels: the buddhi, dharma and sangha, or community; the four immeasurables: love, compassion, joy and equanimity; and the vow of the bodhisattva.

Often New Age people cast away the traditional religions, and I am here to say that there is much richness in these. The *Dhammapada*, which contains quotes from the Buddha, is easy to read and extremely rich. Extensive study and research in these areas has brought me much joy. In Eastern religion the study of the *Rāmāyana*, which is the story of Rama and Sita, is a real treasure.

373   The 22 Sacred Paths of Yoga

The next golden key I have found to be extremely useful is my study of the 22 sacred paths of yoga. I have attempted to follow the path of yoga synthesis, which incorporates the practicing of all yoga paths. There is a chapter on this subject in *Hidden Mysteries*.

374   The Teachings of the Mystery Schools

The next golden key in my spiritual evolution was to enroll myself in nearly every mystery school available on the planet. One after another I would go through their teachings and master what each one had to teach, then I would go on to the next one. I found this extremely beneficial. Much of what I learned from this study is in my books, so I might have saved you an enormous amount of time and energy.

Each mystery school sees the spiritual path through a slightly different lens. Working with so many different lenses has given me insight into a more universal understanding of the spiritual path. This study has been part of my training for not only writing my books, but also for hosting the Wesak celebrations. Nearly every one of the spiritual teachers, ashrams, mystery schools, spiritual texts and spiritual gurus that people are involved with, I too, have been involved with. I feel at home with all of them and honor them all. Immersing myself in the teachings of these mystery schools has been an important aspect of my spiritual development.

The interesting thing about Djwhal Khul's synthesis ashram is that it is the only ashram that has been specifically created to synthesize all seven rays. Though it is only one part of the second-ray ashram, it integrates all seven rays of the Christ. It was created by the Planetary Logos and the master Kuthumi specifically for this purpose. This is why it is such a perfect ashram for me.

The most exciting thing to me about Wesak is how universal and eclectic it is. People come from around the globe, from all spiritual teachers and ashrams or none. I love the synthesis of high-level initiates and ascended beings who attend. The theme of ascension seems to be a unifying principle that all paths can relate to.

375   The "Teachings of the Inner Christ" Mystery School

Another mystery school I was involved with for a while is called the Teachings of the Inner Christ. It was like a combination of channeling and Science of Mind. The woman who started it wrote some very interesting books. Her main teacher was Babaji, who presented a set of teachings geared more to the Western mind. I liked the integration of different approaches that I found in these teachings.

376   The Zodiac, Rays, Tarot, Sephiroth and Archetypes

The next golden key was a concerted effort on my part to become proficient and developed in all twelve rays, all twelve signs of the zodiac, all twelve archetypes, all ten Sephiroth and all cards of the tarot deck. No matter what sign you are, all signs need to be mastered; no matter what ray configuration your monad, soul and personality are connected to, all rays must be mastered and integrated. Go through the material I have written on these subjects and do an inventory of your strengths and where you need some work. Then set up a plan to develop yourself in these areas.

377   The Philippine Healers

Another interesting spiritual excursion was my involvement for a period with the Philippine healers, sometimes called psychic surgeons. In my first session, Alex Orbito stuck his entire hand inside my belly and then pulled his hand out with blood all over it. The wound healed up right before my eyes. This experience had a catalyzing effect on my consciousness.

378   Whole Life Expos

The next golden key has been attending Whole Life Expos. I would use these to make sure that I had covered all areas of training. I would attend certain workshops and lectures, and even though the energies at these events would be incredibly fragmented, during a certain period of my life I found them beneficial. After going to so many, now I am hard-pressed to find much I am interested in. But during a certain phase I tapped into much that was of interest on many levels. In the current phase of my life I am so busy in my service work that I am no longer drawn to attend them.

Spiritual Books, Tapes and Teachings

379   Working with Audio and Video Tapes

This golden key in my evolution was to order audio and videotapes on a variety of spiritual topics. Often when I had the inclination to go to certain workshops or travel around the country or globe, I would order the tapes and videos relating to these topics and places and find that this would give me all I needed. Because of this I have an extensive audio and video tape library. I would also sometimes get audio books on tape that I would listen to in the car because I didn't have the time or inclination to read all those different books. This allowed me to integrate this material while driving. I would also go for walks and listen to the audio tapes. Availing myself of all of these different tools has been a great boon in my quest for a well-rounded education.

380   Studying Diverse Spiritual Teachings

As you know, a golden key that has been instrumental in my spiritual evolution over many years has been studying a diverse range of spiritual teachings. Following are some of the books and teachings that have had the greatest impact on my life.

❖   The Baird Spalding Books

The Life and Teachings of the Masters of the Far East by Baird Spalding provides very interesting reading. These books contain fascinating stories of the lives and higher abilities of the masters as well as profound teachings on living as Christ and God. If you have not read these books, they are must reading.

❖   *The "I Am" Discourses*

I highly recommend *The "I Am" Discourses* from Saint Germain, a series of 13 channeled books from the thirties. I especially like the first four books in the series. I devoured these books, and they connected me to the ascended masters in a way that I never before had been connected.

However, not all of the information in these books is completely accurate, especially in regard to some of the charts, rays and so on. And some of it is a little simplistic, like making all of the ascended masters seem as if they are at the same level and that they all instantly have the same ascended master powers. Although these books are not a complete teaching, they were appropriate for the time in which they were written. They are filled with wonderful stories, and the insights in them will help your manifestation work tremendously. These books had a profound effect on me and they are well worth studying.

The "I Am" Discourses were written by Guy Ballard, also known as Godfre Ray King, who was George Washington in a previous incarnation— and his spitting image. It is interesting that Godfre Ray King, who was George Washington, and Saint Germain, who was Columbus, would get together in Mt. Shasta to bring through these teachings to the United States.

There were two later dispensations of ascended master teachings by Pearl and Innocente, two other channels you might want to check out.

❖   The Alice Bailey Books

The Alice Bailey books, which I have read through and studied almost three times over, are some of the most awesome books on the planet. In some ways they are a little outdated, but there is such a vast wealth of information on the ascended master teachings of the spiritual path and the higher realms that these books are eternal.

The Alice Bailey books probably had the most profound impact on me of any books I have ever read. By the grace of God, I had the benefit of having Djwhal Khul explain them to me as I was studying them, which is a story that will come later.

❖ The Tibetan Foundation Material

Some of the most valuable teachings I have found are the channelings of Janet McClure and the Tibetan Foundation. This organization was started by Djwhal Khul and Vywamus through Janet McClure in the early eighties. She was an incredible channel and brought through much updated information from Djwhal Khul. I ordered all their transcripts and read all of her books. Unfortunately, this organization is no longer in existence. These writings had more of an impact on me than almost anything I have read except for the Alice Bailey books.

❖ The *Yogasūtra* of Patanjali

This is another spiritual text that had a profound effect on me. One of the Alice Bailey books studies it from Djwhal Khul's perspective, which is interesting. It reminds me in many ways of *A Course in Miracles*, though it was written something like four or five thousand years ago.

❖ Self-Realization Fellowship

I went through a phase of immersing myself in Paramahansa Yogananda and the Self-Realization Fellowship. I completed their correspondence course and took the advanced Kriya initiation. I accepted Yogananda as my guru even though in my heart I knew I could never accept only one guru. By that time I was far too eclectic and universal.

❖ The Earlyne Chaney Books and Astara

An important part of my training was studying the books of Earlyne Chaney, who is a fine channel for the ascended masters. If you have not read her books, I highly recommend all of them (she has at least ten). I also subscribed to her three-year correspondence course of the teachings of Astara, the mystery school. I ordered the lessons all at once and devoured the three-year course in six weeks, as was my usual style.

❖ Theosophy

I went through a phase of studying Theosophy and the books of Madam Helena Blavatsky, Annie Besant and especially Charles Leadbeater, who I found much easier to understand. This is an ascended master dispensation and contains some incredible information and stories about the masters.

❖ *The Urantia Book*

The Urantia Book had a big effect on me, though I never actually read the book. It is a massive work, and I have used it as a resource. It has served to catalyze and open up some things for me.

❖ **The Kabbalah and the Tree of Life**

The study of the Kabbalah was a whole other phase of study I put myself through. I was raised in a Jewish family and enjoyed some of the customs, but I didn't feel a strong spiritual connection with Judaism. This didn't change until my late thirties when I began studying *The Keys of Enoch* and everything I could get my hands on relating to the Kabbalah and the Tree of Life. I find the Kabbalah and the Tree of Life to be one of the most profound systems of spiritual growth I have been involved in. It opened up a different world and an entirely new way to tap into God.

❖ *The Keys of Enoch*

This was another book I devoured, and it had a most profound effect on me. Studying the text and glossary of *The Keys of Enoch* opened up a whole new world for me. This is a major work and provides a deep understanding of the nature of the cosmos and our place in it. The information presented merges science and spirituality. In *Beyond Ascension* I share some of the activations I developed from studying this book.

❖ **The World's Religions**

Another very important training project of mine was the complete study of the religions of the world. I received great insight and value from doing this. It provided a foundation for my more esoteric involvement. By being familiar with all religions, then any type of person I would counsel or speak with I could immediately tap into where they were coming from. I could gear my counseling or conversation to whatever path they were on.

❖ **Spiritual Autobiographies**

A course of study I found to be of immense value was reading the spiritual autobiographies of past and present spiritual leaders whom I respected. I found Gandhi's autobiography inspiring. Yogananda's *Autobiography of a Yogi* is one of the best books I have ever read. I was greatly inspired by Swami Sivananda's autobiography and I also enjoyed Earlyne Chaney's autobiography.

Sometimes I would read the autobiographies of sports heroes I admired, such as Magic Johnson or Orel Hersheiser of the Los Angeles Dodgers, who was very spiritual. I have learned an enormous amount from reading these stories. However, the autobiography that has inspired me most is the story of his holiness Lord Sai Baba.

❖ **The Poetry of Kabir**

I have never been a student of poetry, but the poetry of Kabir is so God-infused that it is unlike any poetry I have ever read. Kabir was a poet-saint and one of Sai Baba's past incarnations. I have written about his life

and consolidated some of his poetry in *The Ascended Masters Light the Way*.
I believe you will find his life and poetry as inspirational as I did.

❖ Saints, Teachers and Traditions of the East

During one period of my life I put myself through an intensive training
program of studying the saints from India and studying the Vedas and *Bhagavad-Gita*. I became immersed in studying Ramana Maharshi, Ra-
makrishna, Vivekananda, Sri Sankara, Mahavira and Amritanandamayi Ma
(Ammachi), to name a few. During this time I also studied the teachings of
the Dalai Lama. I very much enjoyed the books of Eknath Easwaran, along
with some of the books of Swami Kriyananda, who was a disciple of Paramahansa Yogananda. I also enjoyed the books of Swami Sivananda, who was a
prolific Eastern writer and whose books I definitely recommend.

I found this course of study to be very illuminating. I believe that one of
the best ways to achieve self-realization is to study the lives and teachings
of the saints and masters who have achieved it. This extensive study led to
the eventual writing of *The Ascended Masters Light the Way*, so in one volume you have available the lives of many great masters.

❖ *The Starseed Transmissions*

Another book that had a very profound affect on me was Ken Carey's
The Starseed Transmissions. I enjoyed listening to the tape set even more
than reading the book, but both are good. There are two other books in this
series, *Vision* and *The Third Millennium*, and Ken Carey has written several
other fine books as well.

❖ *The Mahatma Book*

The Mahatma Book was written by Brian Grattan, who was closely involved with the Tibetan Foundation. The book contains extensive channelings from Janet McClure, founder of the Tibetan Foundation. I highly recommend this book. It offers the reader a range of perspectives and insights
on the revelation of the Mahatma on Earth.

❖ The White Eagle Books

Another set of books that are must reading is the set of books by White
Eagle. They are beautiful channeled material, especially for the beginning
and intermediate student of the path.

❖ The Books of Solara

Another set of books I think worth reading are Solara's books. I don't
agree with everything she says and I personally don't relate to her cosmol-
ogy of the universe, but I think her series of books are definitely worth reading and are quite inspiring.

❖   The Edgar Cayce Books

The Edgar Cayce books have always been a great love of mine. In my opinion he was one of greatest channels who has ever lived on Earth, and if you haven't read the Edgar Cayce material, it is well worth studying.

❖   The Seth Books

The Seth books were the starting point in my soul awakening. Later I went back and read a number of them and found them a little dry at that point in my spiritual progression. But I appreciated the understanding of the oversoul, which I have spoken about in my books.

❖   Ruth Montgomery's Books

Ruth Montgomery is a channel and has written a wonderful series of books. My favorites were *A World Beyond* and *A World Before*. I would recommend all of her books. She has a wonderful style of writing, and early in my progress her books had a great impact on me.

❖   Eckankar

I also went through a phase of training with Eckankar, John-Roger and Darwin Gross as well as reading the books of Paul Twitchell. To be honest, I found the group to be a little cultish. I was simultaneously drawn and repelled. The understanding of soul travel has always been of great interest to me. I studied all the books and got involved with their organization to the point where I felt I had gained what I needed and had achieved mastery. Then I dropped it. Even though I had a push-pull relationship to this particular spiritual path, I did receive some benefits worth mentioning.

❖   The Books of Analee Skarin

At one period I studied a set of books by Analee Skaron, a Mormon who achieved her ascension and wrote some wonderful books about her experiences.

❖   The Extraterrestrial Movement

The extraterrestrial movement became an all-consuming passion of mine for many years and eventually led to the writing of *Hidden Mysteries*. I studied everything I could get my hands on. I would go to the UFO conventions and listen to all the speakers and take notes. I consider this an extremely important slice of the entire spiritual puzzle. Many things clicked into place through this research, and this area of study opened a new aspect of my spiritual path and future mission.

❖   The Sedona Project

Another important catalyst in my healing and manifestation was some work I did with a woman in Sedona who was in charge of a spiritual mission known as the Sedona Project. She was an Arcturian and quite gifted in soul

travel. Going to see her helped me clear all of my alien implants and repair
some of my subtler bodies before I learned how to do this for myself with the
help of the masters.

❖ Tarot and Astrology

I went through another phase where I studied the tarot and astrology
and did tarot card readings for myself and friends. This was another important part of my training, and I took many classes in these areas. I do not
consider myself an expert, but it gave me many insights.

❖ The Study of Healing

Studying healing was an entirely different phase of my training. I
started by getting initiated into Johrei, which has to do with the channeling
of divine light through a connection with Avalokiteshvara, who is a Bud-
dhist derivative (in male form) of Quan Yin. This also tapped me into the
study of Buddhism in a more profound way. Then I was initiated into Reiki.
I also took classes in Rosalyn Bryiere's system as well as workshops with
Barbara Brennan. Hands-on healing is not the main focus of my mission
this lifetime; however, I consider it an essential part of my overall training.

The Ongoing Quest for Spiritual Knowledge

381   Keeping Current with Spiritual Information

The next golden key was staying current with spiritual information.
This lesson was first brought home to me about ten years ago when I was
studying the Alice Bailey material. After I had completed my studies of Bailey, spirit told me that my mind was stuck in 1942. It said that my study of
this material was essential to my spiritual progression, but that I needed to
update and make sure I remained current with spiritual information. It was
this experience that led me to seek information directly from Djwhal Khul,
Lord Maitreya and Melchizedek.

Many people are similarly stuck in the past. They might be stuck in the
Alice Bailey material, *The "I Am" Discourses* from the 1930s, the Edgar
Cayce material or outdated religions. There is nothing wrong with studying
older resources. I am one of the biggest proponents of this. But things are
constantly evolving, and people need to watch that they don't become crys-
tallized in their thinking and fall behind in their awareness.

Do not let your consciousness get stuck in a past time line no matter
how beautiful the teachings are. Djwhal Khul himself said in the Alice Bailey books that his information would become outdated toward the end of the
century. This is why a new dispensation of information is now being given.
It is amazing to me that some of the people involved with these teachings

think that these channels are the only ones who have high-level channeling or telepathic abilities. This would be as if evolution stopped. This is faulty thinking and slows down their spiritual progress.

In my books I have attempted to lay a foundation from these earlier writers who have contributed so much. But I have also updated this material to bring it into the present. And I have shared the dispensation of the future. Study the past teachings, for they will give you a most valuable foundation. then build upon it. This is what I do in this series, *The Easy-to-Read Encyclopedia of the Spiritual Path*.

382   New Information from the Masters

The next golden key has been to give myself free rein to ask questions, investigate, research and try out new ascension activations. Most of the ascension activations in my books came as a result of my searching for them and trying out new ideas that would come to me. After a while the masters, seeing how relentless I was, began to help out. Seek out new activations and new information yourself.

What I have found is that the masters don't volunteer a lot of new information. So use your own creative universal mind to uncover the secrets of the universe. I find that often the masters give a little tidbit and I latch onto it and keep asking questions until the entire subject is illuminated with new information. One time this occurred with Djwhal Khul. While I was asking questions about a creative idea, certain information came through about the holographic computer in his ashram. He said that he wasn't planning on giving this information for another six months. However, I wouldn't let go until he gave me the information right then.

You can see that this is very much a two-way process. I would say that three-quarters of the information in my books has come through my questioning and Sherlock Holmes-like investigation of every idea I could think of. Much information would not have come through had I not been so relentless in my research. I would often check a great many different kinds of activations and only a few would pan out.

Occasionally I would literally tap into the spiritual mother lode. The masters couldn't refuse me if I was wise enough to come up with the right questions. This is how I uncovered the complete process of cosmic ascension and how it works. Once they saw how much we were uncovering in our investigative work, they began to help out more. I think I created a monster, however, because now when I meditate, the masters frequently tell me about another book they want me to write. Melchizedek told me there might be as many as fifty books in this series by the year 2012.

383   Use Many Methods to Uncover Spiritual Information

The next golden key to my success has been my unceasing willingness to pray, meditate and ask questions. I have not been hesitant to ask God and the ascended masters for help. This is how I came up with many of these incredible activations. I would meditate for hours by myself and with my ascension buddies, receiving the energies, praying and asking questions.

I would trust my intuition and my telepathy and write down any question that came to me. Then in meditation I would ask about it. Often nothing would come of it. But at other times my intuition and connection with the universal mind would allow me to tap into some incredible new information and activations, most of which are mentioned in this book. My life became one constant meditation.

384   Record Ideas and Questions

This golden key was to keep a notebook and pen or a mini recorder with me at all times. Then I would write or dictate ideas or questions as they came into my mind. Sometimes I created a log of questions to ask the masters. If I didn't write down these ideas or questions, I would forget them.

385   Fill Your Information Banks

Another golden key has been the understanding that every person has what can be called information banks. These information banks have been slowly but surely filled from past lives and this life. After becoming aware of this, I committed myself to filling my information banks for the completion of my mission. Some channels are limited in their channeling abilities because their information banks are limited.

Getting the Word Out

386   Writing Books

This golden key has been writing my book series. Not only has this been a highly enjoyable process, but it has contributed greatly to my healing.

Books can be written using primarily either the intuitive mind or the rational mind. I use both, but mainly I use my intuitive mind. I do not spend a lot of time planning or organizing. The only thing I need is the title. Once I get the title, that serves as the seed that sprouts and unfolds as I write. Most people make writing a book an impossible task that takes years to unfold. The way I do it is to sit down, attune myself to God and the masters and start typing away. I love writing. It is the most enjoyable part of my day. I go into an altered state of consciousness and am amazed when five hours has gone by. Writing has a healing effect on my physical body as long as I don't overdo it. For me, writing spins the chakras and runs an enormous amount of spiritual current through the body.

It usually takes me only a few weeks to write a book. I get up very early and type for about five hours. Then I call it day for writing and focus on other projects. As I type, chapter titles and the organization of the book unfold. My goal is to write one chapter every day.

One of the best ways to become well-known is to write a book. Books take on a life of their own. They travel around the world and touch thousands of people's lives. So I encourage you to write. Don't go through a lot of elaborate preparations and don't be a perfectionist. Simply come up with an idea and a title for your book, pray—then start typing away. You will be amazed what the masters and spirit will telepathically channel through you. I don't look at it as work. Each morning I can't wait to get up and start writing.

As to the beginning of the book—the title page, table of contents and so on—you can copy what I have done in my books if you want to. Then just write. Even if what you write helps just one person, it is worth it. Even if you do it only for yourself, it is a wonderful exercise. But you never know. What you write might help ten people or a thousand or a million. If you let your creativity flow, you will find writing an exhilarating and uplifting experience. And don't worry about finding a publisher. Just write. I call on Sai Baba to help me get my books published. He and Melchizedek are my book agents—the best in the universe. You can self-publish or find a regular publisher. Books are easy, fun and quick to write if you will let spirit and the masters help you.

387 Advertising

The next golden key has been the process of letting go of my fear of spending money on advertising. In the beginning even the slightest bit of money seemed like too much. But now I am amazed at how much money I spend on mailing things out to people and advertising for the Wesak and my books.

The key is to monitor your advertising very closely to see where the best response is coming from. Ask each person who calls you how they got your number. Then make adjustments according to what is working and what isn't. Target publications that are the best for your type of work. Then make your ads as energized and esthetic as possible in terms of wording and design so they will grab people's attention.

Perhaps the most important thing is to believe wholeheartedly in what you do and know that it is serving the masters and the divine plan. Then be willing to invest in your work. Put your message out to the public in as many ways and as eloquently as you can.

388   Developing My Salesperson Archetype

The next golden key has been the development of my salesperson archetype. I actually haven't had to work on it very much, for I seem to have natural persuasive abilities, especially when it comes to God and the ascended masters.

Sometimes the word "salesperson" has a bad connotation, but I can think of no better word to use. It is important to be able to talk convincingly about what you believe in. When I talk to people and suggest to them that they buy my books and tapes, come to Wesak or have a clearing session, I am not speaking from my personality but rather from my high self. I know that these tools and activities will be highly beneficial to them. I am not really selling anything; rather, I am sharing my natural enthusiasm with people.

Lightworkers need to be able to express enthusiasm for the work they are doing. If you don't sell yourself, who will? Djwhal Khul pointed this out to me one day when he told me that I was highly developed in the persuasive archetype. He said that this was an important skill, but until then I had not thought about this consciously. I had simply expressed myself with my natural enthusiasm.

389   Networking

This golden key is my commitment to networking. This includes sharing information with individuals, fellow spiritual leaders and spiritual organizations around the world. This has been a very important part of my work. No one is an island. Group consciousness is the key to the new age. We are all in this together. Networking with diverse spiritual leaders and groups is an important part of establishing our interconnectedness. Each connection that we make creates a strand of light in the etheric web of the planet.

A project I was inspired to do was to establish a leadership meeting the day after the Wesak celebration in Mt. Shasta. This meeting is for spiritual leaders from around the globe. At these meetings we meditate together and brainstorm to see how we can help each other and the divine plan that we serve. Our goal is to work together as a powerful group body. Can you imagine what could happen if all of the spiritual leaders and groups on the planet began working together and supporting each other? When we unite in one common purpose, there is no limit to what we can accomplish. It is through this group effort that the planet and humanity will ascend. All of us working together can create heaven on Earth.

GOLDEN KEYS TO ASCENSION AND HEALING 11

FINAL GOLDEN GEMS
Keys 390-420

SPECIAL BLESSINGS AND ENERGY PENETRATIONS
LIGHT INFUSIONS
LOVE INFUSIONS AND EXPANSION OF THE HEART
ENERGIES FROM THE DIVINE MOTHER
COSMIC ACTIVATIONS
FURTHER ASCENSION ACCELERATION
INNER-PLANE HEALING
ELEVATED LIVING

Special Blessings and Energy Penetrations

390   Call for the Combined Energies of Melchizedek, Metatron and the Mahatma

This golden key is to call upon the combined flow of energy from Melchizedek, Metatron and the Mahatma. Initially this should be done during brief periods of meditation. Later this can be expanded into longer periods during meditation, but as the combined energy of these three cosmic beings is so powerful (equal to the blessings they bring), one must take this in small doses at first. Then build up to longer and longer meditation periods during which you call in this energy flow. The light and healing energy of this particular process is truly incredible, aiding in every aspect of one's ascension process.

391   Mahatma Energy Increase

This golden key gives you the highest level of energy through the grace of the Mahatma. Each day call upon the Mahatma for an increase of his penetration into your being. This will have the threefold effect of increasing your light, accelerating your evolution and expanding your capacity for world service. This threefold effect will expand as you continue daily to call for an increase in the penetration of the Mahatma energy.

Light Infusions

392   Mahatma Light-Quotient Increase

With this golden key, call upon the glorious energies of the Mahatma to help build your light quotient. The light blessing you will receive at this request will aid you significantly on every level of your being.

393   Anchor God Crystals

Use this golden key to call upon Metatron, the archangel who embodies light itself, for the anchoring of specific God crystals into your being. This has the effect of greatly expanding your light. God crystals can be brought forth from the planetary, solar, galactic, universal, multiuniversal and godhead levels. When making this request, ask for those God crystals that are at the highest potential appropriate for you at this time.

394 Anchor God's Lightbody

With this golden key request an anchoring of God's lightbody into your lightbody and entire being. This will infuse you with untold frequencies of light, raising your light quotient.

Love Infusions and Expansion of the Heart

395 Open the 352 Levels of the Heart

The next golden key has the effect of greatly expanding the heart. Just as we strive to increase our light quotient, we must equally increase our love quotient, as that keeps us in balance and is part of our divine nature and destiny. The Mahatma, who penetrates all 352 levels of God, is the perfect being to ask to increase the 352 levels of our heart. It is within our potential to unfold all these heart levels. This activation also serves to open the levels of the heart within the cosmos of which we all are a part. When we ask for this, it is a good idea to envision it as a holographic image.

396 Build Your Cosmic Love Quotient

This golden key brings the love energy into greater and greater play within one's being and heart. Light needs to be balanced with love, and who better to do this than Sai Baba himself, under whose divine tutelage and guidance I have written this book? Call upon Sai Baba to build your cosmic love quotient, and do this on a regular basis. Sai Baba, being the cosmic Christ, is love personified. By asking him for this divine gift, you will be expanding your own heart and capacity to love in undreamed-of ways. I cannot state how important this is, for without love one cannot proceed far upon the path. The more love one carries, the more godlike one becomes. So call upon Sai Baba to keep building your cosmic love quotient.

397 Expand the Heart

Using this golden key, call upon the divine trinity of Sai Baba, Lord Melchizedek and Lord Buddha to resonate within your heart as one. The combined energies of these three divine beings will further open your heart and infuse you with great love—love to bask in, love to serve with and love to radiate outward to bless the world.

398   Sai Baba's Vibhuti Bath

With this golden key, ask Sai Baba to grace you with an etheric vibhuti bath. The enormous blessing of his vibhuti will fill every level of your being with love, healing and illumination. You can also request an actual physical vibhuti manifestation, though this occurs only when there is a specific purpose and need for it. However, an etheric vibhuti bath is available to all. This is a great blessing from Sai Baba that will fill your being with love and illumination.

399   The Combined Energy of Buddha, Christ and Mary

Use this golden key to ask for the archetypal imprint of the Buddha, Lord Maitreya and Mother Mary. This combined energy carries with it so much love that it is like basking in love itself. This love cannot help but radiate outward, blessing all with whom you come in contact.

400   Love from the Immaculate Heart and the Sacred Heart

With this golden key call to the divine Mother for the immaculate heart and the sacred heart. This will have the effect of bringing you great love blessings—again, enabling you to give forth those love blessings to the world.

401   Love from Core Masculine and Feminine Masters

Using this key, call forth the seven core spiritual hosts: Lord Melchizedek, the Mahatma, Lord Metatron, Sai Baba, Lord Maitreya, Lord Buddha and Djwhal Khul. Equally involve the core seven lady masters. First call in the divine Mother, who embraces the feminine principle itself. Then call in Mother Mary, Quan Yin, the Lady of the Sun, Lady Liberty, the Lady of the Light, Isis and Athena. Ask them to be anchored within your heart; this will strengthen the bond that already exists within you. As your bond increases with these glorious beings, they will pour forth blessings to you on every level. They seek only to be of service and await your invitation.

The expansive nature of their love can only be described as bliss. The gift they give to you through this heart anchoring, you will give to others simply by being deeply infused with this love.

Energies from the Divine Mother

402 Divine Mother Ascension Seat

With this golden key ask that the ascension seat of the divine Mother be installed within your being and in your home. Also request to be taken to the appropriate level of the divine Mother ascension seat in order to attune more fully with the feminine principle of creation.

403 The Rosary from the Divine Mother

This golden key also deeply invokes the universal feminine energy. In the etheric realms there is a most magnificent pink rosary that the divine Mother carries. The essence of this rosary is duplicated and placed around the neck of all who invoke it. It serves to protect, heal and infuse your whole being with love from the divine Mother herself. To receive your own gift of this rosary, simply ask for it humbly and with loving devotion. You can then tune into the divine Mother via your rosary and have her loving, healing, protective presence surrounding you always. In truth, the divine Mother presence is always around us, but this gift deepens our attunement to her and is a wonderful benediction.

Cosmic Activations

404 The Platinum Rod

With this golden key, during meditation call upon Metatron and ask to be touched and blessed by his platinum rod. Platinum is the highest energy color, and to be touched and blessed by Metatron with the divine voltage of this rod is extremely elevating and transforming. Ultimately, the platinum rod is permanently installed as the initiate becomes able to handle and process this rarefied divine energy. However, this will be done by Metatron when the time is deemed right by him. But ask on a regular basis to be touched and blessed by this platinum rod. Each contact prepares the vehicles for higher and higher voltages and divine currents and blesses you with these divine energy streams. So humbly ask Metatron to touch you with his glorious platinum rod.

405 Cosmic Seed Packets

With the first part of this golden key, tune in to Helios and Vesta, who form our Solar Logos. As we become solar beings, our love and wisdom expand beyond the realm of the planetary system into the greater realm of the solar system. Ask for these seed packets of love/wisdom to be anchored within you. They will be of great help to you in this expansion process. When invoked, they will take root and grow within you and aid you in becoming increasingly aware and awake on solar levels.

Taking this process still further, ask Melchior to anchor galactic seed packets within your being. On the next level ask Melchizedek to anchor universal seed packets. Finally, ask the Mahatma for seed packets all the way up to the 352d level of the godhead. These are anchored within one's being to prepare the way for greater and greater expansions through the vast cosmic levels back to Source.

406   Solar Ascension Fabric and God Crystals

Using this golden key, call upon Vywamus nightly before sleep to weave your ascension fabric and anchor solar God crystals into your being. Visualize Vywamus taking his golden hands and, through the power and light of these God crystals, weaving your ascension fabric. Then see yourself being elevated in your ascension through these God crystals and your exquisite ascension fabric. This is a most wonderful way to fall asleep peacefully. Know that this process will continue on the inner realms throughout the night. Request that this be done on all 352 levels of the Mahatma, according to God's will.

407   Sai Baba's Assistance with Your Solar Activation

This golden key is a continuation of the above. Call upon Sai Baba each night to assist in your solar activation. Ask him for this help as well as the blessing of his constant protection and continuing aid in your realization of God on all levels.

408   Ashtar Command Downloading

This golden key is to request downloading from the Ashtar Command. Certain frequencies and information then will be installed within your four-body system to help you function at an increased level of light, love and wisdom.

409   Arcturian Downloading

This golden key is similar to the one above except that you request a downloading from the Arcturians. Therefore the energy installed within your four-body system will be encoded specifically with Arcturian frequencies. Again, this will move you to higher levels of love, light and wisdom.

Further Ascension Acceleration

410   Ascension Activation for your Entire Monad

The next golden key is to request an ascension activation for your entire monad, which includes all twelve oversouls. Remember that you are part of this whole, and the more service work you do for the whole monad, the more you do for yourself.

411   The Light Rod of Buddha for Accelerating Ascension

With this golden key request to be blessed with the light rod of Lord Buddha, who has assumed the position of our Planetary Logos as of Wesak, 1995. The power and blessings of his divine light rod will fill you with such incredible light and love that your ascension frequencies will be greatly heightened. The light rod of Lord Buddha is intimately connected with planetary ascension, since he is now the Planetary Logos. The benefits to your ascension work are too numerous to list. This will greatly accelerate your personal ascension process and that of Mother Earth herself.

412   Your Highest Possible Ascension Wave

Using this key, ask to be placed in your highest ascension wave. As you know, the process of ascension is being done in group formations, or waves. To be sure, each of us is riding the appropriate wave, and all the waves are grace from God and in alignment with the high frequency of Earth's evolution at this time. But as you know, it is my philosophy to move along at the quickest rate possible that is still safe. This makes us more available to do our service work as well as carries us forward on our personal ascension path. With that in mind, simply ask that by the grace of God you are placed in your highest possible ascension wave. Then let go and trust that all is unfolding in perfection within the divine plan of God.

413   Cleansing and Integrating One's 10,000 Soul Extensions

This is a most exceptional golden key. In my ascension process I was guided to move on from asking for the cleansing of my 144 soul extensions to asking for the cleansing of my 10,000 soul extensions. This is because I had completed what I needed to do with the 144 and it was time to expand into a greater grouping.

I am not advising that everyone do this. However, I want to share with you just how vast and continuous the process of divine expansion is. Everything moves onward, upward and becomes more inclusive. Before you invoke this request, you need to know with certainty that you have completed all seven sublevels of your seventh initiation and that you are expanding into higher dimensions. It is wise to verify this.

Then and only then should you begin the process of invoking the cleansing of the 10,000 soul extensions of which you are a part. Always conclude this request with ". . . or as many soul extensions as possible at this time, according to God's will." The benefits are incredibly expansive, but this invocation must be used with great care.

Inner-Plane Healing

414   The Galactic Healers

This golden key is to call forth the divine healing of the galactic healers. One of the departments within the cosmic government is the medical department, which is staffed with superb healers. When they are called into action, they direct cosmic-energy healing currents to us that benefit our physical, etheric, emotional and mental health. All they need from us is our call and a receptive attitude. I cannot encourage you enough to call upon these advanced healers for any healing need you might have. They have had a wondrous effect on me personally, and they always are most eager to help.

415   Combined Energy Beam from Melchizedek, Metatron and the Mahatma

This golden key combines the energy of three great cosmic beings for healing on all levels. Request that a combined energy beam from Melchizedek, Metatron and the Mahatma be directed to any area of your being that needs healing. Request the beaming of this combined energy flow for greater lightness and health in your four-body system. Ask for this so that you can be of maximum service with greater ease.

Remember that those who serve will be only too happy to support you in your service work. They desire to help you attain a healthy and peaceful place within yourself so that you can do your spiritual work. Remember that helping to heal us is part of *their* service work.

Elevated Living

416   Your Master God Blueprint

With this golden key ask Melchizedek for the dispensation regarding a fuller anchoring of your master God blueprint. Do this by asking for mini tornadoes to weave your God blueprint into the fabric of your whole being. This is a most valuable tool for awakening and activating your God blueprint and for bringing forth a higher realization of your part in God's plan.

417   Your Highest Service Work on the Inner planes

Use this golden key to ask God and the masters to help you find your highest and most harmonious area of service work on the inner planes. We all have an inner-plane life; those who are reading these pages have a very active life on the inner planes and are serving in some capacity. It will help you to request to be placed in an inner-plane position where you are most adept, in conjunction with where you are most needed. This will help move you further along your path on the inner planes. It will also help link your conscious mind with the work you are doing there so that you can have memories of doing your inner-plane work.

418   Bilocation

This golden key deals with bilocation. In actuality, all of us who have achieved a certain stage of spiritual evolution bilocate all the time. Whenever we tune in to the masters we send a part of ourselves—an aspect of our awareness—to an ashram of the masters, various ascension seats or inner-plane events. During our hours of sleep, bilocation is as much a part of what we do as rest and dreaming. As we evolve, this process will evolve and we will become ever more conscious of, and adept at, bilocation.

Taken to its ultimate, masters in full manifestation of these powers can manufacture their mayavarupa bodies and actually appear physically to others. This is the case with Sai Baba when he is seen by one group of people at his ashram and another group in an entirely different place—possibly halfway around the world.

Begin practicing bilocation by going to the various ascension seats presented in this book. You can request to bilocate to visit Sai Baba in his ashram in India. You can ask to go to the inner-plane synthesis ashram of Djwhal Khul and to the ashrams of the different chohans. And you can visit Melchizedek in his ashram in the glorious Golden Chamber. Soon you will see how easy it is to bilocate and how God's infinite universe is your playground. You do not have to be clairvoyant or clairaudient to do this. All of you will be able to feel and sense energetically the bilocation experience.

419   Magnify the Effectiveness of Audio Tapes

This golden key relates to magnifying the energies you receive from spiritual audio tapes. When listening to a meditation or affirmation tape, call upon the masters and ask that the effectiveness of these tapes be as if you yourself are speaking the words. This magnifies their effectiveness ten-thousandfold.

Audio tapes are wonderful tools for invocation, affirmation, activation and meditation. When listening to a spiritually inspired talk or lecture, the vibration of the words actually opens the doorway into the very realms from which the words come forth. The words are transmitters of frequency. By taking an active role while listening yet maintaining your receptive attitude, you join with the speakers and combine your energies with theirs. This multiplies those energies by directing them to come from within the core of your own being as well as from the speakers on the tape. By maintaining a receptive attitude, you also remain totally relaxed to receive the word vibration given forth.

Listening in this manner allows you to be both giver and receiver, balancing the male and female, yang and yin, energies. In this way you derive the best possible results from the tape to which you are listening. This is how I make use of meditation, activation and affirmation tapes, and it works wonders for me. I pass it on to you so that you can receive these magnified results when listening to your tapes.

420   The Divine Use of Time and Activities

In this final golden key I remind you to remind yourself that you can use all of your time and activities as opportunities for accelerating your spiritual evolution. If you are working, you can use that work time to run light and healing energies through you simply by asking. While working, I always take a moment to ask Sai Baba, Lord Arcturus and the Arcturians to run their energy through me, charging my four-body system with light and healing.

You also can request that the love energy be run through you. Divine love is a most wonderful healing and protective energy. These energies of love, light and healing will uplift you and keep you energized. You can also send the energies outward so that they can continuously serve those with whom you come in contact.

If your profession is in the healing arts, calling forth these energies will be especially helpful in your work. As I have emphasized many times, not a minute need be lived "away" from God. You can always be practicing the presence of God and running God's energies. You will want to have specific times for silence, meditation and renewal—alone, with your ascension buddies or in a larger group. But connecting with Source is a process that can and should be invoked in all situations at all times. While watching a movie or TV, listening to music or going about your daily activities, ask to receive energies from Father/Mother God or a specific master, and it will be done.

This extends to sleep time as well. All disciples, initiates and masters should go to sleep with the intent of getting closer to God on the inner planes. Ask to sit in the ascension seats, to attend inner-plane classes and to serve. God is a 24-hour-a-day, seven-day-a-week, every-moment adventure in which we are all involved, so why not make the most of every moment by aligning your energies with divine energies at all times? Then there will no longer be "being in meditation" and "not being in meditation." Life itself will be viewed, felt and experienced as one grand meditation-in-action of God.

Blessing and Benediction from the Ascended Masters

The writing of this book, the bringing forth into manifestation through the written word, is itself a great benediction, and Joshua has done us a great service in bringing this forth. It helps to fill the chasm between the ascended master teachings, the New Age movement and Sai Baba's mission of love and God on Earth. Since his mission embraces the Eastern tradition, he has been easily accessible to those of that tradition, particularly in India. Yet his mission and work extend far beyond anything imaginable and therefore his devotees are scattered all over the globe, traversing the various Earth planes and expanding into the cosmos itself.

For all practical purposes Sai Baba is in India, and in the tiny village of Puttaparthi at that. Those he calls come to him. Those who call to him he comes to, as well as those who call him not by name but by devotion and love of God. His work is primarily in India, yet his mission is for the awakening of the entire world. He embraces all true paths, for God encompasses the whole, and it is in that light of wholeness and holiness that he wishes to be seen and known.

He works with the ascended masters; how could he not? And yet so many, even those of very much advancement, have a bit of tunnel vision that must be expanded. This has been the inspiration behind this book and one of its basic motivations. Not a decade or so ago the Eastern masters were eagerly sought after, and thus Sai Baba could more readily make himself known to the seeker. Now many are awakening to their own mastery and are becoming aware of the teachings of the ascended masters and the ascension movement. This is good; it is the divine plan. Yet these same lightworkers are those this glorious avatar wishes to work with in a more eclectic manner, to aid them in their endeavors and help them—and those who are reading these pages—in their planetary and cosmic evolution.

So let it be known that there is no division between East and West except in the minds of humanity and in certain forms of manifestation appropriate to the climate of a specific grouping of souls. In the ultimate sense, however, there is no division, and certainly there is no division between the divine motivation of that of his holiness the Lord Sai Baba and that of ourselves, who are called the ascended masters, and other truly evolved teachers of every path, whether Indian, Asian, Native American or the archangels, elohim and the celestial hierarchy of positive extraterrestrials!

We, like you, have a specific part to play, of that you can be sure. But like an orchestra of many Krishnas/Christs/priests/priestesses, we each sound forth our note, playing our unique tunes upon the divine flute—creating one glorious cosmic symphony! It is the hearing of all of our notes that we seek to unfold within you, and the joining of all true paths of enlightenment under the canopy of the one God of which we all seek to make you aware. Then the path that you travel can be embraced fully — and known as the *one* path. For then there will be no division within your hearts about who to follow. You follow God, Brahman, within your hearts. Then you will find the many masters in our own graded but noncomparative ranks waiting to help you. You also will find those of the angelic line of evolution and the advanced extraterrestrials, who seek to serve those evolving upon the Earth's line of evolution, awaiting with the open arms of light, love and power—Shiva and Shakti—seeking only to help you.

Please do not limit the vastness of Sai Baba, or indeed any of us, by your minds. In the case of Sai Baba, he is one who was born awake, and he thus comes forth to you awake in the knowledge that he is God. Know that he is a true avatar come unto you. However, ask yourselves what this being of awakeness seeks to impart to you. What is it that an avatar of God seeks to tell the devotees, seekers and lightworkers of God? It is really this and only this: that you too are God. The difference between us is the level of unfoldment within our God-selves. What Baba can and does bring to you from his level of God unfoldment of vast expansiveness—which you ponder upon but cannot fully grasp—is his siddhis, or powers, used only in service to you so that you can deepen and expand your own beingness in God, the One.

He wants you to know that he is here much like a mother or father, a sister or brother or a devoted friend who wants to let you know that they are there for you to take comfort in and avail yourself of their assistance. He is here, beloved ones. He is in your hearts, he is in your love, he is in your evolution. Know him there/here within yourselves. Talk to him, write to him, ask him for guidance.

But there is one thing that you must never do with Baba. That is to compare the way he reveals himself to you—the divine gifts of the universe that he brings forth—with how he reveals himself to your brothers and sisters. There are some who need a physical, tangible manifestation to open their hearts to God. These are very tender buds who seek and need to feel and touch the light, for then with tears of devotion they commit ever more to the path of light and love.

Others he has and is close to, connected throughout the vast reaches of time, connected personally within his incarnation as Shirdi Sai Baba or through a lineage of devotion and love that has existed on inner and outer planes. To them he also might give a specific gift as a remembrance and renewal of an ancient relationship. Some he does not give of these things because he gives in other ways, directly through the heart, in dreams and on the inner planes. Those of you who fall into this category know that he is as much with you as with the bearers of certain medallions or rings or vibhuti manifestations.

There is a purpose behind all that he does, but never compare the way he rightly chooses to manifest his purposes or his gifts. One is not greater than the other, but each serves a specific function. If he rouses a man from the sleep of death, it is not because he is better than you, but because that is the best way to wake him up from his earthly sleep and bring him to God. Or perhaps it is because he is fulfilling an ancient agreement to do this in order to demonstrate to humanity the illusion of the death sleep. All of these things and matters you cannot know, but what you must know is that there is a specific purpose behind all that he does and that he is equally available to everyone.

Sai Baba comes to humanity as he is needed and as he is called. He comes to awake and to fulfill a divine purpose. In this purpose there is no division anywhere. There are no distances, no cleavages. Love is the essential key along with devotion to the divine ideals of which he is representative. There are many who think they follow him, but that separate concept of me-ness he outgrew eons ago. So who is it that they/you follow, then? It is your own highest God-self! And to where do you follow it? To an ever greater expansiveness to your own mastership! You are God following your God path within the One Eternal Being of God! This he is here to represent. So do indeed heed his divine call, but realize also that he is a representative who is revealing awakened God to awakening God—and even to sleeping God. That is who he is!

Yet the form serves a great function, does it not? Baba's form allows this cosmically awake part of God to talk with, touch, heal and comfort the awakening and ascending parts of God. In many aspects his teachings are simple. They are little demonstrations of what great love can do. They are attention-getters and wake-up calls. His remote physical location tests the limits of humanity's dedication, devotion and will to sacrifice for the sake of God.

However, do not fall into the trap of thinking that you fall short of this if you do not pilgrimage to Puttaparthi. If you are not among those whose destiny it is to do this—if there is not a specific and definitive lesson to be learned, or a need for you to go there—he will come to you, for you will not

have been called. There are those who feel the stirring to come but then find
blocks at every turn and never make the journey. Know that he himself has
put the blocks there and that you have fulfilled your purpose through simply having the desire to come or by preparing to come. If you are one of
these, do not worry; he is with you anyway. Equally, you are spared many
days traveling, the eating of unfamiliar foods and the drinking of foreign
waters! This we say lightheartedly with laughter and a smile, for it is all a
cosmic play, a play of light and love.

There are some of you who, once there, desire to leave before the
spirit-appointed time. You find yourself a resident of India for much longer
than you had expected or desired, and you have grown frustrated at the
blocks put in the way of your departure. You too should be at peace, for you
are detained until the needed lessons are learned or the perfect exposure to
his incredible love has filled you to your maximum capacity. Perhaps it is
the soil of India herself that keeps you there, igniting memories of long-
forgotten incarnations, or perhaps the need to learn from the holy ones of
India that your soul came seeking in the first place. All Baba asks is your
trust and your faith in these matters and that you know you are ever under
the gaze and guidance of his divine and blessed eye.

As to his purpose and the work that he does, again let us restate that the
height, depth and breadth of this you cannot comprehend—yet how much
does he give to you all! Please be open to receive, and please pay attention
to this book. We specifically asked that it be made known that he works
with us, whom you call the ascended masters. He likewise works with other
cosmic avatars, although it is his privilege to be the only one walking among
you as one of you and simultaneously as the great cosmic being he is. Do not
try to comprehend him personally, but rather unfold the God that you are,
and there he will be. Though he serves vast divine purposes, he has a form,
his mayavarupa form, and walks upon the hallowed soil of Earth in order to
serve in the capacity of teacher and friend. Know that the love, the devotional energy and the light he both is and demonstrates are vast enough to
enfold you all within his aura.

You cannot comprehend Sai Baba personally, for he is, in truth, beyond
the personal, yet can he be known and loved and can serve you and know
you personally through your visions, whisperings and prayers. For this reason has he taken form to walk upon the soil of Earth and thereby bring forth
every possible blessing that is in harmony with divine will. Know that he is
not the apex of a particular religion. All true religions and pathways are of
God, and it is God he represents. He has many disciples but is not a typical
guru in any sense of the word. He is the embodiment of That I AM, the I AM
of Brahma, Vishnu and Shiva. He is the atman, your highest Self, and therefore Brahman, the one Self. Sai Baba lives within you all.

He takes under his wing devotees and students of all paths, all countries, all races, all creeds, all religions. He takes you, the reader, under his wing. For by the very act of reading this book and the devotion therein, of listening to stories of his glorious acts of service, your heart has opened to love, light and godliness. And so your heart has opened to him. He is that which you are in the process of becoming in your cosmic journey within God. Please, beloved ones, take what he has to offer, ask for his help on your journey. He is always available.

Those of you who are familiar with the path of ascension are now more familiar with him. He works with us, the ascended planetary masters and those you call the cosmic masters. Be mindful of the unity that exists between his holiness and ourselves, the masters, for that unity is reflected and must be made manifest upon the Earth. East and West are just different labelings for certain areas on the planet. Viewed from the whole, there is only the whole, and Earth is one planet. Do not divide her. Love, wisdom, enlightenment abound everywhere. They are to be found within the next revelation, the next insight, the next step on the journey.

To those on the ascension path who call yourselves New Age people, we tell you that there is much of what you call new that is hidden within the Eastern and Asian teachings as well as other traditions of the past. This light is hiding there, because in the past it was meant for only the few who were ready. Now the many are ready, so seek out this light. To Americans we would tell you that you walk upon soil hallowed by many hidden mysteries of the Native Americans and upon the hallowed ground that houses many a vortex of light, love and power. Search out these mysteries and seek to bring them out from their hiding places.

As for his holiness the Lord Sai Baba and ourselves, the inner-plane ascended masters, know that there is no place where we are not, and we seek only to serve and to awaken all. There is no division of peoples or paths within our hearts and minds, so beloveds, do not imagine one there. For us there are no distances too great, no situations too steeped in difficulties. If you do not get the answer you seek from us, rest assured that you will get the answer you need and that you are not overlooked.

For the beloved disciples of Sai Baba around the globe, he thanks you for holding his presence before the world in any number of nations and communities. When you gather together in your Sai Baba meetings, he is there in love and light, leading all bhajans. Your work is of great service to his plan. Yet know also that as the world keeps growing smaller through evolution and communication, he must grow larger. Larger in the context of being known and called on to serve those following a broader path than one that is under his name only. Oh, devout followers of his divine and blessed purpose, help to include these other ones so that his mission might expand.

Help make it possible for those on other paths to partake with your groups in meditation, devotion, prayers, bhajans and the wisdom you uphold for him. Do this, however, without asking them, either overtly or subtly, to leave the path that is their destiny.

At this time we are all putting forth this call of unity. We have been greatly aided by Joshua's writing this book for all of humanity in order to integrate the seemingly diverse paths. Again realize that Sai Baba is not in search of followers, but rather those who would partake of the love and light he has to give. He is here to serve each and every one of you and to extend his blessing to all, for you are all children of the One. As the spark is the flame, so atman (your God-self) is Brahman (God, the One), and none exists outside of the whole. He has stepped himself down in form upon Earth so that human beings can see what they are capable of being as more and more light and love are illuminated within their beingness. He is here that humanity might know God. And so it is that he has taken form.

Let his form be of service to you, but limit him not to his form, for that would be a vain attempt to limit the limitless. In that light he asks of you to grow, evolve, expand and live within your own forms, but not to limit yourselves to those forms, for you too have a divine nature that you are only beginning to know. He is here for you in both his form and formless face. He is here that you might see him and take photos of him so that he can transmit to you levels of love and light far beyond the seeing and far beyond those photos.

When you receive darshan and touch Baba's feet, dedicate your devotion to God, not to him personally, for he is here as a representative of the eternal. Yet he is also here in form now, in this vastly expanding period of history. So call on him, for he has already called on you. In the light he brings and the light he is, in the love he brings and the love he is, he performs acts of grace that you might see the works of God revealed. Know that this is why he is here—to reveal God in all that he does. And know how absolutely available he is to you just for the asking.

Know also that you are here to reveal the light and love of God, to act as God in the highest way you know how. Therefore, for all of those pure in heart, we indeed have a shared purpose. Whenever your heart feels dry, your mind overburdened or your health failing, call upon his holiness the Lord Sai Baba and also ourselves, the inner-plane ascended masters. Trust that in whatever way we answer you, your call will be answered and you will not be alone!

A Special Thanks

I would like to give special thanks to Marti Elana Peace for her dedicated work in organizing, editing and putting this book on computer. Her selfless and dedicated work in this regard is much appreciated.

Index of the 420 Golden Keys

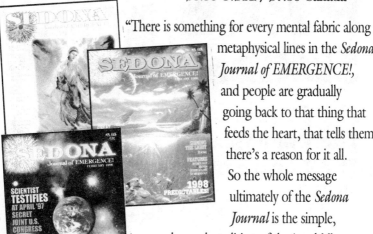

THE EXPLORER RACE SERIES

① the EXPLORER RACE

This book presents humanity in a new light, as the explorers and problem-solvers of the universe, admired by the other galactic beings for their courage and creativity. Some topics are: **The Genetic Experiment on Earth; The ET in You: Physical Body, Emotion, Thought and Spirit; The Joy, the Glory and the Challenge of Sex; ET Perspectives; The Order: Its Origin and Resolution; Coming of Age in the Fourth Dimension and much more!**

574p $25.00

② ETs and the EXPLORER RACE

In this book Robert channels Joopah, a Zeta Reticulan now in the ninth dimension, who continues the story of the great experiment — the Explorer Race — from the perspective of his race. The Zetas would have been humanity's future selves had not humanity re-created the past and changed the future.
237p   **$14.95**

③ Origins and the Next 50 Years

Some chapters are: **THE ORIGINS OF EARTH RACES:** Our Creator and Its Creation, The White Race and the Andromedan Linear Mind, The Asian Race, The African Race, The Fairy Race and the Native Peoples of the North, The Australian Aborigines, The Origin of Souls. **THE NEXT 50 YEARS:** The New Corporate Model, The Practice of Feeling, Benevolent Magic, Future Politics, A Visit to the Creator of All Creators. **ORIGINS OF THE CREATOR:** Creating with Core Resonances; Jesus, the Master Teacher; Recent Events in Explorer Race History; On Zoosh, Creator and the Explorer Race.   339p   **$14.95**

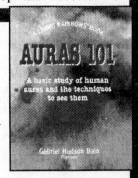

Former U.S. Naval Intelligence Briefing Team Member reveals information kept secret by our government since the 1940s. UFOs, the J.F.K. assassination, the Secret Government, the war on drugs and more by the world's leading expert on UFOs.

Behold A Pale Horse

About the Author

Bill Cooper, former United States Naval Intelligence Briefing Team member, reveals information that remains hidden from the public eye. This information has been kept in top-secret government files since the 1940s.

In 1988 Bill decided to "talk" due to events then taking place worldwide. Since Bill has been "talking," he has correctly predicted the lowering of the Iron Curtain, the fall of the Berlin Wall and the invasion of Panama, all of record well before the events occurred. His information comes from top-secret documents that he read while with the Intelligence Briefing Team and from over 17 years of thorough research.

by
William Cooper

$25.00
Softcover 500p
ISBN 0-929385-22-5

Excerpt from pg. 94

"I read while in Naval Intelligence that at least once a year, maybe more, two nuclear submarines meet beneath the polar icecap and mate together at an airlock. Representatives of the Soviet Union meet with the Policy Committee of the Bilderberg Group. The Russians are given the script for their next performance. Items on the agenda include the combined efforts in the secret space program governing Alternative 3.

I now have in my possession official NASA photographs of a moon base in the crater Copernicus."

Table of Contents

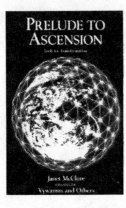

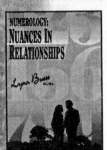

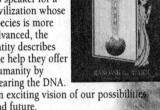